PERSPECTIVES ON GLOBAL CULTURES

Books are to be returned on or before
the last date below.

LIBREX—

⬭ ISSUES ⬭ in CULTURAL and MEDIA STUDIES

Series editor: Stuart Allan

Published titles:

PERSPECTIVES ON
GLOBAL CULTURES

Ramaswami
Harindranath

Open University Press

Open University Press
McGraw-Hill Education
McGraw-Hill House
Shoppenhangers Road
Maidenhead
Berkshire
England
SL6 2QL

email: enquiries@openup.co.uk
world wide web: www.openup.co.uk

and Two Penn Plaza, New York, NY 10121–2289, USA

First published 2006

A catalogue record of this book is available from the British Library

ISBN-10: 0 335 20569 0 (pb)   0 335 20570 4 (hb)
ISBN-13: 978 0 335 20569 1 (pb)   978 0 335 20570 7 (hb)

Library of Congress Cataloging-in-Publication Data
CIP data applied for

Typeset by RefineCatch Limited, Bungay, Suffolk
Printed in Great Britain by Bell and Bain Ltd, Glasgow

CONTENTS

PART 2

SERIES EDITOR'S FOREWORD

'This is not Iraq, this is not Somalia,' correspondent Martin Savidge of NBC News told viewers. 'This is home.' Savidge was surveying the catastrophic landscape left behind in the wake of Hurricane Katrina, one of the worst natural disasters in US history that left more than 1,300 people dead and tens of thousands homeless. In its immediate aftermath, it quickly became evident that the majority of those left in harm's way had lacked the physical or financial means to evacuate, many of them African Americans living in impoverished conditions in low-lying areas especially vulnerable to flooding. Television news images relayed from helicopters circulating above the tragedy were, in a word, shocking. Some journalists made the connection with the consequences of the South Asian tsunami. 'It's amazingly similar, horrifyingly similar. The scene of whole villages gone is very much the same,' CNN anchor Anderson Cooper commented. 'Gulfport, Bay St. Louis, Waveland – it could have been Galle, Sri Lanka. But what makes it different is that this is the US seeing bloated corpses out on the streets for days.' Images of the dead rapidly became iconic symbols of deeply entrenched poverty, neglect and racism. In one news report after another, references to New Orleans as a 'scene from the Third World' (often accompanied by phrases such as 'bodies floating on water reminiscent of Africa') were heard. Angrily defiant statements such as 'I cannot believe this is America' or 'This is not supposed to happen in America' were recurrently quoted, despite the realities of the horrors around them. The global was suddenly being reconfigured as local, a politics of convergence measured in human misery and suffering.

The era of 'globalization', as examples such as this one make all too apparent, is much more than an academic buzzword. In seeking to overcome the limitations of traditional conceptions of it, Ramaswami Harindranath begins *Perspectives on Global Cultures* with an exploration of the contradictions at the heart of the global-local relationship. He explains from the outset that one of the central concerns of the book is to recast the familiar sorts of assumptions underpinning the 'canon' of the established academic literature, not least by recognising the value of contributions from those otherwise displaced by its orthodoxies. For Harindranath, the crucial issue – and one that is often lost sight of in scholarly discussions – is the need to engage with the political and economic imperatives shaping cultural production. Unravelling the globalizing dynamics of representation and subalternity, it follows, becomes a strategic priority. Questions of power assume a vital significance here, he argues, especially with respect to how they are taken up and challenged by voices from the peripheries struggling to articulate the concerns of marginalised communities. In the course of elaborating his theoretical perspective, Harindranath proceeds to present a range of case studies, revolving around topics such as: multiculturalism and 'race', indigenous campaigns over sovereignty and land rights, the aesthetic and political aspects of 'third cinema', and the conduct of nationalist politics in a globalised world. In each instance, he shows us not only why debates about global cultures matter in academic terms, but also how critical theorisations of power can help to open up new possibilities for resistance.

The *Issues in Cultural and Media Studies* series aims to facilitate a diverse range of critical investigations into pressing questions considered to be central to current thinking and research. In light of the remarkable speed at which the conceptual agendas of cultural and media studies are changing, the series is committed to contributing to what is an ongoing process of re-evaluation and critique. Each of the books is intended to provide a lively, innovative and comprehensive introduction to a specific topical issue from a fresh perspective. The reader is offered a thorough grounding in the most salient debates indicative of the book's subject, as well as important insights into how new modes of enquiry may be established for future explorations. Taken as a whole, then, the series is designed to cover the core components of cultural and media studies courses in an imaginatively distinctive and engaging manner.

Stuart Allan

ACKNOWLEDGMENTS

Without Stuart Allan's patience and support this book may have taken a little longer to complete. With his unique brand of unfailing gentleness and humour Stuart persuaded, cajoled, and encouraged me during difficult times, although I am certain I occasionally tested even his seemingly limitless forbearance. I think Stuart, and I hope he finds this book worth the effort.

Through the long gestation period that preceded the more frantic times of the actual writing of the book my interest in it and my general well being were sustained by those I have been fortunate enough to have as friends. I excpress my gratitude to colleagues and companions, too numerous to name here, in Bristol, Milton Keynes, London, and Melbourne.

Students at the University of the West of England and the University of Melbourne kindly offered me the opportunity to discuss my ideas, and enabled me, through spirited debate, to refine the less polished arguments. To them too, I express my appreciation.

R. Harindranath
Melbourne, 2006

To TSR, my mentor, in gratitude and appreciation

INTRODUCTION

As I write this on an early November morning in 2005, the international new sections of newspapers carry reports of race riots in Paris, of anti-American rallies in Buenos Aires at the start of the Summit of Americas, and of the Pakistani President's complaints of what he regards as a lack of generosity by Western donors for victims of the massive earthquake in northern Pakistan. Hardly a day goes by without similar reports on occurrences ranging from inter-ethnic conflicts to declarations of national sovereignty. Such events reveal, in diverse ways, the complexities of the various processes intrinsic to what has come to be referred to as globalization. This book seeks to make a small contribution to the fashioning of academic vocabulary with which to discuss social and cultural marginalization, in what is commonly understood as our increasingly globalized world. Are our conceptual frames adequate for the understanding of the various processes that constitute globalization, in particular the enduring patterns of cultural, political and economic inequality evident across the world? What strategies can and do communities, excluded variously from the purported benefits accruing from globalization, adopt in order to voice their concerns? Such questions animate the discussions in this book.

The provenance of this book can be traced back a few years to the time I taught a course on Global Cultures at the University of the West of England. Instead of merely summarizing the existing debates on various aspects of globalization, the course encouraged the students to engage critically with enduring socio-political and cultural marginality. That was the time of anti-globalization demonstrations in Seattle and Prague, and the students took to the course with alacrity and enthusiasm. Many of the ideas I have attempted to develop in this book had their origins in the discussions I had with students on that course. However, teaching that course at UWE, and similar courses more recently at Melbourne University, has alerted me to the relative paucity in academic literature of accounts and deliberations that are willing to transgress the boundaries of received orthodoxy on the process of globalization. While prevailing debates encompass several relevant developments and attempt to trace their contours, I have noticed that pertinent contributions from outside the Euro-American academia have not been sufficiently explored. Neither have the cultural and political struggles at the margins, both at the global level as well as within local contexts, been adequately acknowledged. Focusing mainly on novel configurations and developments that are seen to constitute contemporary globalization, the majority of available literature has continued to de-emphasize both the persisting patterns of inequality and marginalization, as well as the more recent manifestations that have emerged as a consequence of globalizing processes. Accounts of the increasing fluidity between national borders and of the increase in cross-border mobility for instance, rarely take into account the increase in the number of restrictions being placed on certain communities. The events of 9/11, and subsequent developments, have engendered more nuanced investigations of the 'underside' of globalization, but these continue to remain on the margins of academic discussions.

This book has emerged from these concerns. As I embarked on the process of putting together my ideas and organizing them into a coherent structure, however, I rapidly realized the sheer enormity of the task. It is hardly surprising that theorists and researchers have spent entire careers studying various aspects of the contemporary world. Outlining the various struggles for recognition and redress alone seems a monumental enterprise; engaging with and addressing the complexity – theoretical and political – of such struggles adds yet another dimension to the undertaking. This realization has encouraged me to delimit this project by addressing only a few aspects of the elaborate range of issues.

By way of signalling this complexity, I offer, in Section 1, a conceptual framework with which to grasp the cultural politics of globalization 'from below'. In the first chapter I sketch arguments concerning the need to go beyond the largely programmatic orthodox thinking on globalization in order to examine the intricacies of the global-local dialectic and the politics of cultural production. Chapter 2 negotiates the terrain of cultural difference: expressions of it and their increasing commodification; the damaging consequences of contemporary culture wars; and the ethico-political issue of universalism versus particularism. The politics inherent in representation – both mainstream as well as those from the margins, hegemonic as well as resistant – is the focus of Chapter 3. Rehearsing key moments in the debate on the notion of hegemony, I explore the explanatory potential of the concept of the subaltern and subaltern agency. Following Stuart Hall's assertion regarding marginality as productive, the chapter explores the importance of the loci of enunciation – the positions that inform representations by peripheral communities.

Section 2 presents different case studies, illustrating and exploring the validity of the conceptual themes raised in the preceding section, as well as locating, however briefly, cultural representations and academic contributions from outside the canon. Recent events across the globe have increased attention on national security, and one of the consequences of this development is the renewed focus on multiculturalism, citizenship, and national identity. Chapter 4 traces the complex debates on multiculturalism and the constitution of multicultural citizenship, many aspects of which suffuse representations of sameness and difference, recognition and identity, in the media and other forms of cultural production. One of the best known, and overtly declared, confluences of cultural production and emancipatory political practice is 'Third Cinema', which originated in Latin America and has inspired political film-making, particularly in the developing world. The continuing efforts to refine the political and aesthetic theory of Third Cinema are examined in Chapter 5, along with the intricacies of national cinema or the cinema of nationalism.

Indigeneity is arguably one of the most important markers of economic and political subalternity that rarely gets a mention in academic literature on globalization. Chapter 6 outlines the political role of indigeneity in the national imaginary, and the importance of land and space to indigenous life and aesthetic practice, including figurative art and media representation. The final chapter considers the complex and fraught issue of nationalist politics and culture in the context of the alleged shrinking of the state in the face of the consolidation of the global market. Overall, this book endeavours to present a theoretically informed examination of the politics of marginality and cultural production.

PART 1

ONE GLOBAL CULTURE OR MANY?

It is often the case that works of fiction speak to larger truths. T. C. Boyle's novel *The Tortilla Curtain*, for instance, juxtaposes characters from either side of the US-Mexican border by alerting the reader to the plight of Mexican villagers illegally entering the USA to find manual work. When, at the beginning of the novel, Delaney Mossbacher's car knocks down Candido, the event not only inaugurates a tense and suspenseful story but, more significantly, also precipitates a collision of two worlds. One is that of an environmentally conscious, middle-class liberal American living in a gated community in Los Angeles, and the other is that of an illegal Mexican immigrant who had smuggled himself and his young pregnant girlfriend across the border to search for work as a manual labourer.

These constitute two opposing life-worlds – on the one hand, that of the sensitive nature writer and his realtor wife, a man with leftist sensibilities initially opposed to the notion of a gated community, and on the other a young couple without official papers, members of the largely invisible group of Mexican 'illegals' who form part of the workforce in parts of California. One is the world of plenty, in which the collision with a pedestrian awakens in Delaney a self-reflexive concern for the unknown victim, while at the same time anxiety about potential legal consequences keeps him moving after a cursory glance at the rear-view mirror, retreating into his carefully constructed and guarded domestic environment. The other is a desperate form of existence in which Candido's chances of getting work on the farms are seriously damaged by the broken bones caused in the collision, and he retreats to his makeshift camp in the ravine, concerned about his inability to protect and care for his girlfriend.

The difference however, is not merely between plenty and poverty. What constitutes the expectations of domestic life are different in the two worlds; what Delaney and Candido construe as risk, both avoidable and necessary, are different; their relative positions in the hierarchy of power are different, as are their respective locations in the international division of labour. Their lives, in other words, depict instances of the gulf separating communities that often intersect, interact and sometimes collide with one another, but together contribute to the contemporary form of global culture, economy and politics. The profound differences between Delaney's and Candido's lives are testimony to different worlds – their respective life-worlds testify to the different material realities that underpin the different 'worlds' that constitute contemporary global culture. They illustrate current debates on the cultural and economic aspects of globalization, in particular the interaction between the global and the local, globalization as a process of homogenization or heterogenization, the politics of local cultural production and resistance, and reveal also absences in most academic literature on globalization that ignore, some say wilfully, the consequences of global developments on those sections of the global population that inhabit the lower rungs of the hierarchy.

Academic publication on the subject of globalization has become a veritable publishing industry, with particular names associated with specific debates – Giddens, Beck, Robertson, Castells, Harvey, Jameson – to name only the best known, whose contributions have, through subsequent interventions by other academics and through discussions in classrooms, formed a canon of literature on the subject. The framing of the debates, the very identification of the points of departure in these debates and discussions, the reference to champions of this position or that with regard to a particular issue, as well as the conceptual scaffolding that buttress the frames – all these together, it can be argued, have come to constitute an orthodoxy. Like most orthodoxies it contains tenets possessing the power to offer plausible explanations while simultaneously circumscribing the kinds of issues that the practitioners are willing and able to talk about. This book attempts to bring to the table voices, both academic and cultural, from outside the canon, as well as concerns and anxieties that normally fall outside the purview of received wisdom on globalization. This is not so much a difference in focus as a change in perspective. On the surface, some of the significant issues echo ongoing debates on various issues. Does globalization entail homogenization, for instance? What constitutes the 'local', and what is its role in the process of globalization? In what ways can local and vernacular cultural producers contribute to and interrogate debates on Westernization, global culture, and contemporary forms of capitalist production?

Revealing absences

That prominent conceptualizations of globalization have tended to ignore or neglect the material and cultural realities of communities outside the dominant ones in the West and elsewhere is not a novel suggestion. An instance of such a theorization appears in *Runaway World* (1999), a collection of Reith lectures originally presented, and broadcast by the BBC, at different venues around the world, in which Anthony Giddens claims that, 'We are the first generation to live in this [cosmopolitan] society, whose contours we can as yet only dimly see. It is shaking up our existing lives, no matter where we happen to be' (p. 6). While it serves to highlight the novelty and the magnitude of the changes brought on by globalization, this quote accurately captures the limitations of orthodox globalization theory, exemplifying the intellectual solipsism that inheres such conceptualizations. Burawoy (2000) for instance, takes issue with this claim:

> As we listen to [Giddens] across sound waves, or through cyberspace, or watch him on video, we cannot but wonder how much of globalization talk signifies the privileged lifestyle of high-flying academics . . . But who is the 'we' he is referring to? For whom has risk been extended, tradition disinterred, the family made more egalitarian, and democracy become more widespread? To what slice of Hong Kong's, Delhi's, London's or Washington's population do his sociological obser- vations pertain? Is he talking about everyone or just the new cosmopolitan elite to which he belongs? What does globalization look like from the underside – for example, from Castells 'black holes' of human marginality?
>
> (p. 336)

The pertinence of Burawoy's interrogation of Giddens's apparently inclusive 'we' lies in what it excludes, and by extension, the limitations of such theorizing. For example, exclusive focus on the allegedly novel configurations of contemporary global economy, culture and politics tend to overlook the continuing patterns of inequality. In trying to understand and theorize what is new, be it the knowledge economy, time–space distan- ciation, virtual communities, or 'post-Fordist' production, many theorists of globaliza- tion fail to address issues which have continued to dominate the lives of those who are clearly outside the remit of such conceptualizations.

Neil Lazarus raises a similar point in another context, in response to Martin Jacques's claim that 'our world is being remade. Mass production, the mass consumer, the big city, big-brother state, the sprawling housing estate, and the nation-state are in decline: flexibility, diversity and internationalisation are in the ascendant' (quoted in Lazarus 1999a, p. 35). To Lazarus, such instances of 'undue stress on the portentous- ness and "radical novelty" of contemporary social and economic developments' miss the point.

> It is helpful first of all to examine the content of the term 'our' that Jacques deploys so cavalierly. . . . For it is clear that the subjects of 'our world' do not include those in the core capitalist countries . . . whose livelihoods and security have been undermined by the new strategies of resurgent post-Keynesian capital- ism. Nor does 'our world' include the subaltern classes from the 'Third World'.
>
> (p. 36)

Lazarus belongs to a relatively small group of scholars who have consistently objected to the exclusivity of the celebration of the 'radically novel' aspects of recent develop- ments, and the consequent disregard of those for whom it is the largely unchanging circumstances of their lives that attest to their continuing political marginalization and economic exploitation. This latter group is mainly comprised of what Sivanandan has referred to as those 'massed up workers on whose greater immiseration and exploit-ation the brave new western world of post-Fordism is being erected' (Sivanandan 1990a, p. 6). Lazarus's passionate disavowal of the 'radical novelty' emphasized and celebrated in much writing on globalization is worth quoting at length: for him such moves are problematic

> for in Thailand, Indonesia, Mexico, Kenya, the tide of poor people – landless peasants, or 'rural proletarians' – flooding from the countryside to the cities in search of jobs continues to rise exponentially. In Rwanda, Eritrea, Korea, and El Salvador, the question of the nation-state has never before seemed so pressing or so central. In Brazil, Ghana, Bangladesh, and the Philippines, thoughts of 'diver-sity', 'flexibility', and 'communication' are really of practical significance only to foreigners and indigenous elite classes: to the overwhelming masses of local people, they mostly spell out exploitation in new letters.
>
> (p. 36)

For scholars like Lazarus and Sivanandan such a state of affairs demands a conceptual formulation that accounts for the complex ways in which the changes instituted by novel social developments globally are implicated in the persisting patterns of inequality across the globe.

Giddens distinguishes between 'sceptics' and 'radicals' – for sceptics, according to him, debates on globalization are part of an ideological move within academia and society as a whole, a move which hides the machinations of contemporary global politics and economy, and the neo-liberal ideology that underpins these developments. For those like himself, whom Giddens calls 'radicals', such debates attempt to capture and understand the planetary transformations of the real process of globalization, whose consequences are felt in diverse fields, from everyday life, to the global economy, to environmental concerns. In a more recent encapsulation of his position vis-à-vis globalization (Hutton and Giddens 2000), Giddens distinguishes between two oppos-ing positions on whether or not changes in global economy, politics and culture are continuations of changes from the past. On the one hand, there are those for whom

> the continuities and parallels with the past are much greater than the differences. They argue, for example, that a hundred years ago there was just as much global-isation as there is now. . . . At the other extreme are the 'Gee-Whiz' types, who are so impressed with all the changes happening today, especially those to do with technology, that they see a world breaking quite radically with its past.
>
> (p. 3)

He identifies his position to be closer to the 'Gee-Whizzers', that is, his entire oeuvre on globalization is based on the assumption that the world has changed almost irrevocably from the past.

For Burawoy, Giddens's appropriation of the label 'radical' for himself is problematic. He criticizes Giddens for his distinction between sceptics and radicals that 'deftly forecloses other options [such as] the perspectival globalization of anthropologists', and for arrogating the dubious claim of being one of the radicals (Burawoy 2000, p. 338), which in its turn deftly overturns the generally accepted sense of 'radical' as progressive and leftist, thereby removing from the equation those who emphasize the fundamental inequalities inherent in the process of globalization. Nevertheless, Giddens's self-positioning with the 'Gee-Whiz' end of the spectrum presents a plausible explanation for his stance. Burawoy overlooks the fact that Giddens's focus on the consequences of globalization on the cosmopolitan and the global elite is prompted and informed by his interest in demonstrating the novel aspects of contemporary global social formations and how these evidence a break from the past. Patterns of inequality, both economic as well as enunciative (in other words, marginalized) that either continue from the past or have arisen as a result of recent developments consequently fall outside his lens. Given this focus on a delimited arena, however, the totalizing nature of his thesis is problematic, and attracts criticism such as that of Burawoy – that Giddens's strategy of tracing the origin and development of concepts such as risk, tradition and democracy is 'strangely beside the point' (p. 339).

Tomlinson's notion of cultural globalization as 'complex connectivity through proximity' (1999, chapter 1) is another case in point:

> What connectivity means is that we now experience this distance [between Spain and Mexico] in different ways. We think of such distant places as routinely accessible, either representationally through communications technology or the mass media, or physically, through the expenditure of a relatively small amount of time (and, of course, of money) on a transatlantic flight.
>
> (Tomlinson 1999, p. 4)

And again, 'Jet travel is an intrinsic part of connectivity and, in its increasing commonplace integration into everyday life, demands attention as cultural experience', although he does qualify it later, 'despite its increasing ubiquity, it is still restricted to relatively small numbers of people and, within this group, to an even smaller, more exclusive, cadre of frequent users' (p. 8).

Such acknowledgements of the presence of global inequalities of access to resources pepper his account of globalization and culture and are noteworthy. But his arguments are nevertheless aimed at a constituency which both reads the literature and recognizes itself in it – a constituency that includes Delaney but not Candido. How valid is it then, to refer to air travel as 'an intrinsic part of connectivity' that characterizes globalization?

What is chosen as exemplifying the 'intrinsic part of connectivity' is revealing. The economic and political aspects of globalization which contribute in complex ways to the alleged 'illegality' of the cross-border movements of people such as Candido, whose contribution to US economy and culture and their simultaneous invisibility is explored in Ken Loach's film *Bread and Roses*, is as much part of this connectivity as the jet-setting knowledge workers with specific skills for whom such travel is common-place. One can think of other such instances – the ways in which, for instance, the civil war in parts of Africa such as Angola exemplifies another aspect of the global connecti-vity, in this case through the international diamond trade, or what Naomi Klein (2005) recently referred to as 'disaster capitalism' to describe the corporatization of emer-gency relief and reconstruction of disaster-hit zones. Moreover, it is not merely a question of resources and relative affluence. Issues of race and class intersect, for instance, on who is considered a desirable migrant and who is marked as an 'economic migrant' and, therefore, undesirable. As Stuart Hall (1980) has argued, while 'race' as a socio-historical category possesses a 'relatively autonomous effectivity', it is 'the modality in which class is "lived", the medium through which class relations are experi-enced, the form in which it is appropriated and "fought through" ' (p. 41). Moreover, passport and immigration controls have long been used to police and restrict entry, and have increasingly taken forms of racial and religious discrimination and surveillance since the 'war on terror'. Frequent air or interstate travel is restricted to not only the affluent, but also to those with the right passports and skills.

These perspectives displayed in Giddens and Tomlinson, along with others such as Urry's notion of global 'complexity', in which migration has become fluid across porous borders, while they attempt to negotiate and conceptualize contemporary, complex global changes, appear exclusive in their focus. At times they conform to what San Juan (2002) refers to as 'self-incriminatory', excluding, both in their address and in their focus, communities for whom diverse manifestations of globalization have had more damaging consequences. The 'Gee Whiz' celebration of globalization's novel aspects is severely selective, focusing almost entirely on those aspects of contemporary global processes that are manifested in the experiences of an elite community. These formulations leave out the material realities and cultural manifestations of the funda-mental inequality that patterns contemporary forms of global economy. As Burawoy (2000) notes correctly, of all the 'radicals', who attempt to demonstrate the character-istic ways in which the contemporary world is markedly different from that of the past, it is Harvey (1990, 2003) who comes closest to actually engaging with the economic aspects of the transformation. 'But even he, after documenting the postmodern condi-tion, substitutes for history a plausible but nonetheless speculative Marxist periodiza-tion of capitalism, based on the successive resolutions of the crises it generates' (Burawoy 2000, p. 339).

There is, thus, a widespread ignorance or neglect of non-metropolitan situations in metropolitan knowledge production on globalization that, ironically, claims to speak for and include the entire globe. The conceptual hall of mirrors that makes up the majority of available academic literature on globalization excludes as much as it dazzles. Contributions reflect off each other, and what appears – and are often claimed as – all-encompassing meta-theories that explain the complex processes and con-sequences of globalization actually address delimited areas. Admittedly, and this is a point that needs to be stressed, understanding and conceptualizing the complex, contradictory, shape-shifting, protean processes that the term 'globalization' tries to capture is a mammoth task, as testified by the existence of publications such as Castells three-volume *The Network Society*.

Another point that needs emphasizing is that the existing canon on globalization referred to earlier grapples with aspects of this complex process with more than a reasonable degree of success. Ongoing debates among the contributors to this literature reveal a healthy disagreement, which in turn keeps the debates alive. To reiterate, what concerns us here are the blind spots that belie in important ways the claims that the canon addresses the process of globalization in its totality. This is not merely an academic or an epistemological issue, it is profoundly political too, as it involves a persistent neglect of the 'underside' of globalization.

Such totalizing claims are always problematic, but how is this lacuna to be addressed? There are those like Ahmad (1992) who insist on the centrality of the material inequalities which to them are fundamental to any attempt at understanding and reformulating globalization theories. As Bartolovich (2002) argues, summarizing this position,

> any attempt to rectify the genuine widespread ignorance of non-metropolitan situations in the metropole which fails to address itself to the material asymmetries which both structure and sanction this ignorance, is doomed to failure. It can lead only to further appropriation: cooptation and cloying tokenism at best. The dizzying disequilibria (of power, resources, social agency) exhibited in the contemporary world-system are, as Enrique Dussel among other Marxists, has persistently argued, literally *irreducible* without closing the gaps in *material* inequalities among peoples.
>
> (Bartolovich 2002, p. 12, emphasis in the original)

Without what she refers to as a 'rigorous critique of the imbalances of global political economy' (*ibid.*) any attempt at addressing the diversity of cultural contexts and contests becomes merely gestural, a superficial celebration of cultural difference.

Some scholars in the field of postcolonial studies have been preoccupied with the intellectual dimensions of these global imbalances, particularly in relation to the differences between metropolitan and non-metropolitan forms of knowledge production. This imbalance is characterized by, as Dipesh Chakrabarty succinctly puts it, an 'asymmetric ignorance' sanctioned by institutional practices, 'mandates that while non-metropolitan intellectuals must demonstrate a familiarity with Euro-American scholarships to gain credibility ... the reverse does not apply' (Bartolovich 2002, pp. 12–13).

This sanctioned imbalance in scholarship has resonances in both intellectual production and pedagogic practice. For instance, concepts which are often regarded as innovative and critical seem to lose their edge when considered in the non-metropolitan context. An obvious example of this is the concept of 'hybridity' that has gained currency in critical academic literature relatively recently, in the context of discussions about multiculturalism and identity. Arif Dirlik has observed that the concept is assumed in mainstream scholarship to describe the mixing of metropolitan with non-metropolitan cultures, and rarely as being an effect of cultural features shared, over centuries, by peoples in the non-metropole, as for instance in Latin America (1994, p. 342), where by 'metropole' we mean the Euro-American centres of cultural and intellectual production.

Moreover, the acceptance and sanctioning of ignorance of non-metropolitan cultural forms and conditions of existence contributes to the promotion of particular non-metropolitan academic and cultural texts '(typically ones which in reference or form seem familiar to metropolitan readers) [that] gain extravagant weight – often being subjected to highly decontextualized assessments' (*ibid.*). Further, there is a similar celebration of

> metropolitan cultural forms and works . . . in lieu of less familiar ones, even on matters of most concern to non-metropolitan populations. One notes in general, indeed, that concepts deriving from intellectual circuits outside the metropolitan world often fail to gain currency within this world until put forth, with or without attribution, by metropolitan intellectuals.
>
> (Bartolovich 2002, p. 13)

A major consequence of this is the uncritical acceptance of a melange of concepts, theories and texts that are far removed from the realities of non-metropolitan life. 'The vast discrepancies in "being heard" under current conditions [and] the intimacy of the connection between the "deafness" of metropolitan intellectuals and their location – economic and ideological, not merely geographical' (*ibid.*) needs to be addressed urgently.

It is obviously unnecessary to conceive of this ignorance as a wilful act, nor is it necessary to indulge in *ad hominem* accusations that, by definition, will be both unsubstantiated and unproductive. Nevertheless, this absence of a clearly defined attempt to negotiate the material realities and cultural fall-outs of the process of globalization particularly in, but not necessarily limited to, the developing world, as well as those sections of the population in the developed world yet to benefit from the apparent trickle down of the joys that globalization brings, reveals what is at best a theoretical lacuna in conceptualizations of, and debates on, globalization. Such conceptualizations are, therefore, incomplete as the literature that currently makes up the canon is largely restricted to the understanding of the consequences of globalization on cultures made up by the transnational cosmopolitan elite – the main beneficiaries of the process.

To return to the example at the beginning of this chapter, the available literature on globalization speaks about and to the Delaneys and seldom to or about the Candidos. This absence not only reveals a hierarchization of the contemporary world and the exclusive focus on the top tiers of that hierarchy, but more worryingly, it is normalized in academic literature and in the classroom, thus underlining Dirlik's concern. It therefore, becomes difficult not to share his anxiety about the normative nature of the academic paradigm adopted by even those who engage with the complexity of contemporary global culture, economy and politics.

Using the example of feminist academic interventions on behalf of Third-World women, Mohanty (1994) argues that even in the case of critical engagements with giving a voice to 'Third World' communities, such moves at times ironically reproduce a form of intellectual colonialism. Such interventions made by scholars 'who identify themselves as culturally or geographically from the "west" ' are undermined by 'assumptions of privilege and ethnocentric universality' (Mohanty 1994, p. 199), and serve to 'discursively colonize the material and historical heterogeneities of the lives of women in the third world' (p. 197). Similarly, Bahl and Dirlik (2000) argue that there is no shortage of critics of certain types of modernity,

> unfortunately, the most imaginative of such critics, mostly from Third World locations, go unheard because of an imbalance of power that continues to structure the world. Third World scholars and scientists suffer from the prejudices of media controlled by the powerful who deny a significant hearing to alternative visions of society, indigenous projects, and appropriate technologies as solutions to contemporary problems.
>
> (Bahl and Dirlik 2000, p. 5)

But, as Mohanty herself observes, such castigation of the hegemony of Western scholarship goes beyond merely opposing metropolitan theorizing with academic and intellectual work from the developing world, or from what is considered the margins.

As we have already noted, and as it will hopefully become increasingly clear during the course of the following chapters, it is possible to locate among the theorists based in the West those concerned with the lacunae and inadequacy – with the 'intellectual colonialism' inherent in dominant conceptualizations of globalization. More importantly, as Lazarus (2002) demonstrates, for all the merits of her timely and politically significant intervention, Mohanty's argument is weakened by her reification of the West. 'The word "Western" is used . . . to gloss, qualify, characterize and of course, taint and disparage feminist scholarship that provides her with her subject and critical target. We must then ask of Mohanty . . . why "Western" rather than "Eurocentric" or even "Orientalist"? What does the term "Western" offer that the term "Eurocentric" would not?' (p. 57). Lazarus's concern is that the term 'Western' becomes in such instances, 'an alibi in the determinate absence of a plausible conceptualisation of capitalism and imperialist social relations' (*ibid.*). For him, the simple argument of merely opposing a putative West to the 'Third World' will no longer do.

While Mohanty's intervention is vital to the revision of feminist critical discourse, particularly in relation to marginal or Third-World women, the solution is more complicated than an automatic gainsaying of what is perceived as 'Western' frameworks and epistemologies. Similarly, critical attempts to revise the orthodoxy that has emerged in globalization literature – attempts informed by the socio-historical aspects of cultural production and resistance as well as academic and intellectual discourse from the margins – are not limited to merely resurrecting and bringing to the table voices of the non-metropole. As we see in Chapter 2, the politics of representation and cultural difference enact complexities that undermine any such straightforward opposition of the 'West' with the 'Rest'.

Added to this is the further complication of the commodification, in economic or intellectual terms, of alternative voices and forms. As Brennan (1997) points out, 'What might appear to be gestures of openness to alternatives, or solidarity with marginalized cultural forms and peoples, can all too easily become instead marks of the old, familiar dynamic of *appropriation*' (p. 8). Brennan's complaint is that the transformation of the 'Third World' into objects of consumption dilutes the challenges and potentially radical consequences of cultural and scholarly production from the non-metropole. It is difficult, he argues, for students brought up to consider the Third World in terms of Body Shop or eco-tourism, to appreciate the writings of Ngugi or Kincaid in their historical contexts, as critical engagements with local conditions of life. The relatively recent popularity of one of the forms originating in Latin American fiction, 'magic realism', illustrates his argument that such texts are celebrated more for their genre-busting and as exemplars of mystery and wonder (and marketed as such) rather than as historically relevant creative interventions. These and other such texts – one can, for instance, consider the burgeoning of interest among publishers for South Asian writing in English, or the packaging of alternative cinema – serve only to exoticize cultural production in the margins, thereby dulling their critical edge.

This is noticeable for instance, in the way that non-mainstream music, particularly those genre-transcending forms from the developing world and marginal cultures, is marketed under the nebulous label of 'world music', removing the specific historical, cultural and political resonance of cultural production. To take an example, Salif Keita's work, both with the Bamuko Rail Band and his subsequent output, retains only the vestiges of the complex aspects of the politics of its production in its avatar as yet another variation from the mainstream, in this case 'Mali music'. Dislocated from their historical specificities, through exoticization or scholarly neglect, they cease to have significance as politically relevant cultural forms.

In a similar fashion, the application of academically trendy analytical frames such as psychoanalysis or Deleuzian philosophy to engage with texts such as contemporary Iranian cinema risks taming the film's political significance in relation to the intricate nature of modern Iranian political culture, or of missing the point entirely.

The option open to those interested in rescuing the non-metropolitan from invisibility – those concerned with the plight of the Candidos of this world – is clearly what Cornell West (1990) suggests in relation to cultural workers seeking to address the experience of black and other minority communities in the USA as well as in developing societies:

A new kind of cultural worker is in the making, associated with a new politics of difference . . . Distinctive features of the new cultural politics of difference are to trash the monolithic and homogeneous in the name of diversity, multiplicity, and heterogeneity; to reject the abstract, general, and universal in the light of the concrete, specific, and particular; and to historicize, contextualize, and pluralize by highlighting the contingent, provisional, variable, tentative, shifting, and changing.

(West 1990, pp. 203–4)

This is not new, admittedly, yet 'what makes them novel – along with the cultural politics they produce – is how and what constitutes difference, the weight and gravity it is given in representation . . . To put it bluntly, the new cultural politics of difference consists of creative responses to the precise circumstances of our present moment' (p. 204). We explore in greater detail the cultural politics of difference in Chapter 2.

Wilson and Dissanayake's (1996) lament is pertinent in this context. In their introduction to a collection of essays on the *Global/Local*, they observe that,

this global/local synergy within what we will track as the transnational imaginary enlivens and molests the textures of everyday life and spaces of subjectivity and reshapes those contemporary structures of feeling some culture critics all too commonly banalize as 'postmodern' or hypertextually consecrate as 'postcolonial' resistance. *Too much of cultural studies, in this era of uneven globalization and the two-tier information highway, can sound like a way of making the world safe and user-friendly for global capital and the culture of the commodity form.*

(Wilson and Dissanayake 1996, p. 2, emphasis added)

In the dialogue on globalization voices from one side drown out others, promoting one point of view, one perspective, that is at once both the dominant voice and the voice of the dominant.

The global-local dialectic – a process of homogenization?

Central to the as yet unresolved debate on globalization is the question of the local. For instance, are local cultures, those that do not form part of the 'Western' or 'Americanized' or 'consumerist' culture, in a precarious condition because of the onslaught of global culture? It has been argued that the 'single space' often referred to in connection with theories of globalization

means not only interdependence, but also homogenisation, which is sometimes seen as a threat to the local and to tradition. Jameson has sought to characterise the phenomenon in terms of late capitalism and the transnationalisation of the consumer society and postmodernity [in *Postmodernism, or the Cultural Logic of Late Capitalism*]. Appadurai sees the intersections of the local and the global in relation to the disjunctures in the world economy, changing social, territorial and cultural reproduction of group identity [in *Modernity at Large*].

(Tam *et al.* 2002, p. x)

The notion of homogenization, however, suggests a hegemonic agenda, to which not all theorists subscribe. Tomlinson, for instance, is unconvinced by its thesis of a globally synchronized and standardized culture, promoting and benefiting from the global spread of consumerism. '[T]o assert cultural homogenisation as a consequence of globalization is to move from connectivity through proximity to the supposition of global uniformity and ubiquity . . . [T]his is a precipitate and in many ways an unjustifiable movement' (Tomlinson 1999, p. 6).

He is more forthright in a later essay, arguing against the claim that 'globalised culture is the installation, world-wide, of one particular culture born out of one particular, privileged historical experience'. Arguments that this is 'in short, simply the global extension of *Western* culture' (Tomlinson 2000, p. 23, emphasis in the original) are for him misplaced. His main objections concern the conceptualization of Western culture that such critiques are based on. Firstly, such assumptions ride on 'too broad a generalisation. Its rhetorical force is bought at the price of glossing over a multitude of complexities, exceptional cases, and contradictions . . . A second set of objections concerns the way in which Westernisation suggests a rather crude model of the one-way flow of cultural influence' (Tomlinson 2000, p. 24).

The criticisms raised by Tomlinson about the more simplistic aspects of the notion of Westernization or imperialism seem valid enough, although it must be said that his argument about the 'globalization as the decline of the West' seems far less convincing. Nevertheless, assertions about the destruction of local cultures have at times seemed unsophisticated and insufficiently cognisant of the complex processes involved in globalization and with the global–local dialectic, particularly when made in the context of a straightforward 'West versus the Rest' opposition. It is possible to agree with some theorists of globalization who underline the complexity of contemporary formations of global economy, politics and culture. One such is Featherstone (1996), in whose estimation it is inadequate to regard local cultures as succumbing to Western models of modernity, or to assume that their national formations are promoted on the basis of anti-Western sentiments.

> Rather the globalization process should be regarded as opening up the sense that now the world is a single place with increased, even unavoidable contact. We necessarily have greater dialogue between various nation-states, blocs, and civilizations. . . . Not that participating nation-states and other agents should be regarded as equal partners to the dialogue. Rather, they are bound together in increasing webs of interdependence and power balances. . . . What does seem clear is that it is not helpful to regard the global and local as dichotomies separated in space and time; rather, it would seem that the processes of globalization and localization are inextricably bound together in the current phase.
>
> (Featherstone 1996, p. 47)

Our concern here, however, is with how we should maintain our critique of contemporary global cultural and intellectual domination, without succumbing to the crude generalizations of Westernization identified by Tomlinson and Lazarus. Hall's (2000) intervention in this regard is pertinent. He acknowledges some of the characteristics of 'our friend globalization' identified by others, namely the intensification of old colonial attempts to establish a world market (Held 1999), complex social and economic reorganizations on a global scale prompted by new deregulated financial markets, currency flows and time–space compression (Harvey 1990), 'which struggles, however incompletely, to cohere particular times, places, histories and markets within a homogeneous, "global" space–time chronotype' (Hall 2000, p. 214).

Despite these developments that have significantly altered global relations, however, Hall convincingly underlines an important contradiction in the process:

> The system is global, in the sense that its sphere of operations is planetary. Few places are beyond the reach of its destabilizing inter-dependencies. It has significantly weakened national sovereignty and eroded the 'reach' of the older western nation-states without entirely displacing them. The system however, is *not* global, if by that we understand that the process is uniform in character, impacts everywhere in the same way, operates without contradictory effects or produces equal outcomes across the globe. It remains a system of deep, and deepening global inequalities and instabilities.
>
> (Hall 2000, pp. 214–15, emphasis in the original)

Hall makes a crucial point here, in effect claiming, firstly, that the process of globalization contains a contradictory logic because certain effects such as the growing inter-dependencies and the weakening of state power are common across all societies and nations, yet significantly, this process is uneven. Secondly, the unevenness of the impact of globalization contributes to, even creates, 'deep, and deepening global inequalities', in other words, it both intensifies earlier patterns of inequality while engendering new ones.

Hall's observations on the debate on globalization as a process of homogenization in the economic and cultural spheres is even more germane to our purposes. 'Like the post-colonial, contemporary globalization is both novel and contradictory,' Hall claims. 'Its economic, financial and cultural circuits are western-driven and US-dominated. Ideologically, it is governed by a global neo-liberalism which is fast becoming the common sense of the age. Its dominant cultural tendency is homogenisation.' The process of homogenization engendered by the spread of neo-liberal ideas, however, does not in itself adequately explain contemporary global developments. The complexity intrinsic to these developments is precipitated by the *differences* evident within them:

> [Globalization] has also had extensive *differentiating* effects within and between different societies. From this perspective, globalization is not a natural and inevitable process. . . . Rather, it is a hegemonizing process, in the proper Gramscian sense. It is 'structured in dominance', but it cannot control or saturate everything

within its orbit. Indeed, it produces as one of its unintended effects subaltern formations and emergent tendencies which it cannot control but must try to 'hegemonize' or harness to its wider purposes. It is a system for *con-forming difference*, rather than a convenient synonym for the obliteration of difference.

(Hall 2000, p. 215, emphasis in the original)

As Hall points out, 'this argument is critical if we are to take account of how and where resistances and counter-strategies are likely successfully to develop. This perspective entails a more discursive model of power in the new global environment than is common among the "hyper-globalizers" ' (p. 215).

Here we have a crucial intervention which makes a major contribution to the rethinking of relations between the global and the local without addressing them from the critically unproductive West–Rest dichotomy. Hall is clear about the emergence of neo-liberalism as the underlying ideology that contributes to homogenization in terms of culture, global markets, economic policies, labour relations, and so on. Conceiving of this in Gramscian terms, however, permits the existence of oppositional voices. In other words, although the process is 'structured in dominance', it allows for 'differentiating effects', even opposition, such as the anti-WTO protests in Seattle. Hall's invocation of Gramsci's notion of hegemony is significant in two important respects: it explains the reasons for the homogenization to not be complete, it generates pockets of resistance in the margins which need to be constantly negotiated, and, by emphasizing the discursive nature of power, emphasizes the role of culture – both global and local – in this struggle for hegemony.

It is in this context that the recent emergence of social movements have to be seen – movements in both metropolitan and non-metropolitan communites that challenge dominance. Dirlik (1996) identifies as exemplars of resistance the Chipko movement in India that challenged deforestation, women workers of the *maquiladora* industries of the US-Mexican border, and various indigenous movements which together 'have emerged as the primary (if not the only) expressions of resistance to domination. . . . [L]ocal movements have emerged as a pervasive phenomenon of the contemporary world' (p. 22). The Indian environmental campaign known as the Chipko movement, which began in the 1970s, organized tribal women against deforestation and highlighted the plight of indigenous communities with the political empowerment of women in such communities. This, along with its more recent form of protest against the building of a series of dams on the river Narmada, is an example of a 'local' community-based social movement that coalesces two normally distinct areas of theoretical and political intervention: feminism and environmental activism. As I have argued elsewhere (Harindranath 2000), this effectively undermines the apparent universality of the theoretical boundaries guarded by conceptual formulations which, as a consequence, need to be revised.

To Dirlik, the 'local' is 'a site both of promise and predicament', offering the opportunity and the location for anti-global-capitalist resistance, for challenging the local manifestations of neo-liberal ideology. He distinguishes between a 'critical localism' from

> localism as an ideological articulation of capitalism in its current phase. . . . In its promise of liberation, localism may also serve to disguise oppression and paro-chialism. It is indeed ironic that the local should emerge as a site of promise at a historical moment when localism of the most conventional kind has re-emerged as the source of genocidal conflict around the world.
>
> (Dirlik 1996, pp. 22–3)

Thus, even while it contains the promise of offering resistance and liberation, intrinsic to the local that is complicit with global capitalism is the potential for suppression and conflict. That is its predicament. Ironically, conflicts based on ethnic or religious grounds reify the idea of difference – the 'localism of the conventional kind'.

In ideological terms, modernity and the various projects of modernization such as development have been instrumental in the suppression of the local. What Dirlik terms 'modernist teleology' informed and continue to support development projects, whereby the local, by definition, is considered backward – a site of rural passivity opposed to the dynamic logic of industrialism and urban culture, inhabited by communities in thrall to unscientific beliefs and outmoded customs. The local, in other words, was seen as an obstacle to be overcome in the name of progress. For Dirlik, important intellectual challenges from postmodernism and post-structuralism have played a crucial role in the rejection of modernity's ideological narratives. He locates in the repudiation of modernity's meta-narratives, and the attendant re-examination of the discourses of development as coercion than as teleology, two significant consequences:

> First, it *rescues from invisibility* those who were earlier viewed as castaways from history, whose social and cultural forms of existence appear in the narrative of modernization at best as irrelevancies, at worst as minor obstacles to be extin-guished on the way to development. Having refused to die a natural death . . . they demand now not just restoration of their history, further splintering the already cracked façade of modernity. The demand is almost inevitably accompanied by a reassertion of the local against the universalistic claims of modernism. . . . Secondly [the repudiation] has allowed *greater visibility to 'local narratives'*. . . . The history of modernization appears now as a temporal succession of spatially dispersed local encounters, to which the local objects of progress made their own contributions through resistance or complicity. . . . Also questioned in this view are the claims of nationalism which, a product of modernization, has sought to homogenize the societies it has claimed for itself.
>
> (Dirlik 1996, p. 25, emphasis added)

The challenge to universalist narratives is part of the promise of the local, as it promotes the consciousness of local history and difference and the locations for the emergence of alternative narratives and social movements. The local then becomes the source of resistance and liberation, and of the rejuvenation of discarded histories. On the other hand, the local also suggests fragmentation which, when combined with narratives of ethnic or religious difference, generates separatist impulses and conflicts. Moreover, the local retains earlier forms of exploitation and hierarchization, now further complicated by becoming the site of contemporary global operations of capital. It is an unavoidable fact, therefore, that the proper investigation of the local involves the study of the operations of capital. Take for example the increasing popularity of documentaries (such as *The Take* (2004) which depicts the consequences of Argentina's spectacular economic collapse in 2001, or *Darwin's Nightmare* (2004), an intriguing documentary on the effects of globalisation in Tanzania). These are now shown in cinemas in major metropolitan areas. A similar increase is seen in the audience appreciation of non-metropolitan films such as *Amores Perros, Rabbit Proof Fence* and *The Weeping Camel*, which explore material realities and indigenous histories in Mexico, Australia and Mongolia.

While such films may be taken as either challenging dominant narratives or as engaging with non-metropolitan localities and make visible the 'castaways from history', they, nevertheless, have to work within the capitalist system of production and distribution. Further, as Dirlik argues, 'global capitalism represents a further deterritorialization, abstraction and concentration of capital. In a fundamental sense, global capitalism represents an unprecedented penetration of local society globally by the economy and culture of capital.' A consequences of this is that 'the local understood in a "traditional" sense may be less evident than ever. It is ironic then that capital itself should justify its operations increasingly in the language of the local. The irony allows us to see the local in all its contradictoriness' (Dirlik 1996, p. 28).

The politics of cultural production

The proliferation of local cultural formations, even if penetrated by global capital, offers the opportunity for the expression of difference. As Featherstone observes,

> Rather than the emergence of a unified global culture there is a strong tendency for the process of globalization to provide a stage for global differences not only to open up a 'world showcase of cultures' in which the examples of the distant exotic are brought directly into the home, but to provide a field for a more discordant clashing of cultures. While cultural integration processes are taking place on a global level the situation is becoming increasingly pluralistic.
>
> (Featherstone 1995, p. 13)

One trend in local cultural production is in the form of an intervention on the global, particularly where the global is equated with Westernization. Interestingly, in the arena of local cultural production as a response to the perceived threat of Westernization, two apparently contradictory moves happen, which illustrate the creative tension between the global and the local. This is demonstrated, for example, in the forms of cultural nationalism that have recently emerged in India and China. While these have assumed diverse shapes and ideologies in different localities, the characteristic that they share is that this cultural protectionism happens almost simultaneously with economic liberalization. They, therefore, illustrate Dirlik's observation about the contradictoriness of the local.

For instance, as Fernandes (2000) demonstrates, advertisements selling consumer goods on Indian television straddle this dichotomy – while the advertised products are often made abroad and are internationally known brands, the narrative and the *mis-en-scène* of the advertisement texts refer to local Hindu iconography. Fernandes makes a convincing link between these texts and the rise of right-wing Hindu politics in India.

In the case of China the tension between the local and the global has been manifested in a different way, as a tension between the 'traditional' and the 'modern', leading to a creative chaos, as summarized in Yue Daiyun (1998):

> one side advocated the rethinking of the traditional culture, a restoration of traditional values and attitudes; the other side urged the importation of Western theories and discourses. The rapid transition from tradition to innovation and from Western ideas to Chinese ideas led a dazzling chaos.
>
> (1998, p. 33)

Another response has been a reassertion of local values, riding either on claims of religious exceptionalism, as in the case of protests in New Delhi against the portrayal of a lesbian relationship in the film *Fire*, or as Tam *et al.* (2002) argue, on the basis of recovery of Confucian as part of what has come to be known as 'Asian values':

> [In China] Along with the economic development and the desire to affiliate with the global capitalist system there is the resurgence of a form of cultural nationalism. Hence the local and the global meet in a culturally specific and historically contingent way in contemporary China. The recent revival of interest in Confucianism in China, as well as other parts of East Asia, is indicative of this interaction between the local and the global, as well as on a larger scale of the Asian cultural reassertion.
>
> (Tam *et al.* 2000, p. xiv)

However, the local is not merely a site of particularistic politics or a counterdiscourse to the totalizing logic of the global. Their interaction assumes other shapes too, where the globally dominant discourses inform local cultural practices, complex artistic and intellectual negotiations that require sustained study:

> the complex, multiple and ambiguous relationships of cultural production to cultures that they inhabit demand a multi-faceted inquiry. . . . In East Asia, the interplay between the local and the global has a dimension not only of cultural

reshaping, but also of cultural disorientation. While traditional indigenous culture can be understood as a continuous historical process, contemporary culture is conceived as a phenomenon of transnational formation resulting from the forces of global stratification. In China this is particularly the case. Not only can one find Coca-Cola and McDonald's in almost every city in China, but also the visage of postmodernism in popular music, architecture, literature and theatre performance.

(Tam et al. 2002, p. xiii)

The complex mix of particularistic politics, reassertion of traditions, negotiations with global practices and forms, together constitute the promise and the predicament of the local. The resulting cultural formations may at once, and the same time, address both the local and the transnational. What Benzi Zhang (2002) refers to as cultural diaspora, that is, the presence of Third-World cultural products in 'the global market place previously occupied by the West' (p. 36), demands an inquiry that takes into account local politics, local histories and local social formations, all in the context of the global.

> The ruthless globalisation and sustained local resistance suggests a relationship of opposition; however, beyond the historical opposition, there are other possible relationships between the global and the local. The two processes – the globalisation of the local and the localisation of the global – are both antithetical and convoluted in ever changing configurations.

(Benzi Zhang 2002, p. 36)

To end where we began, the study of global cultures, their local formations and their co-implication with or resistance to the global, needs to acknowledge existing patterns of inequality. It is a question of contextualization, and the context can be summarized, very broadly, in two ways. Firstly, as Hall (2000) points out in relation to the issue of the postcolonial, the term 'post-colonial'

> does *not* signal a simple before/after chronological succession. The movement from colonization to post-colonial times does *not* imply that the problems of colonialism have been resolved, or replaced by some conflict-free era. Rather, the 'post-colonial' marks the passage from one historical power-configuration or conjuncture to another. . . . Problems of dependency, underdevelopment and marginalisation, typical of the 'high' colonial period, persist into the post-colonial. However, these relations are *resumed* in a new configuration.

(Hall 2000, p. 213, emphasis in the original)

Whereas in the earlier configuration relations of power were articulated in terms of the colonizer and the colonized, '[n]ow they are restaged and displaced as struggles between indigenous social forces, as internal contradictions and sources of destablization *within* the decolonised society, or between them and the wider global system' (*ibid.*). The direct rule of the colonial period, in which power was exercised directly through government institutions, has been

> by an asymmetric globalized system of power which is post-national, trans-national and neo-imperial in character. Its main features are structural inequality, within a deregulated free-trade and free capital-flow system dominated by the First World, and programmes of structural adjustment, in which western interests and models of government are paramount.
>
> (Hall 2000, p. 213)

The validity or otherwise of local political struggles, including nationalism, as well as the cultural forms these assume, as in the case of expressions of cultural or ethnic difference, indigenous forms of representation and so on, is contested and negotiated in the terrain that accommodates this structural inequality. Secondly, contemporary forms of global capitalist production, distribution and consumption acknowledge and celebrate difference. Difference, therefore, has itself become in some respects, a commodity or a marketing logic, be it local configurations of the global, such as the global chain McDonald's selling locally appropriate products, or an overt celebration of ethnic or racial 'difference', as exemplified in some of the Benetton advertisements.

> In the process of globalisation, the slogan 'Think globally, act locally' has become the motto of many transnational corporations in their business operations; such a mind-set has also generated a new cultural phenomenon, in the sense that the global is concretised in the local. . . . [T]his is the moment in history when the local and the global are co-implicated in complex and unanticipated ways.
>
> (Tam *et al.* 2002, pp. x–xi)

The stir caused among both academic and the wider community by the publication of Michael Hardt and Antonio Negri's *Empire* (2000) is indicative of the enduring popularity among interested readers of attempts to erect a theoretical edifice that captures the essential aspects of the contested and annoyingly unfixable process of globalization. The book, perhaps understandably, has inspired both adulation and coruscating critique. Timothy Brennan (2003) begins his review with a rhetorical question that chimes with the concerns of this present book: 'what is the predicament of cultural theory today?' He answers by claiming that 'theory has become a code word for relatively predictable positions in the humanities and social sciences, most of which turn on the *ideas* of social transformation, historical agency, the disposition of state-hood (however understood), and the heterogeneity of cultures' (p. 337). Brennan is, however, deeply sceptical of the revolutionary claims of theorists, since their 'ideas have become routine in their very disruptiveness (or the other way around)' (*ibid.*).

This chapter began by positing the concern that a majority of theorizations of the globalization process fall short of acknowledging or taking into account with sufficient seriousness developments on its 'underside'. A consequence of this, it was argued, is the neglect not only of the impact of aspects of globalization on less privileged communities, but also of the political and social struggles within non-Western communities, their histories and alternative voices. Apart from significant exceptions such as Sivanandan (1990b), Wallerstein (1991), and Ahmad (1992) whose critiques of conceptual orthodoxies have been acknowledged in the literature, most theoretical explanations of globalization and cultural homogeneity and difference are guilty of what Brennan asserts is the problem with *Empire*:

> the authors barely nod in the direction of guest-worker systems, uncapitalized agriculture, and the archipelago of maquiladoras at the heart of globalization's gulag. Apart from a handful of passages where they are fleetingly adduced, the colonized *of today* are given little place in the book's sprawling thesis.
>
> (Brennan 2003, p. 338, emphasis in the original)

Further reading

Appadurai, A. (1996) *Modernity at Large: Cultural Dimensions of Globalization*. Minneapolis: University of Minnesota Press.

Skelton, T. and Allen, T. (eds) (1999) *Culture and Global Change*. London: Routledge.

Tam, K. *et al.* (ed.) (2002) *Sights of Contestation: Localism, Globalism, and Cultural Production in Asia and the Pacific*. Hong Kong: The Chinese University Press.

Wilson, R. and Dissanayake, W. (eds) (1996) *Global/Local*. Durham: Duke University Press.

2 | THE CULTURAL POLITICS OF DIFFERENCE

Notions of cultural difference permeate much political practice, be it on behalf of nationalism, state sovereignty, multiculturalism, or the formulation of human rights. Events occur from time to time, which challenge the liberal perception and conception of cultural diversity as pluralistic cohabitation in a 'global ecumene' or a multicultural nation. These events both exemplify the precariousness and significance of cultural politics as well as contribute to the reification of difference that resurrects the divisions between a professed 'us' and an ostensible 'them' drawn along the lines of cultural uniqueness and difference.

The attacks on the icons of American economic and political power on 11 September 2001 are an obvious example, based as they were on a perceived 'enemy', drawing on incommensurable moral imaginaries. The latter engender the politics of 'you are with us or with the terrorists' dichotomy on the one hand, and on the other a projection of an 'evil West' as Islam's 'Other', used to justify the unjustifiable acts of terror. Both sets of cleavages operate to amplify public discourse on the horrific event. As Montgomery (2005) suggests, unlike earlier terrorist attacks that had been referred to as acts of criminality or 'mass murder', in this instance news discourse coalesced to report the event as 'an act of war'.

The 9/11 attacks are considered by some commentators (Roger Scruton, *West and the Rest*) as a watershed event, marking the transition into a new form of global governance predicated upon a deep cleavage of cultural difference between those regions of the globe that enjoy the alleged 'freedoms' of democracy and those that persist under the yoke of premodern values inspired by religious fanaticism. Concurrently, a similar essentialism underlies the self-proclaimed global Islamic community that is seen to subsume linguistically, ethnically and nationally divided groups and is presented as being united against perceived injuries inflicted by a unitary 'West'. These discursive projections of 'enemies' to 'freedom and democracy' or the 'Islamic community' have both, in effect, constructed mutually incomprehensible configurations so implacable that they render a dialogue between the two impossible.

A more recent, and perhaps more subtle, illustration of that kind of cultural politics was witnessed in Australia in May 2005, when an Indonesian court found Schapelle Corby, an Australian citizen, guilty of smuggling drugs into Bali and sentenced her to 20 years in prison. The public outcry in Australia that followed the ruling, and which was reported in the media, invoked the notion of 'difference' in terms of the Indonesian justice system, represented as somehow lacking in comparison to the Australian legal system. Noticeable in the subsequent fall-out was a racially informed invocation of cultural difference, most often wearing the thin veneer of politically correct recognition and acknowledgement of national difference (what Stuart Hall has referred to in another context as 'inferential racism'). At times this spilled over into more overt stances in which Corby – a white Australian – was described as 'one of our own', and thus synecdochically representing Australia and 'Australian values' against an allegedly corrupt and backward Indonesian populace.

A relatively extreme response was the package containing a 'biological agent' sent to the Indonesian embassy in Canberra. As reported in *The Australian*, 'an envelope containing a biological agent has been sent to the Indonesian embassy in Canberra in an apparent reprisal for Schapelle Corby's jailing in Bali' (1 June 2005). Australia's Foreign Minister's warning that such sentiments were counterproductive:

> to continually attack Indonesia and denigrate its institutions and leaders will build up a good deal of anti-Australian sentiment in Indonesia and it will make it very difficult to conclude (prisoner transfer) agreements of this kind, particularly through public institutions like the Indonesian parliament.
>
> (*The Australian*, 1 June 2005)

This is itself indicative of a pragmatic rather than a principled stance against anti-Indonesian attitudes. Another revealing public response was in the form of attempts from sections of the Australian population to withdraw previously pledged support to the Indonesian victims of the Christmas 2004 tsunami as an apparently justifiable response to the Corby judgement.

Entrenched in this discourse is a challenge that questions the ethical and professional validity and legitimacy of the Indonesian justice system while simultaneously representing the Australian-British system as normative. Both individually, in the case of Corby as a white Australian, and collectively, in terms of a perceived lack in Indonesia, this case embodies the politics of cultural difference that animates several contemporary discussions revolving around identity politics, multiculturalism and nationalist discourse. Intrinsic to this is the enduring dichotomy of the West and the Rest, which involves a process of symbolic othering. As San Juan puts it,

> one cannot theorize on the vicissitudes of the 'culture wars' in the United States (or in Europe) without being implicated in their geopolitical resonance, in that

paradoxically normalized excess called the 'Third World' that threatens market stability but makes cultural sublimations ('Western democracy', signifying 'free' elections, 'free' speech, etc., is still referenced as a norm to be emulated) possible.

(San Juan 1998, p. 55)

At least two vectors of the politics of 'othering' converge in this particular instance: one of those is the racialization of the case, whereby the vocal support mobilized around Corby as a *white* Australian and consequently 'one of us'. The other enlists national difference to oppose Australia to Indonesia, in which Corby as an *Australian* provokes a spirited defence against perceived extremes and flaws of the Indonesian judges. In her essay exploring the merits of cosmopolitanism in relation to the dangers of patriotism, Martha Nussbaum asks, in response to Richard Rorty's appeals to shared values in the USA, whether he seems

to argue effectively when [he] insists on the centrality to democratic deliberation of certain values that bind all citizens together. But why should these values, which instruct us to join hands across boundaries of ethnicity, class, gender, and race, lose steam when they get to the borders of the nation? By conceding that a morally arbitrary boundary such as the boundary of the nation has a deep and formative role in our deliberations, we seem to deprive ourselves of any principled way of persuading citizens they should in fact join hands across these other barriers.

(Nussbaum 1996, p. 14)

To take another example: in a grizzly extension of the Rushdie affair of the 1980s Theo Van Gogh, a Dutch film-maker, was murdered in 2004 by a member of the Muslim community in Holland for the alleged crime of blasphemy. Despite, or perhaps because of, the extreme nature of this event, it encapsulates a few of the main conceptual and political issues that are explored in this chapter. Discussions in Chapter 1 demonstrated the pertinence of the concept of 'difference' both at global and at local levels. Animating notions of cultural and/or ethnic difference is culture conceived, conceptualized and expressed in diverse ways. Central to this is both the form and the content of representation. The politics inherent in representation addresses not only content but also seeks to transgress and transform the form of representation, which is frequently incorporated into the mainstream as the logic of the market incessantly recuperates diverse modes of address into its commercial domain. As the discussion in the following chapters demonstrate, cultural production from the margins – be it in the context of multiculturalism, nationalism, or indigenous identity – involves a constant balancing act between the wide appeal of commercial forms on the one hand, and the search for innovative forms that enable the delineation of the complex realities of marginal experience and life on the other.

On the global level, academic publications from different political standpoints such as *Jihad vs. the McWorld, The Clash of Fundamentalisms*, or *The Clash of Civilizations*, together with the political rhetoric that has become prevalent more recently as in, for example, President Bush's infamous 'you are either with us or against us' cleave the world community of nations, peoples, cultures into two. Our critical engagement with the canon of literature on globalization has to consider such developments and the manner in which such intellectual and political moves inform policies and practices involving for instance, immigration, passport control and the treatment of refugees. In the current post 9/11 political climate, this question is fraught with difficulty, punctuated at one end by religious and ethnic fundamentalists whose extreme notions of 'difference' at times lead to extreme acts of violence, as in the murder of Van Gogh. At the other end of the spectrum are those for whom ethnic difference and any proclamation of it are threats to the unity of the nation-state.

As an example of the argument that the active promotion of multiculturalism risks 'balkanizing' the nation, Giroux (1994) refers to Patrick Buchanan's professed fear that cultural democracy is inimical to national unity and the 'American way of life':

> According to Buchanan, calls for expanding the existing limits of political representation and self-determination are fine as long as they allow [white] Americans to 'take back' their country. In this conservative discourse, difference becomes a signifier for racial exclusivity, segregation, or, in Buchanan's language 'self-determination'. For Buchanan, public life in the United States has deteriorated since 1965 because 'a flood tide of immigration has rolled in from the Third World, legal and illegal, as our institutions of assimilation . . . disintegrated'.
>
> (Giroux 1994, p. 33)

The murder in Holland also exemplifies, once again in an extreme fashion, the politics of cultural uniqueness (in this instance conceived along the spurious lines of religious morality), their significance as well as the moral discourses that underpin and are mobilized by them – the battles being fought in the name of cultural representation, embroiled with other issues such as authenticity, voice, propriety and agency, are real and have real consequences. Conceptions of 'difference', inspired by religious extremism or *realpolitik* and drawn along the lines of ethnic, racial or allegedly 'cultural' uniqueness, imbue the politics that separates the 'us' from the 'them', and at times spill over into violence. This is the case not only in the West or the metropole, as demonstrated by the fury of the protests against the film *Fire* in the streets of New Delhi. On that occasion it was the Hindu fundamentalists who protested in the name of the putative 'purity' of Indian and Hindu culture. As we have seen, this is complemented by the suspicion of expressions of difference, and the clampdown of cultural-political expression in the name of national unity and security. Within the national context, it is often the case that dominant, mainstream representations position minorities in certain ways. Challenges to these have had to negotiate a path that stays clear of fundamentalist or 'essentialist' proclamations of uniqueness while at the same time seeking to depict those aspects of experience that are consistently ignored or passed over by dominant forms of representation. The question of difference, therefore, has political, intellectual and symbolic dimensions.

Culture wars

In one of their recent books Hardt and Negri (2004) describe the different responses of two Italian travellers to India: Alberto Moravia, the writer, underlined the differences between Europeans and Indians, concluding that 'the difference of India is ineffable' (p. 127); 'the other writer, Pier Paolo Pasolini, tries to explain how similar India is' (*ibid.*).

> It makes you wonder if the travel companions even saw the same country. In fact, although polar opposites, their two responses fit together perfectly as a fable of the two faces of Eurocentrism: 'They are utterly different from us' or 'they are just the same as us.' The truth, you might say, lies somewhere between the two – they are somewhat like us and also a little different – but really that compromise only clouds the problem. Neither of the two Italian writers can escape the need to use European identity as a universal standard, the measure of sameness and difference.
>
> (p. 128)

Hardt and Negri's argument is pertinent to our discussion as the main issue here is with regard to the question, 'sameness and difference in relation to what?'. 'Euro-centrism' as a critical concept has in recent years come to provide a valuable stance against the excessive normative force of epistemologies and ethical values seen as being specifically European or Euro-American in origin, and bear its imprint, thereby casting alternatives as outside the norm. The location of the colonialist impulse behind the production of knowledge in support of the exercise of imperial power, as in the case of 'Orientalism' (Said 1978) has generated a productive space from which to critique certain kinds of academic and political discourse, and of cultural and material marginalization. This critical position has been mobilized by academic fields of enquiry such as postcolonial studies and cultural studies. It is pertinent to our current concerns in broadly two ways: firstly, it underlines our concerns, outlined in Chapter 1, of the particularistic nature of the totalizing narratives contained in much of the literature on globalization. As we saw, the academic discourse on globalization, the doxa, is restricted to the addressing of selective aspects of the process and the simultaneous neglect of its 'underside'. Further, and even more significantly, since it provides the main impetus to the arguments in the book, addressing this sanctioned ignorance involves locating and focusing on alternative cultural and political practice, be it in the form of perilous nationalism, minority aesthetic, or indigenous challenges.

The 'culture wars' that Giroux (1994) and San Juan (1998, 2002) are concerned with originate in the challenges to such Eurocentric notions of universalism. These challenges punctuate the politics of cultural difference. Cultural production in and from the margins, as expressions of alternative histories and life stories, pregnant with issues of exploitation and neglect, challenge dominant narratives in several ways. 'Dominant cultural traditions once self-confidently secure in the modernist discourse of progress, universalism, and objectivism are now interrogated as ideological beachheads used to police and contain subordinate groups, oppositional discourses, and dissenting social movements' (Giroux 1994, pp. 29–30). Issues including the politics of nationalist discourse, indigenous land and cultural rights, cultural difference and multiculturalism, criss-cross and intersect in complex ways at both the global and the national levels.

> Struggles over the academic canon, the conflict over multiculturalism, and the battle for either extending or containing the rights of new social groups dominate the current political and ideological landscape. . . . Underlying the proliferation of these diverse and various battles is a deeper conflict over the relationship between democracy and culture on the one hand, and identity and the politics of representation on the other.
>
> *(ibid.)*

The intellectual, ideological and cultural assaults on the Eurocentric academic canon are central to this debate, couched in terms of identity, culture and democracy. These challenges have, according to Giroux, led to a reconstitution of cultural politics that focuses on issues of representation, examining the hegemonic functions of discourses, but also various social formations, including race, and 'institutional conditions which regulate different fields of culture' (Bennett 1992, p. 25).

The political dimensions of this struggle over representational practices and cultural politics in the conception of the 'contemporary politics of citizenship' formulated by Hall and Held, as they see it, must address

> questions of membership posed by feminism, the black and ethnic movements, ecology and vulnerable minorities like children. But it must also come to terms with the problems posed by 'difference' in a deeper sense: for example, the diverse communities to which we belong, the complex interplay of identity and identification in modern society, and the differentiated ways in which people now participate in social life.
>
> (Hall and Held 1990, p. 176)

For Giroux, such a politics is crucial as it illuminates the struggles over the question of difference, identity and culture that are central to citizenship in a democratic society. This 'political side of culture' is made even more relevant by the conservative politics advanced by the New Right in the USA during the Reagan-Bush era that inaugurated a

> cultural blitz . . . that has continuously chipped away at the legal, institutional, and ideological spheres necessary to the existence of a democratic society. . . . The New Right has focused on postmodernist, feminist, postcolonialist and other minority discourses that have raised serious questions regarding how particular forms of authority are secured through the organization of the curriculum at all levels of schooling.
>
> (p. 32)

In the conservative discourse of the New Right, the politics of racial and cultural difference is represented in authoritarian populist discourse as a threat to the nation, as a marker for racial exclusivity. The complex ramifications of this politics of cultural difference and representation are illustrated in the ethically and conceptually precarious nature of nationalist politics. For instance, the rise of religious fundamentalist politics in various parts of the postcolonial world and the active participation of women in these developments have posed tricky questions for cultural studies scholars and for feminists. As Ania Loomba notes in the context of the rise of right-wing Hindu politics in India,

> it has surfaced as a major factor in women's relationship to 'the nation' and to postcolonial politics. . . . The crucial point here is that often women themselves are key players in the fundamentalist game: in India women like Sadhvi Rithambara and Uma Bharati have stridently mobilised for Hindu nationalism by invoking fears of Muslim violence. In other words, women are objects as well as subjects of fundamentalist discourse.
>
> (Loomba 1998, pp. 226–7)

On the other hand, however, contestations of existing relations of power include the promotion of alternative visions and other voices. As Stam (1999) argues in connection with debates on multiculturalism in the USA,

> Neoconservatives accuse multiculturalists of Balkanizing the nation, of emphasising what divides people rather than what brings them together. That the inequitable distribution of power itself generates violence and divisiveness goes unacknowledged; that multiculturalism offers a more egalitarian vision of social relations is ignored. A radical multiculturalism calls for a profound restructuring and reconceptualization of the power relations between cultural communities. Refusing ghettoising discourse, it links minoritarian communities, challenging the hierarchy that makes some communities 'minor' and others 'major' and 'normative'.
>
> (Stam, p. 101)

Challenging the attempts to delimit representations of alternatives either through silencing other voices or the foreclosure of debates on the spurious grounds of, for instance, national unity consequently requires two complementary moves: questioning what is presented as the 'norm', while steering clear of the excesses of particularist positioning that so easily follows on into essentialism or fundamentalism. San Juan sees these 'culture wars' in Gramscian terms, as a combination of 'a war of manoeuvre' and a 'war of position' in the struggle for hegemonic power:

> culture wars are emblematic: they signify engagements with the ideological-moral positions that at some point will generate qualitative changes in the terms of engagement and thus alter the balance of power in favor of one social bloc against

another. In modern industrial formations, the struggle is not just to occupy the
city hall, as it were, but also . . . tranform the relations of power, their bases and
modality, on both material and symbolic levels.

(San Juan 2002, p. 167)

While his use of Gramsci highlights the significance of challenging the hegemonic
relations of power, his emphasis on both symbolic and material transformation, that is,
changes to the socio-cultural as well as economic aspects of minority or marginalized
experience underlines the importance of achieving transformation at both levels. The
discursive dimensions of the ideological-moral positions indicative of the global
(im)balance of power have become profoundly marked, particularly in the aftermath
of 9/11. As the subsequent war in Iraq, the terrorist attacks in Spain and elsewhere, and
political repression in places like Chechnya have demonstrated, the mediation of the
discourse on the 'war on terror' and the 'spread of democracy and freedom' has gone
hand in hand with material or 'real' aspects on complex and diverse ways.

Two aspects of the politics of representation immanent in potential and real
challenges to dominant discourses concern us here: firstly, the apparent Eurocentrism
inherent in 'universalist' discourse such as 'democracy' and 'human rights', and
secondly, the racial dimensions of the politics of cultural difference. Benhabib (2002)
begins her exploration of the former by asking 'is universalism Eurocentric?' (Benhabib
2002, chapter 2). Fundamental to the question, for her, is the presupposition that we
know who the 'West and its others' are, which risks homogenizing cultures and civilizations: 'the answer in recent debates on cognitive and moral relativism has turned on a
holistic view of cultures and societies as internally coherent, seamless wholes' (2002,
p. 25). Her complaint is that 'this view has prevented us from seeing the complexity of
global civilizational dialogues and encounters, which are increasingly our lot, and it
has encouraged the binaries of "we" and "the other(s)" ' (*ibid.*).

In the place of what she considers the unproductive explorations of the alleged
tension between relativism (which privileges the local and the particular) and universalism, which promote theses of incommensurability and untranslatability, Benhabib
pleads the case for a dialogue between cultures that are considered not as complete and
coherent wholes, but as unstable, hybrid and 'polyvocal'. 'Politically, the right to cultural expression needs to be grounded upon, rather than considered an alternative to,
universally recognised citizenship rights' (p. 26). Benhabib's vision includes a participatory democracy involving a *dialogic relationship* between different perspectives
inspired by diverse cultural formations and value systems. In the place of an
unproductive dichotomy opposing an unexamined universalism to relativist particularism, her recommendation for addressing the problem of equality is a conversation
among cultural communities with equal powers of enunciation.

In a similar vein, in her response to Nussbaum's (1996) plea for the transcendence of
the parochialism of patriotic fervour into a cosmopolitan universal citizenship, Butler
(1996) presents her case for the continuing validity of universalism, a concept that

requires constant examination and revision, involving continuing vigilance against the privileging of parochial perspectives. We should take cognizance of '[t]he contingent and cultural character of the existing conventions governing the scope of universality [which however] does not deny the usefulness of or importance of the term' (Butler 1996, p. 46). The disparity inherent in existing conventions of universalism, which favour certain groups and specific value systems over others (as for example, 'Euro-centrism'), has been studied and critiqued, for instance in works such as Etienne Balibar (1994), which locates the racist notions intrinsic to ideas of universality. Nevertheless, Butler argues that certain kinds of speech (representations)

> constitute valuable contestations crucial to the continuing elaboration of the uni-versal itself, and which it would be a mistake to foreclose. An example . . . would be a situation in which subjects who have been excluded from enfranchisement by existing conventions (including racist conventions) governing the exclusionary def-inition of the universal seize the language of enfranchisement and set into motion a 'performative contradiction': claiming to be covered by that universal, they thereby expose the contradictory character of previous conventional formulations of the universal.
>
> (Butler 1996, pp. 47–8)

Such a process of enunciation is to Butler crucial in exposing the limitations of current formulations of universality, and for their subsequent revisions and expansions to accommodate these alternatives. The idea of 'performative contradiction' presumes a platform for alternative speech or representation (what Butler refers to as 'cultural translation') that challenges existing norms of universality, thereby enabling their modification. As Butler suggests, this requires us to 'find ways to effect cultural transla-tions between those various cultural examples in order to see which versions of the universal are proposed, on what exclusions they are based, and how the entry of the excluded into the domain of the universal requires a radical transformation in our thinking of universality' (Butler 1996, p. 51).

Such challenges arising from different groups – they could, for instance, be from groups promoting women, or gay rights, or representing the neglected and marginalized experiences of minority ethnic/racial groups – are not meant to be merely acco-mmodated into existing norms of universalism. Crucially, this performative contradic-tion aims to challenge and transform the consensus on which those norms are based. In some important ways, therefore, Butler's recommendations are not so far removed from the premise of intellectual efforts in which this book plays a small part – that the existing conceptualizations of globalization as a process, while they profess to describe it in universal (or 'global') terms, nevertheless exclude significant elements of the experience and consequence of this process including the material, the social and the cultural. Here too, the challenge is not merely to suggest alternatives or underscore the effects of globalization on the non-elite, but by doing so to begin the transformation of our understanding of the process.

In his book on African cinema, Olivier Barlet (2000) answers his own question, 'why should we especially think of African cinema cultures in terms of their unrelenting quest of origins? They throw light on our own search for identity, in a world in which barbarism is becoming entrenched' (Barlet 2000, p. 288). The African tradition of cinema is able to achieve this by exploring the confluence of tradition and the influence of cultural forces from the outside, expressing the complexity of the resulting social forces that Africans contend with. 'Rooted as they are in the questioning of social norms and behaviour, the cinema cultures of Black Africa helps us to come to terms with that uncertainty [we feel about our identity] by challenging our identity-based, nationalist assertions, so that we avoid falling, ultimately, into fundamentalism and stupidity' (p. 289).

This view not only emphasizes the value of alternative storytelling which covers 'other' lives, value systems and social formulations, but interestingly and significantly overturns normal perceptions of Africa as the continent of internecine violent ethnic conflict by claiming that an encounter with African film traditions is potentially a learning experience for those of us from other continents increasingly dealing with the threats of fundamentalism of one sort or another.

> We perceive, as a result, that we have had to pass through the Other to become what we are, and that even today cross-fertilization is the forward-looking solution. Forging one's identity involves the ever-renewed integration of difference: the films of Africa can be seen today as casting a crucial light on *the fate of minority communities living on the outer fringes of our comforts and certainties.*
>
> (Barlet, p. 289, my emphasis)

Notions of universalism, therefore, have to be evaluated constantly in relation to this difference, and the 'performative contradiction' inherent in this ethical-political stance presupposes dialogic relations that involve both speaking and listening – that is, the ability to represent and for representations to be seen, heard and responded to.

Cultural identity and the voice of the Other

Intrinsic to the contemporary forms of the cultural politics of difference and to the New Right is 'cultural racism', which overturns earlier forms of racism based on simpler, more straightforward notions of racial superiority and inferiority, and in which the black 'Other' was constituted as the object of representation, combining fear and desire (Hall 1988). The new cultural racism on the other hand, removes the emphasis from ideas of innate superiority and places it on the notion of diversity, while undermining the latter by arguing that differences in culture and ethnicity threaten national cohesiveness and security. In this formulation, cultural difference is seen as both fixed and insurmountable, and veritable babel of mutually incomprehensible voices and incommensurable value systems, which need to be regulated through the apparently neutral 'national' culture. The racial aspect becomes evident when, for instance, policies based on principles of affirmative action come to be perceived as undermining the principle of 'equal opportunity'. As Giroux notes, one of the ironies of this development is that

> one instance of this hegemonic project is a politics of representation that suggests that whites are the victims of racial inequality. . . . The strategy for such a politics gathered a powerful momentum during the Reagan era with the practice of 'coding' racial meanings so as to mobilise white fears. . . . Another instance of the new politics of racism is expressed in displaying racial difference as a significant aspect of American life, but doing so only to pose it as a threat to be overcome.
>
> (Giroux 1994, p. 38)

Ghassan Hage (2003) provides an insightful and provocative analysis of what he refers to as the 'White paranoia' that, he argues, promotes suspicion of genuine multi-culturalism. Other scholars, such as Robert Miles (1989) and San Juan (2002) have attempted to analyse the political economy of the politics of difference, trying to understand and theorize ethnicity and race in terms of class relations. San Juan for instance, is interested in analysing the development of 'Asian' migrant labour in the West (particularly the USA), emphasizing the need to examine the 'concrete articula-tion between race, ethnicity, and class' (San Juan 2002, p. 148), locating it in the study of the history of race and labour in the USA.

At the start of his analysis San Juan (2002) points out that

> [e]xcept for proponents of the 'Bell Curve' and other reactionary sophistries, the term *race* has by scholarly consensus no scientific referent. It is a socially constructed term embedded in the structures of power and privilege in any social formation. Its signifying power comes from the articulation of complex of cultural properties and processes with a mode of production centered on capital accumulation and its attendant ideological apparatuses to rationalise the iniquit-ous property relations.
>
> (p. 143)

San Juan's explicitly Marxist approach to the examination of the enduring inequities embedded in race relations and in the hierarchy of the labour market enables him to draw a clear link between the overlapping worlds of the Filipina domestic worker and the American family in whose house she works. In a move that focuses on the inter-section of race, class and gender, as we saw in Chapter 1, feminist scholars from the South such as Chandra Mohanty have drawn a clear distinction between the dominant ortho-doxy of Western feminist politics and their interest in the intersections of colour and gender. As San Juan argues,

> [i]nstead of organizing protests around reproductive rights or domestic work, feminists of color have articulated ethnicity and race with their mass actions

centered on political prisoners, rape, and sexual harassment in the workplace and 'ghetto' neighbourhoods, unemployment, and other issues cutting across gender and class lines.

(San Juan 2002, pp. 148–9)

The 'culture wars', then, reveal complex entanglements of diverse aspects of culture, identity and politics, among which are the practices of racialization of culture, the representation of difference, and the reification and essentializaton of cultural difference which either lead to fundamentalist politics or to the conception of multiculturalism as posing a risk to national civil society. Significant in this is the fact that despite arguments that we have arrived at 'the end of history' with the collapse of the Soviet Union, the politics of nationalism and ethnic struggles continue to shape the historical and material realities in different parts of the world. It is possible to ask, with John Comaroff (1996), 'why, when by all accounts they should have died off quietly, have the politics of cultural identity undergone a noisy, worldwide renaissance? Or is it a renaissance? Could it be an entirely new social phenomenon?' (p. 163). He is rightly concerned about theoretical formulations which obscure their own 'politics of *indifference* with reference to the powerless and the truly poor' (p. 164, emphasis in the original). Comaroff's worry that we should be focusing on 'the materialities of power and practice – and especially the practical power of some to silence others' is discussed in detail in Chapter 3. It is worth noting at this juncture that this concern informs those scholars who have been preoccupied with the politics of representation.

Central to the struggle over representation, is Hall's (1988) insightful observation that race and ethnicity are not natural or intrinsic, but that 'Black is essentially a politically and culturally constructed category, which cannot be grounded in a set of fixed trans-cultural or transcendental racial categories and which therefore has no guarantees in Nature' (p. 28). As noted by Julien and Mercer (1988), this insight has enormous significance for critical engagement with diverse artistic and discursive strategies, as the question of being black has been moved from an essential category to that of representation. The cultural politics of representation and otherness, therefore, involves a deconstructive move that interrogates representations of whiteness as the norm, but also enables a constructive engagement in the terrain of multicultural politics. This terrain includes the novel configuration of racism in the USA and elsewhere, which articulates a culturalist version of race, a 'new racism' that construes of racial difference in terms of difference in 'culture' than a question of hierarchy. The consequences, nevertheless, remain the same – the marginalization and ghettoization of specific communities and cultures. As Paul Gilroy has argued, this notion of race as cultural difference conceives culture and cultural identity as fixed and unchanging:

In another context [Frantz] Fanon refers to a similar shift as a progression from vulgar to cultural racism . . . [In this new racism] culture is conceived along ethnically absolute lines, not as something intrinsically fluid, changing, unstable, and dynamic, but as a fixed property of social groups rather than a relational field in which they encounter one another and live out social, historical relationships, when culture is brought into contact with race it is transformed into a pseudo-biological property of communal life.

(quoted in Giroux 1994, p. 36)

Conceiving of cultural difference along the lines of ethnic absolutism not only 'fixes' the relations between ethnicity and culture by essentializing it – that is, in assuming a core cultural 'essence' that distinguishes an ethnic group from others – but this reifica-tion, more damagingly, marks off each ethnic group/culture along racial lines and consequently removes the dialogic aspect of multi-ethnic societies.

In a more recent, radical re-examination of race politics provocatively entitled *Against Race*, Gilroy (2000) seeks to interrogate the academic refusal to engage critic-ally with the exercise of 'biopolitical power' in the management of diverse populations and societies. '[T]his damaging refusal is closely associated with an equally problem-atic resistance to any suggestion that there might be links between those characteristic-ally modern developments and the fundamental priority invested in the idea of "race" in the same period' (Gilroy 2000, p. 7). His investigation of the 'constitutive force of racial divisions' (*ibid.*) takes him away from conceptualizing 'race' in biological terms and towards placing 'a higher value upon the cosmopolitan histories and transcultural experiences whereby enlightenment aspirations might eventually mutuate in the direc-tion of greater inclusivity and thus greater authority' (*ibid.*). Both the realization of these aspirations as well as the challenge of their current Eurocentric premises require, Gilroy argues, a new critical vocabulary on 'race-thinking' and a restatement of its brutal history in the service of nationalism and other exclusivist politics. Proclaiming collective identity and belonging inevitably involves the politics of naming – 'we' and the 'other' – as, 'we are constantly informed that to share an identity is to be bonded on the most fundamental levels: national, "racial", ethnic, regional, and local. Identity is always bounded and particular' (Gilroy 2000, p. 98). 'Nobody,' he laments, 'ever speaks of a *human* identity' (p. 98, emphasis added). The radical premise of Gilroy's book – 'the basic, anti-anthropological sameness' emerges as part of his attempt to imagine a 'political culture beyond the color line', as its subtitle proclaims.

In his excellent analysis of 'the meaning of race' Kenan Malik (1996) raises similar objections to the aspect of racial politics which collapses 'race' into culture by reifying culture and race as immutable, fixed, and essentialist categories. Malik presents a nuanced and closely argued case for the approach to 'race' as a social category rather than the more academically modish insistence of it as cultural difference. The insist-ence on racial difference as constituted by immutable cultural difference is in danger of reproducing in a different form earlier nineteenth-century depictions of biological difference as underlying racial diversity, which were given spurious 'scientific' validity by Social Darwinism. The privileging of cultural difference as an immutable, defining and essential category of putative racial difference collapses 'race' into culture. The argument that such cultural ('racial') differences are fixed and static 'reveals a view of culture as a predetermined, natural phenomenon ... [The] concept of race arises through the naturalisation of social differences. Regarding cultural diversity in natural terms can only ensure that culture acquires an immutable character, and hence becomes a homologue for race.' (Malik 1996, p. 150).

How is this to be contested? What kinds of cultural practice may be mobilized that both challenge existing forms of racializing practice that involves processes of marginalization, as well as providing alternative strategies for representing marginal experience? Cornell West (1990) believes that the new cultural politics that informs such strategies has to steer clear of both simple opposition in the sense of gainsaying whatever is mainstream and dominant, and also the relatively uncritical and the avant-garde which seeks to shock bourgeois sensibilities. Instead, these cultural practices are animated by specific political projects: 'they are distinct articulations of talented (and usually privileged) contributors to culture who desire to align themselves with demoralized, demobilized, depoliticised, and disorganized people in order to empower and enable social action and, if possible, to enlist collective insurgency for the expansion of freedom, democracy, and individuality' (West 1990, p. 204). Since, in pragmatic terms, they are often financially dependent on the very cultural institutions that they seek to critique, their strategy 'puts them in an inescapable double bind. . . . Theirs is a gesture that is simultaneously progressive *and* co-opted' (*ibid.*, emphasis in the original). Given this, West claims, 'The intellectual challenge . . . is how to think about representational practices in terms of history, culture, and society. How does one understand, analyse, and enact such practices today?' (p. 205).

To take a more specific example that combines the political and pragmatic concerns voiced by West, the field of alternative cinema – alternative, that is, to the mainstream Hollywood or national cinema such as dominant Indian cinema or studio-based film production – is confronted by a choice between being self-consciously independent and being commercial. Coco Fusco (1989) expresses the contradictions inherent in the reality of this choice when she claims that

> Independent, non-commercial, supposedly non-exploitative film culture has long depended on maintaining a strict distinction between itself and the commercial sector. As funding sources and political agendas overlap more and more, we can no longer afford to uphold such distinction. These areas function as disjointed echoes of each other. The non-commercial sector is subjected to increasing pressure to be more like the commercial sector, and the commercial sector dips frequently into the non-commercial sector for source material.
>
> (Fusco 1989, p. 8)

A consequence of this dissipation of the distinction between the commercial and independent sectors of cinematic production – and by extension most forms of cultural production – is the need for a radical rethinking of the politics of representation. Adopting alternative strategies of representation, from feminist, anti-racist, marginal, or 'Third-World' perspectives, that challenge dominant codes consequently involves a delicate balancing act between progressive stances and co-option, between being independent of the commercial sector and acquiring adequate funding.

Entangled in the pragmatics of alternative forms of cultural production are more thematic or political issues, such as the representation of cultural difference. Questions relating to the constitution of this difference, and the historical, materialist, 'real' aspects of marginalization that combine in various ways to characterize cultural formations and social experience involve negotiating the marketplace as well as the dangers of essentialist or extremist articulations. In addition to the commercial imperatives of funding assistance, the market is implicated in cultural difference in the way it has begun to commodify cultural difference, once again construed along racial lines. As Stuart Hall argued,

> The thing about modern capitalism is that it loves difference. It can't get enough of it. One of the most important things that happens in modern advertising, is that it's stopped addressing us all as mass consumers, and has us all carefully pigeon-holed. It's not everybody wanting to be like the Joneses, everybody wants to be different.
>
> (Hall 1989a, p. 26)

In her essay entitled 'Eating the Other', bell hooks (2001) recalls Hal Foster's argument regarding the recuperation of the Other in the West. Building on Foster's example of Picasso's use of the 'primitive' or the tribal as 'witnesses' rather than as 'models', hooks argues that while the appropriation of the Other through commodification assuages a perceived lack in white culture, 'concurrently, marginalized groups, deemed Other, who have been ignored, rendered visible, can be seduced by the emphasis on Otherness, by its commodification, because it offers the promise of recognition and reconciliation' (hooks 2001, pp. 427–8). This appropriation of the Other, which masks racial domination and discrimination, is tied up with commodification and consumerism, as evidenced in advertising. 'The world of fashion has also come to understand that selling products is heightened by the exploitation of Otherness. The success of Benetton ads, which with their racially diverse images have become a model for various advertising strategies, epitomize this trend' (2001, p. 429).

Although our current concerns do not allow us to go into this in detail, it is worth taking a slight detour to note here the arguments, for instance, Dirlik (1994) and Lazarus (1999), which explore the constitution of contemporary global capitalism that celebrates and exploits this 'difference'. What Dirlik (1994) has referred to as 'guerilla marketing' is one characteristic feature of this development, which adds another dimension to the relationship between the global and the local, and highlights the process of globalization as involving both homogenization and heterogenization. Evidence of this is legion, as for example the reinterpretation of Confucian and Hindu scriptures for the promotion of capitalism in China and India, or the establishment of the Hindu citizen-consumer in India in the 1990s.

On one level such moves can be seen as evidence of heterogenization and the reinforcement of local cultures, but as Bahl and Dirlik point out,

> such culturalism is fickle, and easily returns to earlier 'orientalist' devaluations of the Other. The Asian economic crisis in the late 1990s was followed by the derogation of the very same Asian value/belief systems, accompanied by the growing opinion that market culture and consumerism are the only means to achieve progress and economic growth.
>
> (Bahl and Dirlik 2000, p. 5)

Equally damaging is the cooption of alternative epistemologies into the logic of the market, as illustrated by the exploitation of the forms of local knowledge and customs that distinguish indigenous communities.

> While looking askance at indigenous beliefs, the powerful do not hesitate to appropriate as their own such beliefs or ways of thinking, which they turn into commodities on a global market to serve not human needs but the greedy search for profits. Hence ... indigenous knowledge produced through centuries of experience is filtered through the market and transnational corporations to be placed at the service of the rich and the powerful, further bolstering claims to Western scientific superiority.
>
> (*ibid.* p. 6)

In his incisive critique of Western intellectual traditions that continue to neglect other knowledges and lifestyles Vinay Lal (2002) essays a deliberately non-Western intellectual practice. He is concerned with how Western frameworks of knowledge contribute to, and legitimize, Euro-American imperialist policies and practices. Three specific practices are typical of these in contemporary global practice of governance, namely, the violence of development initiatives and structural adjustment programmes enforced on the developing world by the International Monetary Fund and the World Bank, the reification of the nation-state in postcolonial countries, and the conceptualization of international human rights on the basis of the individual. None of these, he argues, takes into account with sufficient care non-Western traditions and cultures. Lal might well have added to his list the consumerist ethos that both underpins neo-liberal economic activity as well as the commodification of cultural practices.

Coco Fusco's (1989) concerns about the threat to Latin American cinema's cultural uniqueness and political valence similarly raises questions about the commodification of cultural difference. In the process of examining the diverse ways in which 'subaltern media is positioned, absorbed and consumed' (p. 8), Fusco argues that the rapacious Euro-American film culture, in its constant search for narratives, encroaches upon and eventually subsumes within its narrative logic issues of grave concern to Latin American communities, such as race and representation and socio-cultural history. Along with the resulting increase in attention to these issues, and the contestations they engender, is a commodification that serves to dissipate their primary political focus and rationale. This has repercussions at the level of form and content too: 'It is because of the intensified commodification of subaltern experience that we speak of crossover successes in North America and Europe' (Fusco 1989, p. 8).

Morley and Robins (1995) make an important point about the commodification of local cultural production serving the shared taste regimes of market segments on a transnational, global level. The standardization of cultural production 'reflects the drive to achieve greater economies of scale' (p. 112). In the event, growing world-standardization has resulted in the creation of a

> new cosmopolitan marketplace: world music and tourism; ethnic arts, fashion and cuisine; Third World writing and cinema. The local and the 'exotic' are torn out of place and time to be repackaged for the world bazaar. So-called world culture may reflect a new valuation of difference and particularity, but it is also very much about making profit from it.
>
> (Morley and Robins 1995, p. 113)

By way of foreshadowing the content of the following chapters, politically the notion of cultural difference is strongly implicated in the politics of national identity and multiculturalism. National culture and identity are often inextricably linked to expressions of cultural roots and assertions of cultural purity that provide the foundation for the nation as 'an imagined community'. While such claims have without doubt contributed to both demands for national sovereignty and ethnic cleansing, as for instance in the Balkans, Hall ([1993] 1999) points out that the linking of ethnicity and cultural specificity also underlies attempts to contain 'the proliferation of cultural difference "at home", and the multicultural character of the "new Britain" ' (p. 39), by the aggressive promotion of a putative 'Englishness' that constitutes a retreat into cultural uniqueness and exclusivity. As Gilroy (1987) observed in *There Ain't No Black in the Union Jack*, there has emerged a form of cultural racism that has replaced earlier and cruder ideas of biological inferiority. This new form of racism underpins attempts to create a national imaginary: 'it constructs and defends an image of national-culture, homogeneous in its whiteness yet precarious and perpetually vulnerable to attack from enemies within and without' (p. 50). We see in our examination of multicultural politics and representation in Chapter 4 that this move is by no means restricted to Britain or even Europe. On the contrary, multiculturalism is a much-contested term, both politically and in terms of defining what it captures and entails. Fusco's (1989) observation of the role of media production in the maintenance of 'a regime of multicultural diversity' is pertinent here, particularly the concern that

> in this depoliticised version of the '60s, ethnic identity becomes the focus of ongoing spectacle and aestheticisation, and subaltern popular memory its terrain. This simulation of ethnic diversity keeps each group in a fixed place, since we each have the spotlight only for as long as we express our difference. This process

harnesses nationalist separatism, with its ahistorical notion of race, for the needs of the marketplace.

(Fusco 1989, p. 9)

Fusco's main worry is that the resurgence of 'ethnically oriented marketing' and corporate control over Third-World cultural material in search of profits undermine its political energy and valence.

At first sight the increasing commodification of difference appears to pose an insurmountable threat to the representation of cultural and ethnic difference. If corporate control removes the political edge from such forms of cultural expression, and renders moribund marginal voices attempting to articulate alternative histories and experiences, challenges to hegemonic forms of representation appear futile. However, at the panel discussion, published later in *Framework*, at which Fusco voiced these concerns, Stuart Hall (1989a) invokes bell hooks's argument (made earlier in the same forum) regarding the position of marginality being one of both oppression and silence as well as enabling and empowering. For Hall, marginality is a condition of speech:

> We're now talking about resistance that is not enclosing but one that is open, dialogical. . . . If you look at difference as the commodification of difference, it looks like eating us all in the market and that is a very real possibility. On the other hand if you look at ethnicity and difference as the only place we can now speak from, it's as if we are somehow poised between being totally obliterated, or being in the moment of coming into voice.

(Hall 1989a, p. 25)

This applies to all forms of cultural production, in particular to the cinema of Third-World peoples and of ethnic minorities in the West – that is, 'Third Cinema', cinematic representation that, under its self-avowedly political remit sets out to portray 'voices, people, experiences which have been, over long periods of time, systematically marginalised, systematically displaced from the centre of the cultural industries that have dominated both the west, and through global circulation systems, the cultures of colonised peoples' (Hall 1989b, p. 31).

Such forms of cultural practice are not theoretically informed cultural-political practice, according to Hall, as theoretical positions such as feminism, psychoanalysis and post-structuralism are themselves discourses from the 'centre'. This is a contentious point, as these theoretical frameworks seek to engage critically with the politics of gender and of dominant forms of representation. Hall's, perhaps deliberately provocative, argument is more about marginal cultural producers developing their own critical practice from the position of marginality which, while it is characterized by displacement and silencing, is also a productive space. Significantly, in terms of racial politics, Hall insists on the positionality of ethnicity: 'we couldn't speak about . . . ethnicity without thinking about location' (*ibid.*). 'Location' here refers to more than geographical space; the history of colonization, indentured labour, and patterns of migration are inscribed on it, together with racism – both socio-cultural and institutional. This history is intrinsic to the experience of marginalized peoples, both in the developing world and in the metropoles. Location is centrally implicated in cultural practice from the margins, as it defines marginality and provides its political edge. Hall develops this further in his celebrated essay 'Cultural identity and cinematic representation':

> The practices of representation always implicate the positions from which we speak or write – the positions of *enunciation*. . . . We should think of identity as a 'production', which is never complete, always in process, and always constituted within, not outside representation. . . . We all write and speak from a particular place and time, from a history and a culture which is specific. What we say is always 'in context', *positioned*.
>
> (Hall 1989c, p. 68, emphasis in the original)

This positionality 'marked the speech of people who are coming into representation from the margins', and is centrally imbricated in the politics of representation as it relates to assertions of cultural difference in the case of indigenous communities, racial and ethnic minorities, and other subaltern groups. A consequence of this is the necessity to engage with such representational and cultural practices within the social and political contexts of their production, which has repercussions for both theory development as well as political mobilization.

By way of conclusion, we may note Hall's (1989c) influential discussion of the notion of cultural identity. He distinguishes two distinct ways of conceiving it: firstly, as 'one shared culture, a sort of collective "one true self" hiding inside the many other, more superficial or artificially imposed "selves", which people with a shared history and ancestry hold in common' (p. 69), a putative essence that belies other, more superficial, difference. As Hall observes, conceptions of national identity that formed part of independence struggles were premised on such a formulation, as for example the idea of 'Negritude' proposed by Cesaire and Senghor as a common, unifying feature among all Africans.

This notion of collective cultural identity continues to inform the politics of marginalized communities, enabling the 'retelling' of pasts destroyed by colonization or other forms of oppression. The second position acknowledges differences within this putative unity, allowing for both heterogeneity and for the critique of pronouncements of the alleged unity. Moreover, it also signals the fact that cultural identity is 'a matter of "becoming" as well as of "being". It belongs to the future as well as to the past' (p. 70), that is, it involves the play of history, power and culture. 'Identities are the names we give to the different ways we are positioned by, and position ourselves within, the narratives of the past.'

Here too, power is implicated in the construction of identities, in the sense of the formations of narratives and representations that privilege one form of identity over others. When these inform and are supported by institutional structures in particular social contexts, they contribute to various forms of marginalization. The concept of cultural difference is, therefore, pertinent to political struggles in diverse situations, such as the 'local' with reference to particular locales or spaces with specific historical and power-laden meanings, 'race' and ethnicity in relation to dominant groups in multicultural societies, the culture of nationalism, and the repression of indigenous communities. Among the links between these diverse contexts are a history of subordination and exploitation, and the question of class. Difference, therefore, is also a problematic concept, especially when it is emphasized to the exclusion of other factors such as class or gender. As we shall see in more detail in following chapters, the notion of difference informs the politics of representation in diverse and complex ways.

Further reading

Benhabib, S. (2002) *The Claims of Culture: Equality and Diversity in the Global Era*. Princeton: Princeton University Press.

Dissanayake, W. (ed.) *Narratives of Agency: Self-making in China, India, and Japan*. Minneapolis, MN: University of Minnesota Press.

Gilroy, P. (2000) *Against Race: Imagining a Political Culture Beyond the Color Line*. Cambridge: Harvard University Press.

Hall, S. (ed.) (1997) *Representations: Cultural Representations and Signifying Practices*. London: Sage.

3 | THE SUBALTERN AND THE POLITICS OF REPRESENTATION

Joseph Conrad's *Heart of Darkness*, written at the very end of the nineteenth century, and which famously inspired the film *Apocalypse Now*, is generally regarded as representing Africa and Africans as the 'other world', the antithesis to 'civilized Europe'. The Nigerian writer Chinua Achebe, in a well-known critique the *Heart of Darkness* laments the fact that the 'book . . . parades in the most vulgar fashion prejudices and insults from which a section of mankind has suffered untold agonies and atrocities in the past and continues to do so in many ways and many places today. I am talking about a story in which the very humanity of black people is called into question' ([1977] 2001, p. 216). In a similar vein, Toni Morrison (1987), in her novel *Beloved*, refers to the politics of 'othering' in contemporary USA:

> White people believed that whatever the manners, under every dark skin was a jungle. Swift navigable waters, swinging screaming baboons, sleeping snakes, red gums ready for their sweet blood . . . But it wasn't the jungle blacks brought with them to this place from the other (liveable place). It was the jungle white folks planted in them. And it grew. It spread. In through and after life, it spread, until it invaded the whites who made it. Touched them everyone.
>
> (Morrison 1987, pp. 198–9)

Representations of non-Western, non-White 'Others' have been scrutinized by scholars from a variety of disciplines, ranging from anthropology to cultural studies to film or literary analysis, and these have been inspired by developments in critical epistemologies and philosophical traditions such as post-structuralism and Foucauldian analysis, which have provided the fillip for studying the ways in which discursive strategies or practices of signification have contributed to the exercise and maintenance of power in colonial or modern societies (Said's 1978 seminal study of 'orientalist' depictions of non-Western cultures is a good example). Media research too, has been influenced by similar concerns. More recently, for instance, media researchers examining the depictions of refugees and asylum seekers have pointed to the different ways in which such depictions dehumanize these communities, framing them as 'illegal immigrants' or worse (see, for example, Guedes-Bailey and Harindranath 2005).

The politics of representation, however, also includes practices and modes of cultural articulations, which have been impelled by the logic of resistance to such exercise of power. Cultural forms and artistic expressions from marginal, excluded or subjugated communities, which once played a pivotal role in articulations of national cultures that informed anti-colonial struggles, continue to provide not just resistance, but also alternatives to dominant forms of representation that, for instance, 'frame' our understanding of social and political issues.

For instance, Neil Lazarus ([1992] 2001), in his analysis of 'afropop' underlines the potency, in the Zimbabwean (formerly Rhodesia) struggle for independence, of the 'mbira', 'a legendary instrument found in many parts of Africa . . . strongly associated with Shona [people's] religious and artistic practices'. The musical instrument, which had been 'ruthlessly disparaged' during the colonial period by the authorities and European missionaries, found a new lease of life as part of the liberation struggle when it was revived as a symbolic mobilizing force of national culture

> precisely *because* it was regarded with contempt by the colonial authorities. . . .
> [T]he return to the mbira was not a mere nativist gesture. On the contrary, as
> the struggle intensified, an astonishing fusion of mbira sounds and conven-
> tions, Western instrumentation, and modern means of communication [mainly
> radio] took the war to the remotest regions of the country. The fusion was
> called *chimurenga*, the Shona word for 'struggle', and *chimurenga* came to
> refer both to the war of liberation and to the style of music which spread its
> message.
> (Lazarus [1992] 2001, p. 240, emphasis in the original)

Radio broadcasts from neighbouring Mozambique defied attempts by the then Rhodesian government to jam the signal, to play 'chimurenga' songs by request by listeners in Rhodesia/Zimbabwe.

In our contemporary media-saturated world, where global configurations of satellite and information technology have contributed significantly to what Giddens refers to as the 'stretching' of social relations, and Harvey characterizes as 'time–space compression', and which, through near-instantaneous transmission of the televisual coverage of events across several parts of the world simultaneously, create global, if transitory, communities of audiences, the critical analysis of media representations of events has consequently gained critical validity and political relevance. The analysis of media representations goes beyond exploring the aesthetic aspects of various kinds of texts and the poetics that animate the ways in which the media narrate different stories. Intrinsic to most academic examinations of media texts is the assumption that the media play a crucial role in the shaping of contemporary society, and in the construction and maintenance of certain kinds of knowledge, beliefs and values that underlie modern culture and society.

In other words, the assumed political relevance of representations underpins analyses of media texts. Crucially, the media are seen to be central to the dissemination and circulation of particular ways of seeing and judging the world. By combining words and images to form comprehensible stories, the media *re-present* reality, and this re-presentation involves both a reflection and a construction of the world. The media, it is argued, contribute to the spreading of the values that drive our behaviour, the beliefs with which we evaluate other people's behaviour, the shared ideas which characterize our culture.

This touches on two important points: firstly, when we attempt to analyse representations in the media, we do not examine them as isolated texts, but more as an instance of a wider framework of meaning and values of which that text is an example. What is significant in the continual media depictions of African-Americans as criminals, or more recently, young Arabs or Lebanese as potential terrorists not only in films and television dramas, but also in the news genre, is that they contribute to a discursive formation that is seen to equate black or Arab men with criminal behaviour. The second issue to be noted here is that while this set of representations does not 'reflect' reality, by actively *constructing* a link between criminality and the African or Afro-Caribbean community the media have been accused of contributing to certain kinds of policing. In effect, the argument is that these media representations have engendered a disproportionate increase in the police stopping and searching them. Representations, in other words, can have *real* social and personal consequences.

One of the main reasons for this is the ambivalent status of representations: representations are *constructions*, put together following certain commonly-held conventions and in ways that make sense. At the same time however, these very conventions seem so natural that they become transparent, and appear to reflect reality. As Stuart Hall (1982) has argued, the media, by providing specific meanings and symbolically defining social reality, are implicated in the 'politics of signification'. To Hall, the media do not merely reflect the world, but contribute to the shaping of it: 'representation is a very different notion from that of reflection. It implies the active work of selecting and presenting, of structuring and shaping; not merely the transmitting of an already-existing meaning, but the more active labour of making things mean' (Hall 1997, p. 25). His assessment (Hall 1997) of the politics of representation uses the Foucauldian 'knowledge/power' couplet to examine the ways in which particular representations constitute discursive regimes that have social and political consequences. Representation, in other words, matters. As Beverley (1999) has pointed out, the cognitive authority of certain representations underline their power.

While films of the action and adventure genre such as the *Indiana Jones* series contain problematic depictions of racial 'others' and gender distinctions, war films have traditionally included stronger versions of stereotypes, particularly in their depiction of the 'enemy'. Films such as *Rambo* represent the enemy as innately evil and devoid of moral attributes. By presenting the opposing forces in the war in such simple terms of good and evil, such films ignore the socio-historical contexts of the war itself, portraying the action as just another adventure. What is presented is a militaristic ideology which serves to create a 'we' feeling through the strategy of unification, and legitimizes military intervention in other far-flung places. In the process the 'enemy' are presented as alien Others, embodying evil, with strange cultural practices (which remove them further from what we consider 'normal'), whereas the heroes represent virtue, patriotism, decency, and so on.

Various races and nationalities stand in for the enemy – from the Germans in World War films, to Russians and Vietnamese in films like *Rambo*, to more recently Arabs and Africans in *The Siege*, and *Black Hawk Down*. The racial stereotypes are, as Kellner (1995) points out in his discussion of *Rambo*, 'so crude that they point to the artificial and socially constructed nature of all ideals of masculinity, femininity, race, ethnicity, and other subject positions. These representations are presented in cinematic terms which celebrate the white male power of Rambo against women and other races' (Kellner 1995, p. 67). Crucially, it is possible to identify the overt political ideologies of such films and to locate them within specific socio-historical contexts. Kellner argues for instance, that the Vietnam films (including *Rambo*) are part of an ideological project of remasculinization – that is, the reinforcement of certain physical and psychological attributes which are seen as 'masculine', and of the triumph of American power over its enemies in the Far East in a recreated mythical past. Such films formed part of a media culture which resonated closely with American foreign policy. Kellner (1995) makes a link between the masculine-militaristic ideology of *Rambo* and American policy in the 1980s and 1990s. An important development at this time, especially during the 1991 Gulf War, was the emergence of a particular style of television news reporting in which the use of live footage and other images resembled the stylistic devices of Hollywood films such as *Top Gun*. In textual as well as non-textual terms, this has had several repercussions.

While *Rambo* presents this ideology in a relatively crude and straightforward manner, films such as *The Deer Hunter*, which are ostensibly anti-war, work in a more subtle way. Representations of non-Western peoples in these films for instance challenge their claims of being against war. In particular, the representation of Vietnamese in non-speaking roles as uncivilized torturers of American soldiers (and thereby undermining the Geneva convention covering the treatment of prisoners) in *The Deer Hunter* continues the myth of non-Western peoples as mostly devoid of Western notions of decency, apart from legitimizing American armed intervention in Vietnam. In other words, even the self-proclaimed anti-war film does not attempt to explore the effects of the war on the Vietnamese populace. For instance, *Platoon*, which has been considered an anti-war film, does show through the eyes of a young American soldier, the tragic effects of the Vietnamese conflict on American soldiers, but is largely silent on the tremendous impact the war has had on the Vietnamese population, who merely form the backdrop to the main action.

Consider another example. One of the controversial news stories from the 2003 Gulf War was that of the apparent 'rescue' of Private Jessica Lynch of the US army from a hospital in Nassariya, Iraq. Even more memorable than the actual 'rescue' and the subsequent celebrity status of Lynch was the conflicting nature of the reports: the initial television report on a few channels included live 'footage' shot on night vision camera, a Hollywood-style operation involving Special Forces bursting into a building and saving a fallen comrade. Subsequent reports called this into question, suggesting that what the initial coverage included was an enactment staged for the viewers back home when in reality there was no need to rescue the wounded soldier, since the doctors had attempted to contact the American authorities about Lynch. Even more than the actual veracity of either version of the story, this episode from the coverage of a conflict that had global repercussions is particularly significant for our present purposes. Most importantly, the Lynch story is indicative of the *constructed nature* of the news story, which places it closer to what we generally consider to be fictional texts like feature films, and by extension, enables us to reconsider the assumption that television news 'captures reality on the run'. It also illustrates the bias in news programmes and accounts, which in turn supports a particular ideology.

The ideology or hegemony debate – a small detour

The concept of ideology has had, as the cliché goes, a chequered history. As the American anthropologist, Clifford Geertz (1973) remarked, 'it is one of the minor ironies of modern intellectual history that the term "ideology" has itself become thoroughly ideologized' (p. 193). While it continues to provide a plausible conceptual framework with which to analyse texts, the merits of its evaluative potential, its usefulness as a tool for analysis, and its very nature as a concept, have been undergoing constant revision. In that respect the term is similar to others such as 'world-view' or 'system of values'. Its political validity, however, derives from the extra, crucial dimension of the concept, that is, its link to questions of power and inequality. At the crux of the debate about the value of the concept and analytical possibilities it provides is the question of whether ideology is a 'false consciousness' spread among members of a society in order to enable the continuing domination of particular classes, or if the concept identifies systems of values and beliefs prevalent in a particular society.

The conception of ideology deriving primarily from the Marxist tradition is associated with issues of meaning, power and dominance. Initially, ideology was seen as a distorted way of seeing the world, especially social relations, foisted on the lower classes by the dominant class in order to maintain the status quo. In *The German Ideology* written in 1845 for instance, Marx and Engels present their argument that the economic 'base' of society is closely related to culture and ideology which are constructed to secure and maintain the power of the ruling elite. This argument, which later became known as the 'base-superstructure' model, conceives of cultural and political aspects of society as the superstructure standing on the economic base or foundation. To use Marxist terms, the ruling classes, having control over the means of production, also controlled the means of the construction and dissemination of ideas through the media, arts, education and so on, and are thereby able to impose their ideas on subordinate classes. For such theorists, economic structure thus gives rise to the social structure in capitalist societies, and it is at the level of this 'superstructure' that ideology operates.

This is admittedly a rather crude summary, perhaps even a caricature, of the early Marxist formulation of the concept, but it does highlight some of the flaws which subsequent theorists have underscored. Not only does it suggest that there is a non-ideological position from which to view the world, but in emphasizing the economic base of ideology, and through that the pre-eminence of class, such a conception does not take into account sufficiently issues such as gender, 'race' and national identity. Gender, racial and national ideologies are not necessarily explicable through the use of socio-economic structures alone. At the other extreme we have what Thompson (1990) has called the 'neutral' conception of ideology (p. 57), which presents it as merely a commonsense framework of meaning which enables us to function in our daily lives. This conception, while it contributes in some ways to the investigation of such frameworks, is largely devoid of the critical edge of the earlier account of ideology, and is, therefore, not interested in the relationship between meaning and power.

In his attempt to 'salvage' the critical potential of the concept of ideology, Corner (2001) argues that, despite the potential confusion caused by the attempts to refine it, the concept itself is valuable, and that the sharpening of its critical edge is necessary in order to 'pursue further research and argument about the interconnections between meaning, value, social structure, and power' (p. 532). As he suggests, the economic (or 'material') determinism of the 'classic' version of ideology has been questioned, and it has been argued that ideologies may develop independently of the material base, and even influence it. While continuing to focus on the ways in which systems of meaning – or ideologies – sustain social power, media scholars have continued working on the theoretical aspects of ideology, particularly in terms of how people negotiate and even sometimes oppose certain ideological formations. One consequence of this is the questioning of the notion of ideology as an unchallengeable imposition from above.

Gramsci's notion of hegemony argued that more than force or coercion as the foundation of social power, ruling groups in democratic societies work through seeking and establishing consent among the population to their particular world-view, which is then given the impression of commonsense universality. In the interpretation of Gramsci's reworking of 'ideology' by Laclau and Mouffe (1985), '[i]deology is not identified with a "system of ideas" or with the "false consciousness" of social agents; it is instead an organic and relational whole, embodied in institutions and apparatuses, which welds together a historical bloc around a number of basic articulatory principles' (p. 67). That is to say, power is exercised through the active and constant shaping of what is held to be 'natural' or 'the way things are'.

Two crucial issues are raised here: firstly, the concept of hegemony undermines the notion that ruling ideas are imposed directly on the population. What is emphasized instead is a far more subtle process of maintaining a *consensus* through the shaping of commonsense, everyday assumptions that contribute to the understanding of the social world. For Hall (1997), Gramsci's conceptualization of power brings him close to Foucault: 'Gramsci's notion was that particular social groups struggle in many different ways, including ideologically, to win the consent of other groups and achieve a kind of ascendancy in both thought and practice over them' (Hall 1997, p. 48). This process in which such consent and consensus is obtained is a continuing one. In other words, hegemony is never final, but an ongoing process, which allows for the emergence of alternative world-views, that is, struggles for hegemony, involving a constant process of negotiation regarding the legitimation and justification of particular ways of thinking about society.

With regard to power relations in the construction of collective and cultural identities, it is useful to remember Hall's (1989c) assertion that,

> The ways we have been positioned and subjected in the dominant regimes of representation were a critical exercise of cultural power and normalisation, precisely because they were not superficial. They had the power to make us see and experience ourselves as 'Other'. Every regime of representation is a regime of power formed, as Foucault reminds us, by the fatal couplet 'power/knowledge'.
>
> (Hall 1989, p. 71)

The second significant issue is that, as Forgacs (1984) has argued, for Gramsci the site in which this ongoing process of establishing consensus takes place is culture: ' "Culture" in Gramsci is the sphere in which ideologies are diffused and organised, in which hegemony is constructed and can be broken and reconstructed' (Forgacs 1984, p. 91). Institutions and practices such as education, religion and the media play a vital role, establishing patterns of cultural leadership that are hegemonic. Implicated in this is the politics of representation. The recent 'history wars' in Australia over the veracity of claims that Aboriginal communities had been victims of genocide during the initial stages of the European occupation of the continent, for example, underscores the contestations over 'representation' in education, the ripples from which touch other social and political spheres. In both these instances, hegemonic struggles are often at the level of struggles over representation. As Beverley (1999) has emphasized, the links between power and representation are crucial: 'Power is related to representation: which representations have cognitive authority or can secure hegemony, which do not have authority or are not hegemonic' (p. 2). In the context of the politics of difference, therefore, representation becomes the site of contestation, as for instance the struggle by marginal voices.

One of the critical concepts that have retained prominence among scholars, particularly those interested in interrogating the historical and cultural aspects of colonialism, past and present, is the 'subaltern'. Gramsci's use of the term imbued it with a special political significance, as both a reference to a subordinate group within a society, and an acknowledgement of its potential as an agent for socio-cultural transformation. For him, a subaltern group is 'deprived of historical initiative, in continuous but disorganic expansion, unable to go beyond a certain qualitative level, which still remains below the level of the possession of the State and of the real exercise of hegemony over the whole society' (Gramsci 1971, pp. 395–6). Subaltern groups are on the margins of society, denied their own history in official historical narratives. Such groups, in other words, do not have a 'voice' in the constitutive history of a nation. Etymologically, 'subaltern' refers to a soldier who is below the rank of a captain and, therefore, occupies a lower rung in the hierarchy in the armed forces. In the study of social and cultural formations of colonialism, the term has been used to identify groups who are non-elite, 'lower' in the social hierarchy than both the colonial and the local elites.

It is important to recognize, however, that the subaltern is a *relational* concept rather than a reference to an unchanging ontological condition – that is, its reference to the social hierarchy and to subordination includes, for Gramsci and the scholars who have followed his conceptualization, the suggestion of resistance to and the potential over-turning of established hegemonic relations, and is not an allusion to a fixed and unchallengeable social relations. According to San Juan, 'from Gramsci's point of view, the "subaltern" cannot be conceived apart from the totality of social relations at any given historical conjuncture. In contrast to conventional usage, the "subaltern" is not so much an empirical fact as a theoretical element in understanding order and change in society' (San Juan 1998, p. 87).

The realms of culture and politics come together in Gramsci's arguments about what he saw as the failure of the modern Italian state, stemming from a weakness, installed by the bourgeois leadership's unwillingness or inability to accommodate the 'national–popular will'. The subaltern in this state was the peasant community, whose interests Gramsci argues, were not addressed in the form of any agrarian reform and were consequently left out of the formation of the nation, thus providing a fertile ground for the growth of fascism. The concept of the 'national–popular' is crucial to Gramsci's writing, a notion which he conceived as both cultural and political, engendering, as Beverley (1999) puts it, 'the possibility of a hegemonic or potentially hegemonic bloc of different social agents in a given society' (p. 11).

The primary marker of the division between the leaders and the 'people' was, to Gramsci, language: not only did the 'traditional intellectuals' and the elite speak Italian and the 'people' local dialects, but significantly, there was little secular vernacular literature. For Gramsci then, in Italy 'neither a popular artistic literature nor a local production of "popular" literature exists because "writers" and "people" do not have the same conception of the world . . . [T]he "national" does not coincide with the "popular" because in Italy the intellectuals are distant from the people, i.e. from the "nation" ' (Gramsci 1985, pp. 206–8). In this formulation, traditional intellectuals are seen to collude with the bourgeoisie in the production of subalternity through the practice of representation, which continues the marginalization and servitude of the subaltern classes. The subaltern is thus a result of the ideological practice of the bourgeois intellectual, and is deprived of a historical force, or agency to transform social conditions.

The critical element that provides the potential for transformation of subalternity is, for Gramsci, the self-awareness of the subaltern class, which is a necessary prelude in the move from serfdom to liberation, from the economic to the political. This is what he alludes to as 'the passage from the "objective to the subjective", and from "necessity to freedom". Structure ceases to be an external force which crushes man, assimilates him to itself and makes him passive; and is transformed into a means of freedom, an instrument to create a new ethico-political form and a source of new initiatives' (Gramsci 1971, p. 367).

The subaltern and agency

The challenge for us is to extrapolate from Gramsci's concerns the issues of representation and praxis or agency, in other words, to locate in his conceptualization of the subaltern echoes that resonate with our present concerns and our contemporary historical situation. In the words of San Juan (1998), 'Can we describe what used to be called the "Third World", now renamed the "global South", as subaltern? Only, I think, in a provisional sense. If "subaltern" signifies lack of historical initiative, disintegration, and dependency of recent independent nation-states, yes' (p. 98).

The issues of representation and agency coalesce in contemporary manifestations of subalternity, as demonstrated in the proclamations made on 'debt forgiveness' in the recent round of the conference of the Group of Eight industrialized countries (G8). Not only are these developments made on the basis of perceptions of the problems in contemporary Africa as seen from the vantage point of a metropolitan, industrialized elite, but more damagingly, the diagnosis rests on dubious assumptions about governance in Africa. At best, these are incomplete evaluations. Crucially, for our purposes, the prescription, the declarations of debt cancellations (or 'forgiveness', which has its own connotations of deviance and norm) and the ethical stances that underpin them, have not taken into account the interpretations of their problems by African intellectuals and leaders. Their call for global trade being freed from local subsidies currently being offered by the USA and Europe to their farmers, for instance, is largely ignored. On the contrary, the debt relief is conditional and prescriptive.

The subaltern, once again, is denied a voice, and they are ideologically interpellated into a continuing position of subjugation and marginality. This is not to deny the debilitating power of crippling debt, which itself has a complex history whose contours are beyond the scope of this book, but to question both the prescription and the discourse that characterize the announcements of the G8.

The 'white man's burden' seems to continue well after formal independence, and it appears to ignore both the historical conjunctures of global debt, as well as the interests of Africa. And, for all its declared intentions, this development appears to be an instance of what Diawara terms 'Afro-pessimism':

> There is a globalized information network that characterizes Africa as a continent sitting on top of infectious diseases, strangled by corruption and tribal vengeance, and populated by people with mouths and hands open to receive international aid. The globalization of the media, which now constitutes a simultaneous and unified imaginary across continents, also creates a vehicle for rock stars, church groups, and other entrepreneurs in Europe and America to tie their names to images of Afro-pessimism for the purposes of wider and uninterrupted commodification of their name, music, or church.
>
> (Diawara 1999, p. 103)

The subaltern in Gramsci's formulation suggests the importance of social and political contestation in the realm of culture more than in the economic, merging representation with agency. The complexity intrinsic to this is revealed when we consider the two meanings of the term 'representation', namely political representation (that is, 'who speaks for or on behalf of the subaltern?') and representation as signifying practices, in other words, what Hall identifies as 'meaning producing practices' (Hall 1997b, p. 28) such as cultural and artistic production, alongside the question of the subaltern's ability toward achieving social transformation. The issues of culture and politics come together in the representation–agency dialectic, in which the potential for emancipation is realized through the subaltern finding a voice that both challenges dominant representation and provides as an alternative world-view, Judith Butler's notion of 'performative contradiction' referred to in Chapter 2. As San Juan (1998) argues, the practice of representation and emancipatory politics involves intentionality on the part of the subaltern: 'Of primary importance in this debate on the politics of difference and identity is the salient question of agency, the intentionality of transformative practice, enunciated in concrete historical conjunctures' (p. 9).

With regard to the subaltern, the issue of representation becomes particularly tricky: in essence, if the subalternity is characterized by the denial of a voice, as Gayatri Spivak (1988a) famously asked, 'Can the subaltern speak?' If not, how justified are intellectuals and cultural producers in their attempts to speak *for* the subaltern? San Juan presents the predicament succinctly: 'the issue of subaltern speech as an artificial construction precipitates the urgent dilemma of whether we can truly speak for others. . . . If these others (usually the alien, foreigner, pariah) cannot speak for themselves, dare we speak for them?' (p. 101).

It is possible to discuss this difficulty in terms of the intellectual's or artist's responsibility to present the voice of the subaltern transparently, to perform the role of a conduit for subaltern interests and representations. Nevertheless, the danger of denying the agency to the subaltern persists when it is represented by others, a practice that could well extend the process of producing the subaltern. If subalternity is produced through representation, Beverley asks, 'how can one claim to represent the subaltern from the standpoint of academic knowledge, then, when that knowledge is itself involved in the "othering" of the subaltern?' (Beverley 1999, p. 2). Or, as Khare puts it in the context of anthropological representation, 'Given the unavoidability of some form of cultural hegemony and power discourse when representing the Other, the practical question now is whether such a power and privilege can be consciously rendered genuinely reciprocal (and put to good use), rather than be totally eliminated' (Khare 1992, p. 5).

Spivak's question needs to be considered in this context, as the speaking subaltern is no longer a subaltern, in her view, and subalternity is in addition defined by it not being *adequately* represented either in academic knowledge production or in artistic practice. Representing the subaltern entails the risk of assuming a vanguard stance in the place of subaltern agency, even in the case of activists acting on behalf of the marginalized. Spivak (1988a) is concerned about the precariousness of what she calls 'paradoxical subject privileging', whereby those who 'act and speak' silence those others who 'act and struggle' (p. 275). The question of 'who represents the subaltern?' here merges and confuses the two ideas of representation in the practice of speaking of and for the subaltern. The crucial question for Spivak and those critics in the field of postcolonial studies is about the politics and boundaries of representation – in particular, how one can know and represent the other. Spivak (1988a) provides the example of the practice of sati or widow sacrifice in colonial India, in which the Indian woman as the subaltern is denied a voice yet is represented differently by the imperialists working to outlaw the practice as an instance of 'white men saving brown women from brown men' on the one hand, and on the other the nationalist intelligentsia's attempts to resist imperialism, who insisted that 'the women actually wanted to die' (p. 297). Entrenched between the 'benevolent' overtures of the colonial power and the discursive practices of nationalist struggle, the Indian woman, according to Spivak, couldn't speak, represented as she was by the two opposing dominant narratives.

Spivak's, and by extension postcolonial studies scholars' preoccupation with the discursive dimension of the subaltern question has been critiqued by those like San Juan (1998), for whom a critical approach should include an engagement with historical conjunctures and structural factors that contribute to the marginalization and exploitation of the subaltern, which in turn is a preamble to political and emancipatory projects. '[Orthodox postcoloniality's] reduction of political economy, of the facts of exploitation across the categories of race, gender, and class, to the status of discourse and intertextuality has cancelled the possibility of the intervention of social subjects and collectivities in the shaping of their lives' (San Juan 1998, p. 9).

Despite the validity of such critiques (see also Ahmad 1992, and Dirlik 1997) the concept of the subaltern has contributed to the effective and creative interventions into academic knowledge production. One such is the Subaltern Studies project that began in India, with the express intention of excavating from the traditional inscriptions of history (both colonial and national) the voice of the subaltern, once again identified as the peasant, specifically in relation to that community's contributions to anti-colonial independence struggles.

Defining 'subaltern' as 'a name for the general attribute of subordination ... whether this is expressed in terms of class, caste, age, gender and office, or in any other way' (Guha 1988, p. 35), or as 'the demographic difference between the total Indian population and those we have defined as the elite' – the elite were 'dominant groups, both foreign as well as indigenous' (1982, p. 8) – Ranajit Guha, one of the founding members of the Subaltern Studies Group sought to locate the 'small voice of history' (1996). In his 1982 essay 'On some aspects of the historiography of colonial India', Guha sets out his project as the examination of the 'historical failure of the nation [India] to come to its own, a failure due to the inadequacy of the bourgeoisie as well as of the working class to lead it into a decisive victory over colonialism' (p. 43). For him, this failure stemmed from the fact that it was neither a bourgeois-democratic revolution nor one instigated by the working class or the peasant community. The initial impetus for his research came from concerns about the failure of Indian nationalism to realize the social and political transformation that was considered a necessary part of the independence struggle.

Plagued by communal politics inaugurated by the trauma of partition of India and Pakistan, the inability of the traditional Marxist left to contribute to national development, and the enduring poverty and other socio-economic problems, Indian scholars turned to a revisioning of the history of the anti-colonial movement. Significantly for our current purposes, Guha's revisionist historiography initiated the study of the subaltern, particularly in the field of postcolonial studies.

It is important to recognize too, that Guha's project involved the recovery of the subaltern voice that had been submerged in historiographic discourses concerning India, to represent it as a subject of history, and to restore to it the power of agency through an analysis of its role in the independence struggle, a role that transcended and translated the national liberation discourse installed by the national elite. As a politically informed academic practice, this exercise has tremendous relevance to our contemporary time, as Beverley (1999) has argued,

> that means that subaltern studies cannot be not simply a discourse 'about' the subaltern. What would be the point, after all, of representing the subaltern *as* *subaltern*? Nor is subaltern studies simply about peasants or historical pasts. It appears and develops as an academic practice in contemporary setting in which globalization is producing new patterns of domination and exploitation and reinforcing older ones. . . . Subaltern studies is not only a new form *of* academic knowledge production then; it must also be a way of intervening politically in that production on the side of the subaltern.
>
> (Beverley 1999, p. 28, emphasis in the original)

For Beverley, subaltern studies as an intellectual and political project has contemporary relevance:

> If we are indeed in a new stage of capitalism in which the teleological horizon of modernity is not longer available – either because it has been achieved, as in the

hypothesis of the 'end of history', or because it will be indefinitely deferred – then what is required is a new way of posing the project of the left ... [S]ubaltern studies entails not only a new form of academic knowledge production or self-critique, but also a new way of envisioning the project of the left in the conditions of globalization and postmodernity.

(Beverley 1999, p. 3)

Gramsci's conceptualization of culture as the site of contestation, where struggles for hegemony take place, not only entails the assessment of the mechanisms through which subalternity is created and maintained in both historical and contemporary settings, but also signals it as the space for challenges and alternatives to hegemonic narratives and representations. The subaltern in Gramsci has the potential for trans-formative practice, as in the case of Lazarus's discussion of the role of the Zimbabwean 'mbira' in the independence movement. Implied in this are firstly, the subaltern as an agent, not merely a victim of dominant forms of representation, and secondly, cultural practice as the principal mode of challenge. Gramsci's notion of culture anticipates the reversal in the status of culture from being an autonomous sphere, as presented in, for instance, the Weberian model, to culture being now attributed agency by theorists such as Frederic Jameson, for whom this shift is indicative of a new stage of capitalism in which postmodernism is the 'cultural logic' of globalization. Jameson's argument is that in 'late capitalism', which characterizes contemporary forms of globalization, culture overlaps with the social and political spheres, so much so that they can be seen as marked by struggles over representation.

To argue that culture is today no longer endowed with the relative autonomy it once enjoyed as one level among others in the early moments of capitalism (let alone in precapitalist societies) is not necessarily to imply its disappearance or extinction. Quite the contrary; we must go on to affirm that the dissolution of an autonomous sphere of culture is rather to be imagined in terms of an explosion: a prodigious expansion of culture throughout the social realm, to the point where everything in our social life – from economic value and state power to practices and to the very structure of the psyche itself – can be said to have become 'cultural' in some original and yet untheorized sense.

(Jameson 1991, p. 48)

To understand and theorize this development requires, for Jameson, a new form of 'cognitive mapping', to which, it can be argued, the subaltern studies project contri-butes. As Beverley argues, 'subaltern studies might be seen ... as an effort to articulate against that which is hegemonic in globalization' (1999, p. 15). Similarly, the effort of the subaltern, either in the form of artistic practice, or as new social movements, can be seen as articulations against what is currently hegemonic, globally as well as locally, as subaltern articulations embodying 'the intentionality of transformative practice' (San Juan 1998, p. 9).

Recently, however, the issue of agency has been much debated and, in the hands of some theorists, has had its transformative potential dissipated. Framing the question of agency, therefore, requires us to recuperate it from the excessive preoccupations of a few dominant cultural theorists. Dissanayake rightly points out that 'our emphasis should be on the historical and cultural conditions that facilitate the discursive production of agency' (Dissanayake 1996a, p. ix). He distinguishes between two principal notions of agency: liberal humanism, which locates it in the autonomous human subject who transcends historical and social factors, and operates as 'the originator of action and the locus of truth', and which consequently 'ignores cultural differences and the role of social formations and ideological discourse in the constitution of agency' (1996a, p. xii). The other is what he terms 'structural', which exaggerates the play of the text and proposes 'a decentred agency that is determined by the power of discourse and the interpellative force of ideology' (1996a, p. xiii), and therefore denies the autonomy of the subject. Both, according to him, overstate their case. It is important to recognize the role of representation and discourse in the formations of identities and subjectivities, that is, to acknowledge that we act as social subjects and not as completely autonomous individuals, and that being a social subject entails being discursively constituted (and, therefore, as we saw earlier, representation *matters*). To argue, however, that this causes the loss of *any* autonomy is to go to the other extreme, as by denying agency by locating the subject in discourse this position declines marginal communities such as minorities, women, or gays the power to act and transform.

What is critical here, as Dissanayake suggests, following Butler (1990), is the distinction between being *constituted* by discourse and being *determined* by it, as representation and signification accommodate agency. Butler's argument is that the post-structuralist position regarding the subject, that it is constituted in discourse, does not entail it being

> determined by the rules through which it is generated, because signification is not a founding act, but rather a regulated process of repetition that both conceals itself and reinforces its rules precisely through the production of substantializing effects. In a sense, all signification takes place within the orbit of the compulsion to repeat; 'agency' then, is to be located within the orbit of the compulsion to variation on that repetition.
>
> (Butler 1990, p. 145)

In the present context, agency understood as the ability to destabilize existing discursive regimes involves, in Butler's terms, both revealing what the repetitive representation conceals, as well as promoting a variation on or alternative to that repetition. The revisionist project of the Subaltern Studies Collective is an example of this, as it sought to resuscitate or recover the role of the subaltern in the history of anti-colonial struggles, a role which had been left out of conventional, elitist historical accounts. While this is an example of critical interventions into the production (and repetition, through canons) of academic knowledge, there are instances in cultural practice too, as for example films such as Van Peebles's *Sweet Sweetback's Baadasssss Song* (1971), which seeks to interrogate stereotypical representations of blacks in dominant Hollywood narratives.

Dissanayake's starting premise that 'I conceive of the human agent as the locus from which reconfirmations or resistances to the ideological are produced or played out.' (1996a, p. x), therefore, has scholarly as well as political relevance. It is difficult to disagree with his view that 'What is urgently required is a theory of agency that recognizes that agents are shaped irreducibly by social and cultural discourses and that they have the potentiality to clear cultural spaces from which they could act in accordance with their desires and intentionalities' (p. xvi). This theoretical and political re-evaluation of agency however, does not necessarily guarantee enunciative authority, that is, that it gets a hearing.

To anticipate the argument in the following chapters, political cinema from the so-called 'Third World' is constantly marginalized in metropolitan centres in the context of the global economy of film production and viewership. As Shohat and Stam argue in their excellent essay (1996),

> Although arguably the majority cinema, Third World cinema is rarely featured in cinemas, video stores, or even academic film courses. The yearly Oscar ceremonies inscribe Hollywood's provincialism: the audience is global, yet the product promoted is almost always American, the 'rest of the world' is being corralled into the restricted category of the 'foreign film'.
>
> (1996, p. 148)

Other forms of the vast and diverse cultural production of the Third World, like music, are treated similarly, grouped under the nebulous title of 'world music'. Articulations from indigenous communities or the Fourth World peoples, again, rarely register in the transnational imaginary, other than in specialist film festivals or commodified in the art market.

If the struggle for enunciative authority is one problematic issue with regard to subaltern agency, the other is with regard to the political legitimation of this authority, in particular, questions of essentialism and inclusion. How legitimate is it for the subaltern to speak on the basis of an exclusive experience or history that provides the essence of subaltern identity? Likewise, how does subaltern representation include or exclude issues such as gender and sexuality? Given that essentialism is anathema to cultural theorists, especially but not only because of its suspect epistemology as well as its potential to lead to political and cultural fundamentalism, these issues are central to the exploration of subaltern agency.

Spivak's solution to this dilemma is to call for 'strategic essentialism', an invitation to cultural and academic practitioners repeated by Stuart Hall in the context of ethnic minorities in the West. The 'strategic' element is to be interpreted in political terms, as a pragmatic approach to destabilizing dominant, authoritative discourse with the intention of achieving political and social change. Representations by refugee communities of their experience of exile and repression encapsulates this move, as it simultaneously attempts to undermine the inadequacies of being represented in the dominant media, while selectively portraying experience that synecdochically stands for exile and 'refugeeness'.

For Guha (1983) the subaltern experience of history was relatively less theoretical than that of dominant groups, and more particularistic – a simple inversion that was predominantly reactive, demonstrated in responses to the 'high semioticity' of the cultural markers of superiority and deference (such as dress codes, food taboos and linguistic forms) which framed peasant rebellion in India. 'It would be quite in order to say that insurgency was a massive and systematic violation of those words, gestures, and symbols which had the relations of power in colonial society as their significata' (Guha 1983, p. 39).

Conceiving subaltern resistance

If, as in Beverley's concise formulation, Subaltern Studies is the study of power 'who has it, who doesn't, who is gaining it, and who is losing it', (1999, p. 1), and subalternity is closely related to the politics of representation and discursive regimes in a social situation where power involves a process of negotiation and consent, what does the challenge to hegemony entail? What constitutes counter-hegemonies and counter-discourses? This problem becomes particularly acute when we consider the post-structuralist suspicion of 'essences', or conceptions of a unitary subject or collective. In the absence of such 'essentialized' constructions of cultural identity, on what grounds can the subaltern begin to articulate alternative histories and life stories? This crucial question underlies notions of subaltern agency and is related to both conceptions of the subject as well as, in terms of the loci of articulation, to Hall's observation regarding marginality as a productive space, mentioned in Chapter 2.

With regard to the first issue of the subject, Kathy Ferguson's (1993) notion of 'mobile subjectivities' presents a creative way of capturing for the subaltern an enunciative agency. Ferguson is particularly interested in feminist theorizations of gendered subjectivities, which she considers 'mobile' in the sense of being constantly interpreted and reinterpreted. They are consequently unstable and fluid, resisting essentialization, but, importantly, are also 'standpoints of a sort, places to stand and from which to act' (Ferguson 1993, p. x). This provides, at least, a momentarily firm platform for the subaltern, for the initiation of a counter-hegemonic move. For Ferguson herself, it is an important step towards addressing the excesses of post-structuralist challenges to a unified identity and the consequent denial of political agency, which she feels has been counter-productive to the practice of resistance: 'Just when feminists, minorities, gays, and lesbians are seeking to assert their identity, some of the theorisations associated with postmodernism seem to cut the ground from under their feet by denying agency and positing a passive and totalising subjectivity that is at the mercy of discursive power' (Ferguson 1993, p. xv).

Spivak (1988) attempts to address the problem of strong anti-essentialist dis-avowal of subaltern agency by promoting the idea of 'strategic essentialism'. As Radhakrishnan has argued this is a problematic move as, by suggesting it, he feels that Spivak is trying 'to have it both ways: neither the pure contingency of nothing but strategy without the comfort of identity effect; nor a naïve essentialism that believes in itself' (Radhakrishnan 2003, p. 161). To him it is a cautious exaltation of political practice which attempts to sustain an ethical doubt over the constitution of the subject. To Beverley, on the other hand, Spivak's promotion of 'strategic essentialism' is indica-tive of the tension between a post-structuralist deconstruction of ideas such as nation and nationalism on the one hand, and a constructive advocacy of political agency on the other. What Guha has called the 'politics of the people' is caught up within this tension. In terms of the politics of nationalism, as we see in Chapter 7, critiques of its constitution focus on the conceptions of national culture by elites, which excludes subaltern and marginal constituencies. Conversely, subaltern agency and political praxis are at times articulated through nationalist politics.

In recent times, this has been evidenced in anti-apartheid struggles in South Africa, and in nationalist resistance in East Timor. In both instances, it has been the 'people' who have both borne the brunt of oppression and silencing, and it has been these subaltern groups who contributed in various ways to the struggle against existing powers. Acts of repression have included not only physical incarceration and violence, but also cultural silencing.

The imprisonment of the Indonesian writer Promodeya Ananta Toer is a case in point, even if, in his case, the alleged sedition was, at least initially, against the Indonesian authorities and not necessarily in the context of East Timor. In the case of South Africa, as Narismulu (2003) demonstrates, cultural repression involved marginalization of black intellectuals and writers, and of women's literary and artistic contributions that challenged, along with apartheid practices, deaths in custody, patriarchy and neo-colonialism. Narismulu begins her essay with the charge that in contemporary South Africa, 'the voices of the subalterns who made up the critical mass in the South African reistance struggle were sidelined by the negotiated settlement and the related deals struck between the old regime and the new order, all underpinned by the financial imperatives of neo-liberal globalization' (Narismulu 2003, p. 57). This move to the right, she claims, has included the co-option of sections of the trade union movement and civic groups, with the result that 'over the past few years, subaltern voices have returned to the margins and are only dimly perceived in the statistics of HIV-Aids, tuberculosis, cholera, infant mortality, rape, violence, murder' (ibid.). This is a severe indictment that goes to the heart of postcolonial, in particular, post-apartheid, politics.

Even more significantly, the case of South Africa illustrates Spivak's recent contribu-tions to the question of political agency. In her assessment of contemporary global capitalism and the 'new subaltern' it engenders, Spivak (1999) engages with the constituents of the New Empire, in which earlier forms of imperialism are rearticulated in 'free trade' agreements, in developmental policies, and in aid programmes. The gendered subaltern, among the most marginalized communities, is currently caught up in the global capitalist imperatives, as indicated in 'credit baiting', the provision of credit to women in the developing world by initiatives encouraged by the World Bank and NGOs, but without sufficient infrastructural support.

In the context of the emergence of this new subaltern, as Didur and Heffernan (2003) argue, Spivak has acknowledged the inadequacy of her earlier formulation of 'strategic essentialism' as necessary for political struggles, and has begun to suggest alternatives. Spivak's (2003) distinction between responsibility-based (subaltern) and rights-based (Northern) cultures begins this process. While recognizing the value of conceptions and declarations of universal rights, Spivak is explicitly critical of the relationship between human rights initiatives and development projects, which to her are emblematic of the unequal relations between the North and the South. In many ways this replicates dimensions of the exercise of colonial power and its exclusion of the subaltern. She sees current aid and development workers as latter-day Minute Men of Thomas Macaulay, and as epigones of colonial middle-class administrators. Redressing this inequality of power involves for Spivak (2003), initiating dialogues with 'responsibility based cultures' of the subaltern, which sustain an understanding of those 'parts of the mind not accessible to reason', and which, consequently, are 'inaccessible to us as objects and instruments of knowledge' (quoted in Didur and Heffernan 2003, p. 7). This imaginative, non-rational space is available to us, like language, which is 'outside us, in grammar books and dictionaries', but also within us in the sense that we use it to understand and communicate to the world outside.

Recuperating these spaces involves accessing those forms of subaltern knowledge in an effort to revitalize the imperative of 'responsibility' among those of us caught up in the imperatives of global capitalism. The overlaps between Spivak's recommendation of a dialogue between 'rights-based' and 'responsibility-based' cultures and Benhabib's plea for the establishment of a dialogic relationship between different perspectives and diverse cultures is a useful reminder of the need for an engagement with globalization's 'other', the subaltern, and the 'underside' in order to begin the process of comprehending the complexity that the process involves.

The concept of the 'subaltern' then, offers us the possibility of engaging with the complexities and entanglements intrinsic to the politics of representation. These include, as elaborated in subsequent chapters, discourses of nationalism; racial or ethnic difference and multicultural politics; political cinema; and indigenous politics.

Further reading

Beverley, J. (1999) *Subalternity and Representation: Arguments in Cultural Theory*. Durham: Duke University Press.

Gandhi, L. (1998) *Postcolonial Theory: A Critical Introduction*. Edinburgh: Edinburgh University Press.

Loomba, A. (1998) *Colonialism/Postcolonialism*. London: Routledge.

San Juan, E. (1998) *Beyond Postcolonial Theory*. New York: St Martin's Press.

PART 2

4 | MULTI-CULTURES, NATIONAL AND TRANSNATIONAL

Initially concerned by his son's apparently impulsive removal of all vestiges of teenage life from his bedroom, and subsequently bemused by the son's sudden piety and abrupt turn to Islam, Parvez the hard-working, Pakistani-English taxi driver finally loses his temper and his patience at the end of Hanif Kureishi's sensitive short story, 'My Son the Fanatic' (1997). The story neatly reverses the stereotypical view of second generation immigrants as being more assimilated into the host culture than their parents. It is Parvez who is the whisky drinking, pork-pie eating agnostic from Pakistan, and his son Ali the pious Muslim who castigates his father for his 'Western' ways:

> 'The problem is this,' the boy said. He leaned across the table. For the first time that night his eyes were alive. 'You are too implicated in Western civilisation.'
>
> (p. 125)

Terrorist attacks in London and elsewhere in 2004 and 2005, which have initiated concerns regarding the fundamentalist turns among Islamic youth in Europe, North America and Australia, make Kureishi's depiction of Ali impressively prescient. Radicalization among Muslim youth is contributing to the current debates on the complexion of multiculturalism in such societies. This development reveals the validity of the observation by Morley and Robins (1995) regarding not only the need for countries in Europe (and by extension, North America and Australia) to re-examine their national identities following the arrival of the Third World as immigrants into the First World, but also that '[t]ime and distance no longer mediate the encounter with "Other" cultures. This drama of globalisation is symbolised perfectly in the collision between Western "liberalism" and Islamic "fundamentalism". . . . How do we cope with the shock of confrontation?' (p. 115).

Morley and Robins have in mind the 'Rushdie affair' as an instance of such confrontation, but their point is if anything even more accurate in the current global politics, and underlines the significance of their argument against a retreat into 'fortified identities' (or Tradition) in favour of 'Translation', whose responsibility 'means learning to listen to Others and learning to speak to, rather than for or about, Others' (p. 115).

Public perceptions, media representations and declarations by, and debates among, political leaders have together launched a re-examination of cultural difference and national belonging, of national values and citizenship, and policies on immigration and police action. The significance of allegedly 'home-grown' terrorists participating in the 7 July attacks in London has transmuted into scrutinizing the legitimacy of representations of cultural and religious difference and their impact on national identity, as well as the emergence of a transnational Islamic imaginary which is presumed to underpin acts of terrorism and of 'terrorist cells' in the West. If 11 September 2001 was a rude awakening to the existence of global terrorism, 7 July in its turn pointed to the existence of 'the enemy within'.

The broadcast by Al Jazeera (rebroadcast on the ABC TV news on 3 September 2005) of excerpts from the video diary of one of the alleged suicide bombers involved in the bombing of the London underground, proclaiming an Islamic war against the 'West', has added a further fillip to such fears. As an instance of the formation of political subjectivity in which 'race' is one signifier along with religion, this exemplifies the trend in contemporary social formations that Jameson (1991) referred to as 'neo-ethnicity', and Baumann (1991) as 'neo-tribal'. The recent controversy in Australia in connection with female Muslim students wearing the 'hijab', construed by one politician as 'an iconic emblem of defiance and of difference' (ABC Radio National, 28 August 2005) inadmissible in the post-9/11 world, in particular the 'secular state' of Australia, is indicative of the complexity of cultural and religious identity in multicultural states.

From another perspective, what was referred to as 'Katrinagate' – George Bush's perceived incompetence in dealing with the aftermath of the devastating floods in New Orleans and the ensuing neglect of a significant proportion of the city's inhabitants, mostly poor and black who were unable to flee the city in time – reopened scars on the national imaginary regarding the treatment of African-Americans in the USA. If concerns regarding the presence of diverse cultures and their attendant relations to the 'national culture' involves questions of 'difference', the controversy following hurricane Katrina links 'race' to economic inequality. Critical here are discussions of multiculturalism that, using a Marxist analysis, explore the relations between 'race' and economic exploitation (San Juan 2002; Sivanandan 1990a,b). For instance, San Juan builds on Wallerstein's (1991) insight into the role of ethnic or cultural differentiation in the organization of capital–labour relations – the 'ethnicization of the workforce' – to argue that '[w]ithin the boundaries of the US nation-state, ethnicization of the workforce has proceeded along with occupational hierarchization' (San Juan 2002, p. 140). In addition, the controversy surrounding the aftermath of hurricane Katrina recalls the distinction that James Baldwin draws, in a conversation with Margaret Mead, between African-American experience in the north-west USA, and the southern states, in particular Alabama and Mississippi.

When I went south, I was a grown man. . . . I found myself in Montgomery, Alabama, and it wasn't the spirit of the people which was different or which surprised me, because by the time I was thirty-one, I had given up expecting sanity from most white Americans. Essentially, I knew most white Americans were trapped in some stage of infantalism which wouldn't allow them to look at me as though I were a human being like themselves. But I didn't expect what I found in the South, either.

(Baldwin and Mead 1971, p. 23)

What this underlines is Nancy Fraser's (1997) contention that the politics of multiculturalism includes both cultural difference and redistributive justice. Among the myriad political, ethical and theoretical questions that arise from these developments is that of the constitution of multicultural states, and of communities within such states that on the one hand, proclaim their 'difference' from the national mainstream, and on the other, are marginalized and/or criminalized on the basis of perceived cultural or religious 'difference'. In the context of our present interests, it is possible to locate a clutch of issues that combine urgent ethico-political concerns surrounding the issue of 'multiculturalism', namely, the debates and disagreements about the meaning of the term, the diverse manifestations of multiculturalism in different national contexts, the politics of 'recognition' and representation and of cross-cultural dialogue, and of the constitution of transnational diasporic communities. Inherent to these is the matter of identity – both the formation of ethnic and cultural identity and how this impacts on notions of national identity – and of economic equality, which links 'race' and ethnicity with patterns of migration and labour.

Contestations and debates

Far from being a clearly articulated and succinct concept that captures the multivalent politics of immigration and national identity, 'multiculturalism', as argued by numerous scholars, is a much debated term, the interpretation and usage of which often proclaims the political perspective of the user. In his opening remarks in the collection of essays on the debates around 'multiculturalism' Bennett (1998) succinctly sums up the diverse positions that have come to inhere the concept:

'Multiculturalism' is fast following 'postmodernism' from the isolation ward of scare quotes into the graveyard of unusable, because overused, jargon. . . . [C]ultural analysts now construct taxonomies of 'multiculturalism', distinguishing such species and hybrids as 'conservative or corporate multiculturalism, liberal multiculturalism and left-liberal multiculturalism', 'critical', or 'radical', 'polycentric', and 'insurgent' multiculturalisms.

(Bennett 1998, p. 1)

While its overuse in multiple contexts by diverse groups has robbed it of its significance and meaning, the self-conscious use of quotation marks suggest the ongoing debates and attempts to engage critically with the term. Homi Bhabha (1998) for instance, argues that

> Multiculturalism – a portmanteau term for anything from minority discourse to postcolonial critique, from gay and lesbian studies to chicano/a fiction – has become the most charged sign for describing the scattered social contingencies that characterise contemporary *Kulturkritik*. The multicultural has itself become a 'floating signifier' whose enigma lies less in itself than in the discursive uses of it to mark social processes where differentiation and condensation seem to happen almost synchronically.
>
> (1998, p. 31)

The synchronic social processes of 'differentiation' and 'condensation' that the use of the term discursively contributes to – that is, the ways in which the term is used to designate difference and sameness – provide the political and ethical charge to the debates on the notion of 'multiculturalism'. The 'leaking' of different realities into each other, in Salman Rushdie felicitous phrase to describe the politics of multicultural Britain, points to the presence of the 'third world' in the 'first world', informed and propelled by labour shortage and economic migration, with the consequent dilution of a putative homogeneous national culture by the presence of minority communities and cultural difference. This, along with other developments resulting from the arrival of new, 'coloured', immigrants, such as housing and other local government policies have, according to Radhakrishnan (2003) led to

> mainstream discussions of multiculturalism [being] part of an opportune and instrumentalist strategy to contain the crisis in the name of and from the point of view of the dominant regime. . . . Mainstream discourse on multiculturalism, with its assimilationist ideology, has clearly opted for the avand-gardist course of action, and as a result we have seen a rapid proliferation of diversity workshops, heterogeneity seminars, and sensitivity sessions in academic and corporate sectors.
>
> (p. 32)

Radhakrishnan's point here is that the perceived threat to national unity and culture is being contained through strategies at delimiting 'difference' by assimilating it into the mainstream. A casualty of this strategy is the ethically sound dialogic project between the mainstream and the marginal that results in the transformation of the constitution of the national and the mainstream. He finds the mainstream discourse on multiculturalism problematic as it reproduces the trope of the dominant culture, an unspecified 'majority' and its many 'Others', a constellation of 'minorities', a relationship which, he argues, requires problematizing and deconstruction. The urgency and importance of this task is underlined by Etienne Balibar's argument that in the context of discrimination in multicultural communities 'the racial/cultural identity of "true nationals" remains invisible but is inferred from . . . the quasi-hallucinatory visibility of the "false nationals" – Jews, "wops", immigrants, *indios, natives*, blacks' (quoted in Bhabha 1998, p. 31).

The opinions expressed by the former British minister Norman Tebbit exemplifies the suspicions of multiculturalism vis-à-vis national cohesion among conservative politicians and academics:

> Multi-culturalism is a divisive force. One cannot uphold two sets of ethics or be loyal to two nations, any more than a man can have two masters. It perpetuates ethnic divisions because nationality is in the long term more about culture than ethnics [*sic*]. Youngsters of all races born here should be taught that British history is their history, or they will forever be foreigners holding British passports and this kingdom will become a Yugoslavia.
>
> (*The Guardian*, 8 October 1997, quoted in Hesse 2000, p. 3)

Tebbit's perception of multiculturalism as a threat to national unity and identity, Hesse (2000) points out, reveals certain assumptions and prejudices: he considers multiculturalism as an alien influence arising from outside the nation; his conception of the term warrants a dissolution of cultural differences in the service of performative fidelity to a constructed 'Britishness', a national identity which in turn is conceived as being constituted by its history and cultural uniformity. Recent debates in Australia, for instance, on the role of education in inculcating 'Australian values' among 'immigrant' children, are testament to the persistence of such prejudices and assumptions about non-Western cultures.

For Hesse, such arguments embody an instance of the instability of meanings that characterize 'the broadly uncharted relational terrain between the *multicultural* and *multiculturalism*' (Hesse 2000, p. 2, emphasis in the original). Despite the increasing presence of multi-cultures in Western democracies which allows for the discourses of celebration, or condemnation, of multiculturalism and cultural or ethnic difference emanating from diverse political points of view, the discourse reveals the abiding presence of colonial hierarchization of cultures in which the dominant (Western) culture is presented as the norm. As Radhakrishnan argues,

> constitutive of that political configuration [of debates on multiculturalism] is the colonial formation of the *multicultural* as a signifying relation. The multicultural is a signifier of the unsettled meanings of cultural differences in relation to multi-culturalism as the signified attempts to fix their meaning in national imaginaries. The multicultural always refers contextually to the 'western' and 'non-western' cross-cultural processes involved in establishing the meanings invested in the racially marked incidence of contested cultural differences.
>
> (Radhakrishnan 2003)

While multiculturalism was construed in the period between 1960 and 1980 as 'the incidence of harmonious cultural differences in the social, particularly where this meant the decontestation of "race" and ethnicity and their conflation with the individualist ethos of nationalist liberal-democracies' (*ibid.*), the challenges posed since the 1990s on the nature of national social formations by the presence of diverse ethnic communities within national borders have disturbed this conception of a harmonious co-presence of multi-cultures. A consequence of this, according to Hesse, is that multi-culturalism has been transformed into a critical concept, in either a celebratory mode or one of censure. To Hesse, the contestation around the discourse of multiculturalism reveals not only the politics of cultural and ethnic difference, but also specific political positions regarding these differences within national boundaries.

The politics of multiculturalism and the different conceptualizations of the term it gives voice to have been commented on by a number of scholars. The quotation marks that punctuate each 'species' of multiculturalism are for Bennett (1998) indicative of the contested nature of the term that in turn reveals the politics that the term signifies and stands for, not just within academia, but even more significantly, in the ways in which it informs government policies in Europe, North America, and Australia in areas of bureaucracy ranging from immigration and education to housing. As Bennett points out, however, the contestation is not merely at the margins of the multicultural imaginary, but also within it.

> In the disparate domains in which the term has circulated during the past three decades . . . 'multiculturalism' has served variously as code for assimilationism and cultural separatism; campus Marxism and ethnic nationalism; transnational corporate marketing strategies and minority competition for state resources; radical democracy and cosmetic adjustments to the liberal-democratic status quo.
>
> (Bennett 1998, p. 1)

For Shohat and Stam (1994) the term 'multiculturalism' has no essential meaning attached to it. Rather, it is an 'empty signifier', that is 'polysemically open' to diverse interpretations mobilized and informed by different political agendas, as a result of which they argue the case for locating it in the centre of a debate on the nature of democratic liberal Western societies. Positioning themselves against what is to them the 'co-opted version' of multiculturalism, an instance of which is the corporate sponsored 'United-Colors-of-Benetton pluralism, whereby established power promotes ethnic "flavours of the month" for commercial or ideological purposes' (Shohat and Stam 1994, p. 47), they prefer to use the term in a critical sense, in order to radically interrogate existing power relations. What is significant in the debate, for Shohat and Stam, is the conceptualization of multiculturalism in relational terms, that is, as a 'substantive and reciprocal intercommunalism' that conceives multiculturalism as 'a notion of ethnic relationality and community answerability' (p. 47). Both the neo-conservative fear of multiculturalism as a threat to the unity of the nation as well as the liberal-pluralist model of separate but cohabiting ethnicities, in their view, are inadequate.

That the inequitable distribution of power *itself* generates violence and divisive-ness goes unacknowledged; that multiculturalism offers a more egalitarian vision of social relations is ignored. A radical multiculturalism, in our view, has to do less with artefacts, canons, and representations than with the communities 'behind' the artefacts. In this sense a radical multiculturalism calls for a profound restructuring and reconceptualization of *the power relations between* cultural communities.

(Shohat and Stam 1994, p. 47, emphasis added)

Shohat and Stam's insistence on the *relational* aspects intrinsic to multicultural states underlines the importance of conceiving such societies not merely as a collection of disparate ethnicities or cultures, and shifts the focus more to the interrelations between these groups, thereby linking minoritarian communities. They recommend the formation of 'active intercommunal coalitions' (*ibid.*), arguing that cultures, com-munities and nations do not exist in isolation from one another, but in a complex and interrelated web of relationality, characterized by mutual awareness and dialogic relations.

Different contexts, diverse conceptions

The conceptual disagreements that the term 'multiculturalism' is immersed in inform, and are reflected in, the policies adopted in different states to tackle cultural diversity and difference engendered, particularly in Europe, North America and Australia, by successive waves of migration. Careful considerations of who constitutes a desirable migrant, as opposed to an undesirable alien, animate immigration and multicultural policies, and these considerations have differed in different locales. According to Hesse (2000), the conservative attitude to non-white migration into Britain, represented by Norman Tebbit, is complemented by the liberal conception of changes brought to British nationalism and identity by the arrival of Afro-Caribbeans and Asians, which 'was less inflexible, more tolerant, more open to accommodation of cultural differ-ences' (p. 6). Post-war non-white immigration, Hesse argues, as well as the public perceptions of national identity were carefully managed through assimilationist pol-icies, at least until the 1960s, in which the new arrivals were expected to fit seamlessly into a utopian construction of a putative 'British way of life'. The logic underlying this formulation conceived of ethnic difference as being dissolved and dissipated through successive generations.

Post-1960 immigration and multicultural policy moved towards 'integrationism', a version of assimilationism, was 'coaxed into existence', a 'publicly sponsored cultural one-way ticket from the "coloured immigrant's" veil of ignorance to participation in a good society' (p. 6), a move predicated upon assumptions of the 'passivity, malleability and inferiority of Black and Asian cultures' (*ibid.*) that permitted the illiberal prefer-ence of visions of British 'good society' over the rights and desires of new immigrants.

As Anthias and Yuval-Davis (1992) note, the assumption of cultural differences gradually dissolving over generations in the melting pot of a putative national culture was, by the 1970s, considered no longer valid: 'multiculturalism emerged as a result of the realization originally in the USA, and then in Britain, that the melting pot doesn't melt, and that ethnic and racial divisions get reproduced from generation to generation' (1992, p. 158).

A modified version of integrationism located mainstream culture as the national one, with a constellation of ethnically and racially demarcated minority cultures that overlapped with national culture minimally. This version

> constructs society as composed of a hegemonic homogeneous majority, and small unmeltable minorities with their own essentially different communities and cultures which have to be understood, accepted and basically left alone – since their differences are incompatible with the hegemonic culture – in order for the society to have harmonious relations.
>
> (*ibid.*)

Both the conservative concerns regarding the dangers posed by 'alien' communities to the cohesion of a putative national culture – the 'culture wars', as well as the politics of representation that animate assertions of cultural difference and attempt to depict the experiences of minorities engage with this notion of harmony among incommensurable, discrete cultures within the nation-state.

This, however, is not restricted to the Euro-American context alone. The conception of national identity in states incorporating ethnically and racially diverse postcolonial communities such as India, Malaysia and Singapore includes elaborately conceived proclamations of 'unity in diversity', in which the media play a prominent role. An example of this is the serial *Under One Roof*, which attempts to depict a microcosm of Singaporean multi-racial society, promoting values of inter-racial harmony. The programmatic aspects of the slogan 'unity in diversity' attest to the statist construction of a unitary national imaginary that incorporates and contains difference within it even as the state acknowledges and celebrates difference. Given their shared history as Malaya under British colonial rule and the similarity of the make-up of their multi-racial citizenry, the cases of Malaysia and Singapore, specifically the discursive or aesthetic politics of multicultural nationhood that also includes a degree of differentiation between the two states, is a particularly interesting example of the management of multi-cultures in the interest of national identity.

India, with its teeming multitude of languages, religions, castes and ethnicities, presents an interesting example of the contribution of colonial bureaucratic practices to the formation of post-independence nation-states, according to Chakrabarty (1998). For him, the lack of a recognizable Indian ethnicity in the British creation of the Indian public sphere has had the consequence of making the construction of a putative 'Indian' unity a problem in the postcolonial state. 'Modern ethnic consciousnesses in India have been fashioned under circumstances in which the politics of cultural difference have been of pre-eminent value' (p. 104). This will be explored in greater detail in Chapter 7, but it is worth noting here that the prominence of cultural and ethnic difference has had repercussions at the political level. Kohli (1990) points out, in particular, the mobilization by elites of diverse ethnic groups drawn along linguistic, religious, or racial lines in different regions of the country: 'the Maharashtrians in Belgaum; the Sikhs in Punjab; Hindus versus Muslims in various parts of the country; the Gurkhas in West Bengal' (Kohli 1990, p. 18). On the socio-economic level too, assertions of ethnic difference and their recognition by the state in affirmative action policies have challenged the idea of national unity, according to Tharoor (1997), as the 'damaging consequence of well-intentioned social and political engineering means that, in the five decades since independence, we have failed to create a single Indian community. Instead, we have become more conscious than ever of what divides us: religion, region, caste, language, ethnicity' (Tharoor 1997, p. 122).

In Britain, 'race relations' as a progressive way of negotiating racial and ethnic difference and non-white immigration not only valorized 'their aesthetic permanence in the national way of life and psychological role in providing an important sense of self-worth for individuals from those communities', but also, as Hesse notes, informed pedagogic policy and practice in schools fashioned largely around learning about and consequently respecting diversity conceived as 'a dialogical mosaic rather than as fixed, monological coordinates' (Hesse 2000, p. 8). A consequence of this, he argues, has been an understanding of racism and inter-racial tensions arising merely from ignorance and not from deep-seated social and economic reasons, but merely from ignorance or lack of adjustment among minorities (for more details, see Braham *et al.*, 1992). In the words of Phil Cohen, this multicultural 'illusion is that dominant and subordinate can somehow swap places and learn how the other half lives, *whilst leaving the structures of power intact*. As if power relations can be magically suspended through the direct exchange of experience, and ideology dissolve into the thin air of face to face communication' (quoted in Hesse 2000, p. 8, emphasis added). Hesse rightly emphasizes the need to take seriously 'local memories' and, in Foucauldian terms, 'subjugated knowledges' in an attempt to form coalitions involved in the 'co-production in knowledge formation' by way of challenging hegemonic and dominant valorizations of multiculturalism and national identity. Crucially, this demands engagement in representation, both political and aesthetic.

In contrast to Britain, where the schools were the primary institutions for debates on multiculturalism, claims Hesse, the fact that in the USA the institutional site for this contestation was the university has meant that, 'the figuration of multiculturalism in the United States has produced much greater social reverberations and contested theoretical elaborations' (p. 13), particularly in response to the 'culture wars' of the 1980s and 1990s, expanded the notion of cultural difference to include gender and sexual politics.

Shohat and Stam (1994) raise concerns regarding multicultural politics in the North American context, and the variety of responses from diverse groups and administrations, each with its favorite metaphors, many of the culinary: 'melting pot', 'ethnic stew', 'tossed salad', 'Bouillabaisse', 'stir-fry', 'gumbo'. For neoconservatives, multiculturalism is code for 'left opposition', and 'people of color', both ideal scapegoats now that the cold war is over.

(p. 46)

While nationalists find use for 'orginary metaphors' such as cultural roots and wellsprings, and reveal an ambivalent attitude to multiculturalism, incorporating both ideas of co-option into the national imaginary as well as potentially contributing to national change and rejuvenation of national culture, liberals, aiming to 'invoke the well-behaved "diversity" dear to college brochures', prefer 'ceramic metaphors like "gorgeous mosaic", culinary metaphors like the "smorgasbord experience" ' (p. 47). However, they dissociate themselves from radical conceptions of multiculturalism that seek to interrogate the Eurocentric versions. Shohat and Stam find that in Canada multiculturalism is transformed into 'cosmetic government programs' that attempts to soothe the concerns of indigenous communities, separatist movements in Quebec, as well as those of African and Asian immigrant groups. In Latin America, in the mean time, 'intellectuals worry about a new "multicultural" neo-colonialism' (p. 47). Underlying their recommendation of the creation of 'active intercommunal relations' is, as we saw earlier, a conception of multiculturalism as ethnic or cultural relationality, rather than as discrete communities.

In the Australian context too, the end of the Second World War instituted changes in immigration policy, commencing the recruitment of immigrants 'from the "darker shade of White" regions of Southern Europe and the Mediterranean' (Hage 2003, p. 55) that required, as an appeasement of the 'white' Australians troubled by the apparent cultural difference embodied by the new arrivals, the institution of aggressive assimilation policies. As an attempt to address white paranoia, claims Hage, ' "Assimilation" carried a clear message to the White population: migrants will not perturb or change Australia's Anglo-Celtic culture. It is the migrants who have to fit into it. For the incoming migrants, "assimilation" was more a general ideological directive to assimilate than a set of "assimilationist institutions" provided to produce a desired outcome' (Hage 2003, p. 55).

In what amounts to a parallel to developments and debates in British multicultural policy, the recruitment, from the late 1960s onwards, of 'immigrants from an even "darker shade of white" ', it was discovered that new migrants 'did not shed their previous cultural practices and they did not become indistinguishable from the population of British origin. At least not as quickly as expected' (Hage 2003, p. 57). Following this discovery and the emergence of ethnic enclaves in various Australian cities, 'assimilationism' was replaced by 'integrationist' policy, which, as in Britain, claimed to recognize the new arrivals as culturally different, but counted on later generations becoming 'fully Australian', that is, 'one of us'. Moving in Australian cities, one could witness the formation of ethnic streets and enclaves. However, as Hage points out, integrationist immigration policy marked, 'the first state/bureaucratic recognition that Australia was no longer a homogeneous White European society; it did now contain non-English speaking communities (the non-assimilated first generation) whose needs required special government policies' (p. 58).

To Hage, present debates and policies signifying contemporary versions of Australian multiculturalism are indicative of the 'paradoxical homogenisation' of the diverse meanings of the term 'multiculturalism' as it has come to be affiliated with the process of globalization. In particular, the meanings have been homogenized around the American sense of the term, that is, 'cultural pluralism and identity politics. That is mostly what it means in Australia today, but this has not been always the case' (*ibid.*).

The similarities and differences in the constitution of multicultural policy and politics in North America, Britain and Australia together testify to the enduring significance of the notion of cultural difference among populations cohabiting within a national space. Stephen Castles *et al.*'s (1996) observation on the Australian state's intervention on behalf of a national imagined community is relevant to most multicultural states: 'Multiculturalism is based on a construction of community through a celebration and fossilization of differences, which are then subsumed into an imagined community of national cohesion' (p. 365). On the one hand, as we have seen, the state's response has been to negotiate difference through various strategies of controlling perceived 'excesses' of expressions of difference, ranging from 'assimilating' difference into the national imaginary and a putative 'national culture' that simultaneously proclaims a distinctive American or British or Australian identity, to integrationism, and the liberal rhetoric that constitutes a rather empty celebration of diversity. Debates on the constitution of multiculturalism, on the other hand, have also included the politics of identity, or 'identity politics' as it has come to be known, which informs expressions of cultural distinction and of marginal experience, both of which are closely bound up with histories of racism and exploitation.

Negotiating sameness and difference

In the context of national politics and culture, identity politics, an engagement with multiculturalism from the perspective of the 'other', epitomize the struggle of the local against the global, the particular as opposed to the universal, the marginal versus the mainstream. In some ways this struggle embodies contestations over the definition of national identity and the hegemony of majority (elite) culture – what San Juan refers to as 'majoritarian consensual culture' (2002, p. 7). He quite correctly alludes to the central problem that '[w]hat the current multiculturalist orthodoxy (of left or right varieties) elides . . . is the history of the struggles of people of color – both those within the metropolis and in the far-flung outposts of finance capital.' (p. 8).

The political rationale for the struggle however, often conceals profoundly disquieting issues that have continued to plague affirmations of ethnic or cultural distinction.

For instance, the debates on declarations of ethnically specific identities reveal justified suspicions of essentialism that underlies the search for cultural 'roots'. As Bennett has noted, the conceptual confusion surrounding the term multiculturalism also characterizes identity politics. It is, as he points out, 'protean' as the other, coterminous concepts such as 'race', or ethnicity: 'Signalling essentialism, separatism, withdrawal from the liberal-democratic polity on one hand, it can signify complicity with "culturalism" and identity-consumerism thought to be promoted by liberal-pluralist and corporate, "Benetton-style" multiculturalism on the other' (D. Bennett 1998, p. 5).

Gilroy (2000) too, draws attention to 'the exceptional plurality of meanings' that the new popularity of the term harnesses, which, while they are adapted from 'highly specialised language' attesting to an unfortunately rare but happy instance of academic contributions to political and cultural activism, 'are condensed and interwoven as the term circulates'. The problem, however, is that,

> We are constantly informed that to share an identity is to be bonded on the most fundamental levels: national, 'racial', ethnic, regional, and local. Identity is always bounded and particular. It marks out the divisions and subsets in our social lives and helps define the boundaries between our uneven, local attempts to make sense of the world.
>
> (p. 98)

Gilroy's complaint is that in such assertions of the particular, the universal, in terms of 'human identity' is lost. He shares Butler's (1995) concern regarding the growing acceptance of the inter-changeability of the concept of 'identity' with cultural specificity. While it enables and even demands an examination of 'the perilous pronoun "we" ' and the processes of inclusion and exclusion that clearly implies, the difficulty with the concept, for Gilroy, stems from the fact that identity is 'something of a problem in itself', particularly when it involves the policing of group boundaries and is evident in articulations of group solidarity that give voice to ideas of belonging. To return briefly to the Hanif Kureishi story 'My Son the Fanatic', the disagreements between father and son highlight differences of opinion regarding the issue of belonging, specifically to do with the boundaries marking British-Pakistani/Islamic identity.

As Gilroy argues, 'Calculating a relationship between identity and difference, sameness and otherness is an intrinsically political operation. . . . [Consequently,] identity becomes a question of power and authority when a group seeks to realize itself in political form' (p. 99). Whether this group constitutes an ethnic community, a nation, a class, a movement, 'or some unsteady combination of them all', conflicts based on declarations of exclusive identity and inter-group incompatibility abound in the contemporary age. While its starkest configuration is perhaps evident in the opposing sides of the West against Islam's polarity, 'identity' is also the basis of inter-ethnic conflict in, for instance, Rwanda, as well as in nationalist politics (as in the former Yugoslavia, or currently in Chechnya), and subnational separatist politics (one can think of a number of examples here: Sri Lanka, India, Indonesia, Spain, Canada). Consequently, it is difficult to argue with Gilroy's assertion that

> Identity is thus revealed as a critical element in the distinctive vocabulary used to voice the geopolitical dilemmas of the late modern age. Where the power of absolute identity is summoned up, it is often to account for situations in which the actions of individuals and groups are being reduced to little more than the functioning of some overarching presocial mechanism. . . . In this light, identity ceases to be an ongoing process of self-making and social interaction. It becomes instead a thing to be possessed and displayed. It is a silent sign that closes down the possibility of communication across the gulf between one heavily defended island of particularity and its equally well fortified neighbours, between one national encampment and others.
>
> (Gilroy 2000, p. 103)

Gilroy's concerns regarding the politics of particularism and identity attest to the dilemmas that attend minority representation and multiculturalism. Specifically, the issue of 'sameness and difference' is intrinsic to the politics of ethnic and racial minorities that seek to challenge attempts at assimilation into a national culture. Identities asserted on the basis of difference predicated on 'pre-social' allegiances tend to overreach themselves into counter-productive stances that, on the grounds of incompatibility and mutual incomprehension, animate against cross-cultural dialogue. Gilroy's call for the acknowledgement of 'anti-anthropological' sameness and 'human identity' has to been seen in this context.

However, within the politics of representation and the significance of representing 'otherness', the question remains as to what constitutes justifiable assertions of difference. Once we acknowledge the precariousness of the concept of identity we are confronted with the complexity of the politics of representation that simultaneously explores the social and cultural aspects of minority immigrant experience including for instance, racism, while conceding enough to 'human identity'. Negotiating this political and conceptual morass requires an exploration of the nature of identity formation, of the politics of recognition, of the dialectic of the particular and the universal, and of the promotion of subaltern voices.

Gilroy (2000) among others, has insisted on the discursive and intersubjective aspect of identity formation. The intersubjective element of the formation of individual and collective identity is founded upon interaction with the world. The crucial question however, is 'how selves – and their identities – are formed through relationships of exteriority, conflict, and exclusion' (p. 109), a process that involves the acceptance of differences both within and between identities. Like Benhabib (2002), Gilroy insists on the feature of dialogue in identity formation and maintenance that at once points to the need for a dialogic Other and allows for the instability of identities. 'The Other, against whose resistance the integrity of identity is to be established, can be recognized as part of the self that is no longer plausibly understood as a unitary identity but appears instead as one fragile moment in the dialogic circuits' (Gilroy 2000, p. 109). He uses Debbora Battaglia's (1995) useful phrase 'representational economy', part of her argument that 'there is no selfhood apart from the collaborative practice of its figuration. The "self" is a representational economy: a reification continually defeated by mutable entanglements with other subjects' histories, experiences, self-representations; with their texts, conduct, gestures, objectifications' (Battaglia 1995, p. 2).

Two related points can be raised here. Firstly, as Radhakrishnan points out in his exploration of what he calls the 'perspectival legitimacy of representation' (Radhakrishnan 2003, p. 33) the issue of representation is strongly implicated in multicultural politics, particularly in relation to the perspective from which the 'multivalent realities' that constitute a multicultural society are voiced and arbitrated. Crucial here is the absence of dialogue in the configuration of multiculturalism from the perspective of dominant (national) culture:

> The multiculturalist initiative as sponsored by the dominant culture sidesteps the question of what it would mean for the dominant regime to be narrativized and rendered visible from the points of view of the many and the unassimilated. Rather than pose the issue in dialogic and relational terms, the unilateral dominant mandate on behalf of multiculturalism fixes the many as the object of a paternalistic benevolent representation. The 'multi-' continues to carry the mark of alterity within a dominant model that refuses possibilities of reciprocity and mutual narrativization. In other words, nothing has changed in the house of Euro-America.
>
> (Radhakrishnan 2003, p. 33)

The unequal power relations that are intrinsic to this lack of dialogue and 'mutual narrativization' renders, for Radhakrishnan, the dominant perspective invalid because it is one-sided. His call for subaltern representation stems from this insight.

The other issue relating to Gilroy's point about the discursive dimension of identity formation is its links to Charles Taylor's discussion of 'the politics of recognition'. In his influential essay (1994a), Taylor presents his argument that 'our identity is partly shaped by recognition or its absence, often by the misrecognition of others, and so a person or a group of people can suffer real damage, real distortion, if the people or the society around them mirror back to them a confining or demeaning or contemptible picture of themselves' (Taylor 1994a, p. 25). In his treatment of the term 'recognition', Taylor combines two different meanings: that of *equal* recognition that is conceived in terms of equal rights and dignity for all citizens, thereby the politics of universalism on the one hand, and the recognition of *difference* that discerns the distinctiveness of cultures. Paradoxically, the recognition of difference is couched in the language of the universal, in that it is declared as a general – that is, universal – rule, thereby universalizing the particular. Central to his argument is the validity of *both* meanings as, while the first sense of the term ensures equal treatment of all citizens within a multicultural democracy and guards against prejudice, the second militates against assimilation.

'Where the politics of universal dignity fought for forms of non-discrimination that were "blind" to the ways in which citizens differ, the politics of difference often redefines non-discrimination as requiring that we make these distinctions the basis of differential treatment' (Taylor 1994a, p. 39).

Recognition and identity

In terms of formations of identity, Taylor links two elements of his philosophy: the dialogic model of identity as formed and maintained through intersubjective 'webs of interlocution', and his insistence on the dual recognition of equality and difference. In an earlier book (1989), he describes his conception of the 'web of interlocution' in terms of the connection between the self and language,

> I am a self only in relation to certain interlocuters: in one way in relation to those conversation partners which are essential to my achieving self-definition; in another in relation to those who are now crucial to my continuing grasp of languages of self-understanding – and, of course, those classes may overlap. A self exists only within what I call 'webs of interlocution.'
>
> (Taylor 1989, p. 36)

Taylor's insight has contributed a specific philosophical and political valence to the exploration of cultural rights and citizenship in multicultural societies. The sameness–difference dialectic, along with his conception of the formation of the self and the centrality of recognition to it, reasserts the significance of representation and provides a framework for the analysis of cultural formations and discourses. In a few instances, as in Dallmayr (1998), Taylor's framework has been utilized by theorists engaging with issues of culture on a global level, conceiving global society as multiculturalism writ large.

Despite the value of Taylor's contribution, however, it has been critiqued for its over-emphasis on recognition and a relative disengagement with redistribution, and for its insufficient attention to inequalities inherent in patterns of cultural recognition. With regard to redistributive justice, Nancy Fraser's (1997) contributions have been widely regarded (Benhabib 2002; Radhakrishnan 2003) as offering a useful corrective to Taylor's neglect of it. In Fraser's conception, two paradigms of justice imbue demands for recognition and redistribution. These constitute the focus on firstly, cultural injustices (the recognition paradigm) that seeks to redress inequalities and problems associated with patterns of representation, communication, and interpretation, and secondly, socio-economic injustices in the form of exploitation, marginalization and deprivation. The main thrust of Fraser's argument is the relevance of both paradigms in the demand for social and economic equality as well as recognition of cultural difference. Both paradigms together are constitutive of claims for justice in a multi-cultural society. Four kinds of collective identity formation are mapped on to the two paradigms: 'race', gender, class and 'despised sexualities'. What Fraser achieves is a useful analytical distinction between the politics of difference and heterogeneity, and the demands for distributive justice that seek to remove economic differentials in the name of equality, while emphasizing the interrelationship between both. In other words, while the two paradigms appear contradictory, Fraser insists on a dialectic link between them, conceiving them as analytically distinct but interlinked domains.

In his defence, Taylor does consider briefly the inequalities inherent in the uneasy balance between non-discrimination and difference, in which attempts to accommodate difference within a presumed homogeneous national culture often reveals asymmetries of power, whereby the hegemonic subsumes the non-hegemonic, the minority and the subaltern. Radhakrishnan (2003) however, is unconvinced about the adequacy of Taylor's avowal of power differentials. For him 'the politics of recognition has to be articulated with and informed by the politics of subalternity', since 'some cultures have been recognized more than other cultures; some cultures have had recognition as a *fait accompli* while others have had to struggle against heavy odds' (Radhakrishnan 2003, p. 54). Given this context, Radhakrishnan argues, the politics of recognition 'needs to be played out between the utopian and trans-ideological invocation of a relational universalism and an active and critical awareness of the representational failures and injustices of the status-quo' (*ibid.*).

In a recent instance of the fairly regular revisiting of the 'Bell Curve' controversy making dubious links between racial difference and intelligence, a Canadian-Australian law professor's attempts to publish a paper applauding the wisdom of the now defunct 'White Australia' immigration policy caused a predictable stir in the media and in the public imagination (see *The Australian*, and *The Age*, 21 September 2005). Discussions of this case have interrogated the content of the professor's argument against the purported investment in racial equality and in favour of an apparent 'racial realism' promoting 'Anglo-Australian' ethnic homogeneity in response to the perceived threat of the emergence of an Asian-Australian managerial ruling class as well as what he calls the 'less intelligent' and alleged criminal tendencies of African immigrants. Quite apart from the obvious racist content of this argument and the spurious 'scientific' data that it rests on, debates about this startling anti-multicultural position that argues in favour of terminating non-white immigration have included questions of academic freedom and freedom of expression in a liberal democratic society.

The defence of free speech in this context, while it is an admirable call for the guarantee of universal equality – what Laclau and Mouffe have referred to as 'the egalitarian imaginary' – and the place for multiple voices in a democratic debate, overlooks the inequality inherent in the power of enunciation, that is, the coordinates of power that allows or denies access to modes of address. Declarations of equal access to free speech are unfortunately not a guarantee of it. In other words, in terms of Taylor's dual modes of 'recognition' of equality and difference, marginal voices lack the enunciative power of the hegemonic bloc, with the result that the dialogue between cultures is unequal. How ideal-typical then, is Taylor's assertion that 'democracy has ushered in a politics of equal recognition' (1994a, p. 30)? And, to return to a question we posed in Chapter 2, what is the 'sameness' and 'difference' intrinsic to Taylor's politics of recognition in relation to? As we have seen, sameness construed in terms of a putative equality is problematic, given the issues of power relations that undermine it. Difference, on the other hand, conceived in terms of expressions of authenticity that facilitate mutuality or reciprocity in the dialogic, 'interlocutionary' construction of identity, raises the uncomfortable issue of what constitutes authenticity, and of how and by whom it is to be represented.

Radhakrishnan's insistence on *multilateral recognition* is, therefore, crucial, as it seeks to address the unevenness of the realization of 'cognitive human landscape' that continues to marginalize communities and subjugate knowledges. The call for multilateral recognition, however,

> is not in the name of the authenticity of any one group's self-image, but in the name of a categorical and systemic fairness and openness that rigorously guards against the possibility of 'recognition' becoming the exclusive function of any one particular gaze. It is rather like an anti-trust provision against cognitive and epistemic monopoly and control.
>
> (Radhakrishnan 2003, p. 55)

Extending Spivak's assertion about whether the subaltern can speak, Radhakrishnan argues that subalternity is constructed through unilateral misrecognition that fixes the subaltern in the gaze of the other. Subaltern understanding of its own experience, in other words, works only through its objectification by the elite and the mainstream. He makes a crucial distinction between subaltern demands for recognition and Taylor's argument regarding enunciations of 'authenticity' as marking difference.

Since objectification of their experience by elite culture interferes with subaltern self-understanding, such constituencies are no more in touch with their 'authenticity' than other groups.

> As a matter of fact, it is this hasty and sloppy coupling of subalternity with authenticity that has depoliticised the subaltern cause and rendered it ever more vulnerable to the histrionics and theatricalizations of the dominant culture. The issue rather is that there is a 'relative inside space' that pertains to every group including the subaltern, and in the case of the subaltern, the integrity of this space has been violated over and over again, and it is the right to speak for that interiority that is in question.
>
> (Radhakrishnan 2003, p. 56)

In other words, the issue is one of addressing the non-reciprocal recognition of the subaltern. Subaltern demand is for participation in a dialogue, for mutual and reciprocal recognition. It is 'for permission to narrate a certain story from a certain place and a certain position, so that the story and "where it came from" can be made sense together' (*ibid.*). The politics of representation alluded to here involves the recognition of subaltern expressions as arising from particular historical and social locations – the 'locus of enunciation' – that contain within them the various coordinates that constitute subaltern culture, including racism, and economic and social inequality – more than a question of an alleged authenticity, therefore, the struggle entails locational or perspectival legitimacy. Moreover, it also involves safeguarding the legitimacy of subaltern cultural expression, since 'when the self-image of a dominant culture meets up with the self-image of a subaltern culture on a world historical stage, the former all too easily destroys all subaltern defence on behalf of itself and prescribes its own mode of cognition as the answer to the subaltern question' (p. 57). This is why, according to Radhakrishnan, 'The politics of recognition has to be articulated with and informed by the politics of subalternity.'

This raises several epistemological issues. Firstly, with regard to the status of experience in relation to formations of cultural identity and representativeness, identity politics has been conceived differently by different frames of reference that either privilege the notion of inherited essences or the constructivist critique of essentialism. As Mohanty points out,

> the essentialist view would be that the identity common to members of a social group is stable and more or less unchanging, since it is based on the experiences they share. Opponents of essentialism often find this view seriously misleading, since it ignores historical changes and glosses over internal differences within groups by privileging only the experiences that are common to everyone.
>
> (Mohanty 1998, pp. 202–3)

Whatever position is adopted, however, the question of belonging is 'unavoidable as we translate our dreams of diversity into social visions and agendas' (*ibid.*). Secondly, the potential for disagreement between dominant and subaltern representations of experience and the consequent incommensurability between them prompts the subject of relativism that damages mutual recognition. To quote Mohanty again, cultural plurality is both a political ideal and a

> methodological slogan. . . . It is necessary to assert our dense particularities, our lived and imagined differences, but can we afford to leave untheorized the question of how our differences are intertwined and, indeed, hierarchically organized? Could we, in other words, afford to have *entirely* different histories, to see ourselves as living – and having lived – in entirely heterogeneous and discrete spaces?
>
> (1998, p. 130, emphasis in the original)

Thirdly, examining the value of enunciative practice involves, as Frow (1998) avers, both positionality and the set of 'ethical and political questions: Who speaks? Who speaks for Whom? Whose voice is listened to, whose voice is spoken for, who has no voice? Whose claim to be powerless is a ruse of power?' (Frow 1998, p. 63). This clearly echoes Spivak's concern about the representational politics of the subaltern explored in

Chapter 3. In his analysis of subaltern speech, San Juan asks, 'If the hegemonic censor always screens thought and culture overdetermines speech, can we even claim to represent ourselves justly and with adequate fidelity? If these others (usually the alien, foreigner, pariah) cannot speak for themselves, dare we speak for them?' (San Juan, p. 101).

Building on the Alcoff's (1991–92) attempt at suggesting an ethics of enunciation, Frow (1998) underscores the importance of appraising the 'enunciative modalities' of subaltern representation. Critical in this context, for him, is Alcoff's concern that the practice of being spoken for compounds the marginalization of subaltern groups by denying them their own voice. Her linking of 'social position and the semantics of utterance' by way of examining the politics of speaking is for Frow a way around the complexity of subaltern representation, although he concedes that the relationship between position and meaning is complicated. The essential problem of 'positionality' underlying the ethico-politics of enunciation is that 'whereas the act of speaking for others denies those others the right to be the subjects of their own speech, the refusal to speak on behalf of the oppressed, conversely, assumes that they are in a position to act as such fully empowered subjects' (Frow 1998, p. 65).

In her invocation of the notion of 'polyvocality' Benhabib, as discussed in Chapter 2, promotes the idea of a dialogic relationship between different cultural formations as a way of negotiating the unproductive dichotomy between the universal and the particular. The seemingly intractable problem of cultural difference and relativism explored by Mohanty and others such as Gellner (1985) stems, as Mohanty argues, largely from considering cultures holistically as internally consistent and homogeneous wholes, which Benhabib sees as inimical to cross-cultural dialogue, as demonstrated in Chapter 2. Eric Wolf memorably called such division of a 'totality of interconnected processes' into a set of discrete and coherent 'billiard balls' invariably turned 'names into things' (Wolf 1982, p. 6). Benhabib's insistence on the 'polyvocality' of all cultures reconceives them as 'multilayered, decentred, and fractured systems of action and signification' (2002, p. 25), thus undermining theses of untranslatability and incommensurability that underpin arguments about the incompatibility of relativism and universalism.

For Benhabib, debates on multiculturalism offer concrete social situations with which to engage critically with representation and dialogue. As a measure of the dialectic relations between particularism and universalism, for instance, she argues that 'politically, the right to cultural self-expression needs to be grounded upon, rather than considered an alternative to, universally recognized citizenship rights' (p. 25). This goes to the heart of the matter as it presents subaltern expression not merely as simply oppositional, but as providing a critical and significant perspective on the necessary debates on citizenship in multicultural societies.

Subaltern aesthetics

Referring to the heated debate on race and celebrity prompted by the display of an African-American sports star in an Italian pizzeria in Spike Lee's film *Do the Right Thing*, Shohat (1995) argues that 'On the symbolic backgrounds of the mass media, the struggle over representation is homologous with that in the political sphere, where questions of imitation and representation easily slide into issues of delegation and voice' (Shohat 1995, p. 166). This is especially pertinent in the national public sphere in which debates on 'political correctness' have to deal with the contradictory impulses of, on the one hand, rejections of biologistic or essentialist determinations of 'race' and identity by academic theory and on the other, the practice of affirmative action whose premise includes identifying groups along essentialist lines.

Raising the politically pertinent issue of whether the 'experience of oppression confer[s] special jurisdiction over the right to speak about oppression' (p. 167), Shohat reformulates Spivak's famous question to ask 'can the nonsubaltern speak?', by way of alerting us to the fact that

> anxieties about speaking are asymmetrical. Those who have been traditionally empowered to speak feel relativised simply by having to compete with other voices. Made aware of their own complicity in the silencing of others, they worry about losing a long-taken-for-granted privilege. The disempowered or newly empowered, on the other hand, seek to affirm a precariously established right.
>
> (Shohat 1995, pp. 167–8)

This is a crucial point with regard to discussions of minority or subaltern representation and the corollary challenge to dominant or mainstream discourse. In the realm of the media, this amounts to the issue of counter-hegemonic practices that engage with and provide alternatives to hegemonic representation, particularly those that contribute to the persistence of old stereotypes, or in formal terms, co-opt new racial minorities into old systems of stereotypical representation.

The film *The Siege* (2001) presents an interesting example of the aesthetics and politics of cinematic representation. While, as has been widely recognized, the film tries to depict the theme of Arab terrorists without demonizing the community (exploring for instance the injustice inherent in the internment of Arab-Americans following a terrorist attack in the USA), the narrative logic of the film nevertheless sets up unproductive dichotomies in which the trope of Arab terrorists is used uncritically. The film depicts an American general following orders from a special senate committee and ordering martial law in a major American city following a series of hijackings and destructions of buses and the bombing of a Federal building. The enemy in this case is within the USA, but still an outsider, a member of the non-Western community in the form of Arab Muslims living in the city.

Of the two Arab characters with speaking parts in the film – the many other Arabs are depicted as a mass of people – one is an FBI agent and, therefore, a 'good guy' who briefly loses his faith in American values when his son is taken into custody along with the rest of the Arab population, and the other represents, as a trope, Islamic fanaticism. The film has a fairly conventional ending of a mainstream Hollywood thriller, when the main villain is killed and order is restored in the city. The final clip confirms Samir as the main culprit – an Arab who duplicitously exploits his relationship with his well-meaning white partner Sharon, callously kills her, and quotes from the Koran to justify his intention to kill large numbers of people (who are, ironically, protesting against the detention of Arabs – such is the extent of Samir's evil nature).

In a different type of exploration of inter-racial relationships, the film *The Sheltering Sky*, based on a novel by the same name, follows the journey of a young American couple, Kit and Port, through North Africa in 1947. During the course of this journey Port (the man) is killed in the Sahara, while Kit (the woman) is apparently kidnapped and raped by a Tuareg community, a narrative deeply reminiscent of the erotic confusion suffered by the main female character in *A Passage to India*. Like the heroine from that film whose encounter with the 'sensuality' of India manifests in fantasies of rape, Kit too is overwhelmed by the sexual 'power' of Belqassim, the Tuareg chief. Such encounters have been seen by film analysts as 'analogous to the West's confrontation with the violent and vital sexual vigour of the Third World' (Loshitzky 2000, p. 54). Representations like these, which depicted the developing world and its peoples as possessing a sexuality that was simultaneously threatening and attractive, formed part of colonial discourse. Films such as *The Sheltering Sky* reproduce colonial representations of 'the other', that is, the colonized non-Europeans. The danger of the encounter between a European woman and a colonized man for instance, is represented in Kit's eventual descent into madness. This is despite the depiction of Kit as the dominant partner in her relations with Belqassim – her whiteness appears to guarantee superiority over the chief from an 'inferior' race.

Needless to say, such depictions of Arab communities and cultures simultaneously reflect and contribute to the current global concerns about terrorism that have on occasion descended to the level of Manichean dichotomies of alarming simplicity. In terms of the politics of multiculturalism too, such portrayals reverberate with stereotypes in an disquieting manner. For example, as Peter Manning (2003) has demonstrated through the analysis of Sydney newspapers, communities that are incorporated into the wide rubric of 'Arab' are sometimes portrayed as external and internal threats to Western societies, reinforcing the 'them' and 'us' divide among different ethnic groups. 'Arab young men, in particular, are seen as especially threatening, wanting "our" Caucasian women, and not policed sufficiently by their own communities who lack either values (respect for women) or interest (accepting responsibility) for these men' (Manning 2003, p. 69).

It is debatable whether the political economic imperatives of Hollywood cinema sanctions politically relevant engagements with multiculturalism and 'race'. It is legitimate to ask whether the increase in the number of black actors in mainstream Hollywood cinema is an indication that things are changing? While it is true that black actors have started taking on central roles in mainstream cinema, the question of casting is more complicated, as Shohat (1995) argues. On the one hand, the recent emergence of African-American actors playing central characters improves on the history of black representation in Hollywood, in which 'Euro-Americans have historically enjoyed the unilateral prerogative of acting in "blackface", "redface", "brownface", and "yellowface", while the reverses has rarely been the case' (p. 170), and in which 'dominant cinema [was] fond of turning "dark" or Third World peoples into substitutable others, interchangeable units who can "stand in" for one another' (p. 171). Conversely, recent developments by which African-Americans, or Latino/a actors are permitted to 'represent' their communities is 'hardly sufficient if narrative structure and cinematic strategies remain Eurocentric. An epidermally correct face does not guarantee community self-representation' (p. 172).

As Shohat demonstrates, the simple replacement of white performers with black actors does not adequately deal with the problem of the ideology of race. In order to counter racist discourse it is necessary to go beyond dominant codes of representation and fashion a different film aesthetic which both suggests the possibility of a different kind of storytelling, and while doing so explores the lived experiences of black and other ethnic minority communities in the West, and the complex nature of what it means to be black in the West. Increased awareness of the media's role in society has resulted in attempts to undermine the hegemony of dominant media representation. Stuart Hall (1981) for instance, argues that the issue of racism and the media 'touches directly the problem of ideology, since the media's main sphere of operations is the production and transformation of ideologies. An intervention in the media's construction of race is an intervention in the ideological terrain of struggle' (Hall 1981, p. 8).

Asserting that classical Hollywood narrative 'often articulates time and space through recourse to a discriminating gaze toward American blacks' (Diawara 1993, p. 13), Diawara (1993) presents a complex argument on the representational variations in African-American cinema. In exemplary black American independent cinema, he argues, the space and time coordinates of filmic narrative violate dominant mainstream narrative forms, contributing to what he refers to as the new 'Black aesthetic'. In films such as *Boyz 'N the Hood*, and *Daughters of the Dust*, he claims, Hollywood's cinematic and political focus on the development of white characters and people ('White times') is undermined through their non-linear treatment of time and spatial narration in an effort to reconstruct African-American cultural history and explore the material conditions of everyday life in black America. Whereas the repetitiousness and cyclicity of 'space-oriented narratives' such as *Daughters of the Dust*

> can be said to center Black characters on the screen, and therefore empower them, the Black-times narratives [in films like *Sweet Sweetback's Baadasssss Song* and *Boyz N the Hood*] link the progress of time to Black characters, and make times exist for the purpose of defining their needs and their desires.
>
> (Diawara 1993, p. 13)

Films by other American and British film-makers – black and Asian – such as Spike Lee (for instance, *She's Gotta Have It, Do the Right Thing*), Gurinder Chadha (*Bhaji on the Beach, What's Cooking?*) and Mira Nair (*Mississippi Masala*), have centred on the lives of ethnic and racial minorities in the West, examining the uneasy politics of 'race' in terms of both the inter-relations of these minorities as well as the complex politics of racism.

Crucially, a significant, and for Diawara a necessary, characteristic that most of these films share is their independent financing, which by placing them outside the political economy of Hollywood studio production, enables them to 'investigate the possibilities of representing alternative Black images on the screen; bringing to the foreground issues central to Black communities in America' (Diawara 1993, p. 5). Such films are able to 'put on the screen Black lives and concerns that derive from the complexity of Black communities. Independent films provide alternative ways of knowing Black people that differ from the fixed stereotypes of Blacks in Hollywood' (p. 7).

Merelman (1995), in his exploration of the depiction of black experience in black cultural expression, feels that *Boyz 'N the Hood* is unsuccessful as a filmic critique of white oppression and as a 'coherent counter-hegemonic statement' (p. 109), since such films lack an overt political content that confronts racism in the USA:

> The film's concentration on the sheer *insulation* of black life reveals the *consequences* of white domination but not the actual process of white domination, nor of black reaction to whites. Instead, the films dwell on the self-destructiveness of the black community, a perspective that reinforces white perceptions of black weaknesses and unworthiness.
>
> (Merelman 1995, pp. 112–13)

this, for him, is clearly problematic. Conversely, Spike Lee's films he argues, consistently engage with racial politics, tackling the sometimes explosive contact between white and black communities. *Do the Right Thing*, for instance, provides, for Merelman, 'a powerful and insightful depiction of racial attraction and racial antagonism' (p. 117), as depicted in the key scene in which the character Mookie, played by Lee, has to choose between loyalty to his racial group or his Italian-American employer, Sal. In this scene 'Lee arrays arguments in favor of an "hegemonic" decision' – that is, Mookie's loyalty to Sal – 'against arguments in favor of a "counter-hegemonic" decision' in the form of Mookie's commitment to his black neighbours (*ibid.*).

Importantly, Merelman echoes Diawara's point about the significance of independent production in his observation that Lee's ability to continually tackle racial politics in his films stems from his relative financial independence from Hollywood, which allows him to write, produce and direct his projects. In a controversial statement about the uniqueness and purity of black cultural expression Lee declared: 'Black cinema is written, produced, and directed by black folks. And usually all three of them have to be Black for the film to stay Black' (quoted in Merelman 1995, p. 113). For all its political valence, Shohat and Stam (1994) object to such pronouncements of 'epidermically suitable representatives' of specific communities, and the 'ethnic insiderism' that it implies. The crucial question for them is '[h]ow can scholarly, curatorial, artistic, and pedagogical word "deal" with multiculturalism without defining it simplistically as a space where only Latinos would speak for Latinos, African-Americans about African-Americans and so forth, with every group a prisoner of its own reified difference?' (Shohat and Stam 1994, p. 343).

Gray ([1995] 2001) submits another set of queries with regard to black representation in multicultural societies. His concern is with the reductiveness of the argument for changing industrial and financial conditions to enable black representation in television by black producers. He proposes instead a historically contextualized analysis of the circulation of social meaning of black representation in terms of its cultural and political significance, arguing that 'our contemporary moment continues to be shaped discursively by representations of race and ethnicity that began in the formative years of television' (Gray 2001, p. 442). He locates contemporary representations of African-Americans within configurations of race politics in the USA, claiming that assimilation, pluralist and multicultural frames provide different discursive spaces. For instance, *The Cosby Show*, while being historically significant in its inauguration of particular aesthetic constructions of black cultures, is for Gray nevertheless limited as it focuses almost exclusively on middle-class mobility, individualism, and consumerism, and neglected to explore the complexities inherent in the social and cultural diversity among African-Americans.

Transnational identities and the media

In his analysis of the 'Rushdie affair' following the publication of Salman Rushdie's *The Satanic Verses*, and the fatwa declared by Ayatolla Khomeini, Chetan Bhatt (1997) argues that the debates exemplify the contradictions intrinsic to political discourse in Western liberal democracies: for example, between particularism and universalism, and around adjudications on the rights of minorities. In the case of the Rushdie affair, however, the pro-Islamic demonstrations against the alleged blasphemy committed by Rushdie, as well as arguments defending principles of free expression – particularist interests colliding with universalist rights – transcended national boundaries. As Bhatt argues:

> The local spaces of community and nation are importantly transgressed during the affair by Muslim social movements. . . . [However, it] threw up transnational social spaces that were not altogether diasporic, since they involved affiliations between life-worlds from different national social spaces that had nothing in particular to do with earlier national or continental origins.
>
> (Bhatt 1997, p. 110)

Bhatt's comment alludes to yet another dimension of the constitution of multicultural identities, namely, that the presence of the Third World in the first, the patterns of migration and the routes that trace, complicates the notion of cultural identity in such a way as to problematize the simple correlation between 'race' and culture. The term 'diaspora', which productively engages with the complexities of migration and the formation of cultural identities, has itself come under theoretical scrutiny. Bhatt's observation that the alliances constituting anti-Rushdie movements, not only in Britain but also in India and Pakistan, cannot be conceived as 'diasporic' is indicative of the debates on the concept of diaspora.

On the one hand, 'diaspora' as a concept supplies a necessary epistemological tool with which to negotiate the complex convolutions that contribute to the experiences and identity formations among minority groups. It is a productive concept that allows for conceiving identity as being constantly renewed and constructed, and not fixed in terms of 'race' or community, or religion (Gilroy 1993; Clifford 1997). On the other hand however, as Lewellen (2002) observes, 'currently there is considerable controversy about how "diasporas" should be defined in an era of globalization' (Lewellen 2002, p. 160). Until recently, Safran's (1991) identification of the characteristics of diaspora communities was generally accepted as a useful taxonomy. Chief among these was the notion of a common ancestral homeland – 'roots' in Clifford's formulation – that the community's ancestors were dispersed from, the myths and folklores that form a collective, idealized memory of 'home', and a commitment to homeland as an imagined space encouraged by cultural alienation from the host cultures. As Lewellen points out, later approaches to diaspora that have included a more general understanding of it as ethnicity and group cohesion also underline the importance of a real or imagined homeland which, as an apparently defining category, raises a few conceptual difficulties.

> Many Jews do not view Israel as a homeland in any but a historical sense. And what is one to make of the Black diaspora, which, for most, has no specific homeland, only a sort of generalized Africa? Diasporas may have multiple centers, such as may be found among Jamaicans, Haitians, Dominicans, and many others living in New York or Miami.
>
> (Lewellen 2002, p. 161)

These 'multiple centers' reveal the historical trajectories of migration, often marking diverse groups within the same diasporic community depending on whether they are once, twice, or multiple migrated or displaced (see Mehta 2003). In such cases, the notion of homeland presents a problem. Describing the divergent routes and histories of migration that make up the Indian diaspora for instance, Mishra (1996, 2002) makes a distinction between 'old' and 'new' diasporas, marked respectively by migration as indentured labour and by economic migration – the 'diaspora of plantation labour', and the 'diaspora of late capital'. The second moment, mostly post-1960s,

> is very different from the traditional nineteenth – and early twentieth – century diaspora of classic capital, which was primarily working class and connected to

plantation culture [examined in great detail by V. S. Naipaul in his novel *The House of Mr. Biswas*]. The diaspora of late capital has now become an important market of popular cinema as well as a site of its production.

(Mishra 2002, p. 236)

As Gilroy (1993, 2000) has brilliantly argued in the case of the 'Black Atlantic', the complexities that such heterogeneous histories of mobility bring to diaspora formation requires a rethinking of place, geography and genealogy in terms of hybrid and non-territorial identities:

> As an alternative to the metaphysics of 'race', nation, and bounded culture coded into the body, diaspora is a concept that problematises the cultural and historical mechanics of belonging. It disrupts the fundamental power of territory to define identity by breaking the simple sequence of explanatory links between place, location, and consciousness.

(Gilroy 2000, p. 124)

In Clifford's (1997) formulation, diasporic communities retain a creative tension with national spaces and identities, constructing public spheres and forming collective consciousnesses that transcend national boundaries and form alliances with similar others elsewhere.

Akin to the debates around multiculturalism, disputes on the conceptual validity of 'diaspora' testify to significant aspects of minority politics. As Gilroy (1994) has observed, '[Diaspora is] more than a voguish synonym for peregrination or nomadism.' In terms that recall Doreen Massey's reference to the 'power-geometry' that informs migration, Gilroy declares that '[l]ife itself is at stake in a way the word suggests flight or coerced rather than freely chosen experiences of displacement. Slavery, pogroms, indenture, genocide and other unnameable terrors have all figured in the constitution of diasporas and the reproduction of diaspora-consciousness' (Gilroy 1994, p. 204).

Besides the light it throws on the constitution of diasporas, Gilroy's comment is relevant in the context of ongoing debates in the media and in the political sphere on the status of refugees, and the recent escalation of fears of terrorism informing protective measures being adopted in Western countries. From another perspective, in their examination of 'Tradition' as challenged by 'Translation', that is, the confrontation between national identity constructed in terms of heritage and that which takes account of the multicultural and multi-ethnic nature of national culture, Morley and Robins (1995) assert that 'It is in the experience of diaspora that we may begin to understand the way beyond empire. In the experience of migration, difference is confronted; boundaries are crossed; cultures are mingled; identities become blurred.' The unsettling, recombinant and hybrid nature of diaspora experience, they argue, following Stuart Hall, challenges Tradition. 'The experience of diaspora, and also of exile, as Edward Said has powerfully argued, allows us to understand relations between cultures in new ways. The crossing of boundaries brings about a complexity of vision and also a sense of the permeability and contingency of culture' (p. 123).

Practices of cultural production, in particular, television and film, have been well researched (see for example, Naficy 1993, and Shohat and Stam 2003). As we saw earlier, the cinema of Gurinder Chadha and Mira Nair, as well as the novels and films of Hanif Kureishi offer explorations of ethnic minority experiences and inter-generational disputes within diasporic communities. Mehta's (2003) essay on Mira Nair offers an exemplary analysis of her film *Mississippi Masala*, in which the director 'depicts the complex relations between two nonwhite minorities in the United States, the Indian and the African American, prompting reflections on issues of race, color, and identity' (Mehta 2003, p. 154). Broadcast television provides a more complex cultural sphere. Naficy, for instance, divides 'minority television' into three categories: 'ethnic, transnational, and exilic' (Naficy 2003, p. 346), where 'ethnic television' is produced by indigenous minorities 'located here and now, not over there and then'. Potentially, these programmes appeal to a wide variety of audience groups as they are made in English. 'Transnational television' includes programmes made and imported from the 'homeland', as well as those made under the auspices of American and other multinational corporations to cater to particular ethnic or linguistic groups. Finally, 'Exilic Television is by definition produced by exiles living in the host country as a response to and in parallel with their own transitional and provisional status. . . . They tend to encode and foreground collective and individual struggles for authenticity and identity, deterritorialization and reterritorialization' (Naficy 2003, p. 347). Both trans-national and exilic, unlike 'ethnic' television, are examples of 'narrowcasting', as they are restricted in their audience appeal by the fact that their language is not English.

From the other end, that is, from the perspective of consumption of media and other cultural production, there has been a dramatic increase in the number of research studies on the relations between audience engagement with texts, both transnational and 'ethnic television', to use Naficy's term, and diasporic identity formation. These studies are specifically interested in locating the role that the media play in the constitu-tion of collective identities among communities that are located in particular sites but are linked through the diasporic imaginary to other similar ethnic groups located in geographically distant sites. The 'route and root' combination here is further compli-cated by location, and by what that signifies in terms of the politics of recognition involving ethnic communities and host cultures.

Contemporary diasporas are often construed as occupying a 'third space', 'beyond space and time, and beyond the situated practices of place and the lived experience of history' (Michell 1997, p. 534). This is clearly problematic, as it disavows the pertinence of the historical configurations of migrationary routes and overlooks the politics of location. The tropes of nomadism, creolization and hybridity, while they gesture towards the potential of such positions to critically transgress notions of identity that are premised on essentialized conceptions of territory and identity, nevertheless end up denying the importance of geography, as Carter (2005) argues.

In many of these accounts borders are traversed, boundaries are dissolved and space is something that is overcome. Space is invoked, but often left un-interrogated. In particular, the diaspora literature tends to discount the re-territorialising elements of diasporic practices, a shortcoming that I argue is largely due to the lack of interconnectedness between the theoretical literature on diaspora and empirical research on 'actual' diasporas and their specific geographies.

(Carter 2005, p. 55)

The diverse studies on diasporic audiences attest to and reflect this problem. As I have argued elsewhere (Harindranath 2005), Gillespie (1995), in a valuable and timely study of television viewing and cultural identity among Punjabis in a London suburb, successfully avoids the pitfalls of construing diasporic cultures in terms of 'authenticity' or 'purity' by attempting to adopt a dynamic conception of culture and identity, locating for instance, facets of inter-generational difference in television viewing and response to programmes. Unfortunately the study still ends up reifying 'ethnicity' as a defining characteristic in audiences' 'reading' of television. Gillespie's recommendation of a 'multi-sited' ethnography as a way of engaging with the complexities of diasporic identity formation is however, extremely valuable. Mishra (2002) acknowledges the contradictions and ambivalences that constitute diasporic groups: 'the diasporic social selves that I have in mind here are not some ideal, perfect community or communities but are in fact marked by strong ambiguity and self-contradiction, by a double-subjectivity, a double consciousness' (Mishra 2002, p. 238).

As noted earlier in this chapter, Mishra makes a crucial distinction between 'old' and 'new' Indian diasporas, and he argues that the Non-Resident Indian ('new') diaspora, unlike the 'old' group, plays a key role in Bombay cinema's 'gaze back' at them as a lucrative international market, contributing thereby to the adoption of specific textual strategies. In a similar move, Ray (2000), in his study of the reception of Hindi films among Fijian Indians in Australia, concedes the existence of 'different diasporic Indias', arguing against a monolithic conception: 'in fact, it is the very globality of the concept that needs to be contested and read as a sign of ahistoricity and ethnocentrism that so often underwrites the perception of postcolonial societies' (Ray 2000, p. 141). This debate underscores the complexity and ambiguity that are inevitable characteristics of most diasporic groups.

Reflecting on the question of the contemporary resonance of multicultural demands, Benhabib (2002) suggests various reasons. These include a 'reverse globalization process' involving migration from the non-West to the West, where new arrivals are confronted with values and principles of liberal-democracy, the emergence of nationalism as a powerful divisive force in Eastern Europe following the dissolution of the Soviet Union, and the 'unintended consequences of the redistributive politics in capitalist democracies and the rise of protected status identities for cultural groups through such policies' (Benhabib 2000, p. 114). The resulting complexities in terms of governance and identity politics, that is, the tussle between notions of universal citizenship rights and cultural difference, demand new ways of conceiving multiculturalism. Shohat and Stam's (1994) recommendation of a 'polycentric multiculturalism' suggests a way forward. As they see it, their formulation avoids the flaws in liberal pluralist conceptions of multiculturalism as it conceives it in terms of relational power, clearly sympathizes with the disempowered communities and promotes minority representation towards interests of a dialogic inter-relation between communities, and suggests a way to transcend narrowly defined identity politics in favour of 'informed affiliations' based on shared social inclinations and justice. Issues of sameness and difference, universalism and particularism, as we saw earlier, underscore the precariousness of multicultural and identity politics.

Further reading

Bennett, D. (ed.) (1998) *Multicultural States: Rethinking Difference and Identity*. London: Routledge.

Gilroy, P. (1993) *The Black Atlantic: Double Consciousness and Modernity*. Cambridge: Harvard University Press.

Goldberg, D. (ed.) (1994) *Multiculturalism: A Critical Reader*. Oxford: Blackwell.

Shohat, E. and R. Stam (eds) (2003) *Multiculturalism, Postcolonialism, and Transnational Media*. New Brunswick: Rutgers University Press.

Shohat, E. and R. Stam (1994) *Unthinking Eurocentrism: Multiculturalism and the Media*. New York: Routledge.

5 | THIRD CINEMA

One of the films that attracted critical attention in 2005 for its portrayal of an apparently 'true' story was *Hotel Rwanda* (dir. Terry George, 2004). An unusual film in that its subject matter was the internecine conflict between the Hutus and the Tutsis that resulted in a genocide in Rwanda, which, as a general area of concern hardly registers in Western film-making ventures, *Hotel Rwanda* succeeds in both raising the profile of the tragedy and referring to the complexity of the role of the UN in the conflict. Despite these merits, however, the film's scope is limited by its address. Narrated as a bio-pic relating the events from the perspective of a heroic hotel manager who managed, in spite of his initial reservations and his concerns for the safety of his family, to save hundreds of innocent civilians from the massacre, the film's perspective is limited to tracing the dangers faced by the family and their eventual escape to safety across the border.

In terms of narrative style and structure *Hotel Rwanda* exemplifies dominant cinematic codes. For instance, the initial intimations of the conflict are presented as destabilizing the state of equilibrium, represented by close family members gathering around a dinner table. The film follows established conventions of mainstream narrative cinema, depicting the conflict in terms of how it affects the plight of the family, through to the family's eventual break for freedom in the final suspenseful minutes of the film. The sense of the film conforming to the practice of mainstream thriller genre film-making is underlined by the ending, when, seconds before their flight across the border the hero's family are reunited with his young niece and nephew orphaned in the conflict. This is so because the film rarely engages with the complexities of the conflict itself, and the narrative structure and its final closure focuses on the family of the hero, in whose plight the conflict provides the context and the reason for disequilibrium. By retaining as the ending the resolution of the family's dilemmas and difficulties as they cross the border the film offers a happy conclusion, without commenting on the situation they leave behind in Rwanda, where the conflict and the massacres continued long after.

Even though its subject matter is ostensibly an African conflict, far removed from the normal preoccupations of dominant Hollywood narratives, the film captures the constraints faced by film-makers wanting to address 'serious' issues concerning the developing world, the South, without challenging normative ways of telling the story. Consequently, the critical edge of such interventions is dulled by the representative conventions they follow.

Compared to films such as *Once Were Warriors* (dir. Lee Tamahori, 1994), or *La Haine* (dir. Mathieu Kassovitz, 1995), *Hotel Rwanda* appears a 'typical' Hollywood adventure, transplanted from the cityscapes of New York or Los Angeles to Kigali. The former's attempt to explore the contemporary realities of Maori life in urban Auckland, while it similarly focuses on the challenges faced by members of a family (including domestic violence, unemployment, and alcoholism), nevertheless presents a more intricate and nuanced picture of the complex negotiations that are part of the formation of contemporary Maori identity. *La Haine*, a stylistically adventurous film that examines the institutional and cultural racism in contemporary France, uses a multi-racial group of youthful friends to consider the politics of multiculturalism and the continuing marginalization of ethnic minorities in French society.

It is possible to argue that these two are political films, as opposed to *Hotel Rwanda* whose treatment of its potential deeply political topic as a conventional narrative robs it of serious comment. A crucial question that emerges here is whether stylistic innovations that seek to undermine conventional or dominant narrative strategies are essential for the engagement with serious political issues. Can Ken Loach's *Bread and Roses* (2000) be considered a political film for its scrutiny of the 'invisible' lives of the illegal Mexican labour in the USA – in this particular instance, Mexican women working as cleaners in Los Angeles – despite its fairly conventional structure and its inclusion of a romantic attachment among two of its protagonists? Similarly, Bahman Ghobadi's Kurdish film *Turtles Can Fly* (2004) combines comedy with pathos in its use of the experiences of a group of children (played by non-actors) as an allegory to indict war. While it does not employ a mainstream narrative that ends on a neat resolution, neither is it interested in formal innovation.

What distinguishes a politically committed film from a commercial film that follows established codes of narrative and realism? What is the transformative potential of film-making as cultural practice? Questions like these animate discussions of what has come to be called 'Third Cinema', a form of film-making practice with explicit commitment to political comment and social transformation. As Mike Wayne (2002) points out, 'The term Third Cinema designates a body of theory and film-making practice committed to political and cultural emancipation' (Wayne 2002, p. 211). Understandably, given its emphasis on the interaction between theory and practice, Third Cinema as a term and as a critical examination of creative output has undergone constant revision since its inception, and can be said to retain its stature as a contested category.

Influenced though it was by developments in Soviet cinema of the 1920s, Third Cinema's commitment to stylistic challenge and political transformation emerged in the 1960s era giddy with the success of the Cuban revolution, the victory of Vietnam in the conflict against the colonial French rule, and the triumph of national independence struggles against colonial powers. In this political and cultural context it was relatively easy to imagine a tri-continental (that is, between Latin America, Africa and Asia) revolutionary practice in both politics and aesthetics, and Third Cinema consequently became one of the diverse manifestos that fuelled emancipatory politics. Initially coined by Fernando Solanas and Octavio Getino as part of the theoretical accompaniment to their 1968 film *The Hour of the Furnaces*, the term Third Cinema was one of the militant manifestos of the 1960 and 1970s that sought to engage politically and stylistically with the practice of film-making, calling for a social and aesthetic revolution that would culminate in the making of films addressing social concerns and contribute to changing them.

In the case of Solanas and Getino the call was for militant guerrilla documentaries or 'unfinished' cinema that radically neutralized the hegemony of Hollywood or dominant European hegemony, including capitalist modes of cinematic production (Martin 1997). In a later essay (Solanas and Getino [1983] 1997) they argued that 'The model of the perfect work of art, the fully rounded film structured according to the merits imposed by bourgeois culture, its theoreticians and critics, has served to inhibit the film-maker in the dependent countries' (Solanas and Getino 1997, p. 48). The alternative, to them, is a ceaseless search for innovation in terms of form that will enable a critical and politically relevant intervention: 'the existence of revolutionary cinema is inconceivable without the constant and methodological exercise of practice, search, and experimentation' (*ibid.*).

Glauber Rocha ([1982] 1997) similarly argues for an 'aesthetic of hunger' that articulated and engaged with social issues in Brazil, a new form of cinema that distinguished itself from 'industrial cinema', which to him represented 'untruth and expoitation' (Rocha 1997, p. 61), whereas Cinema Novo 'is an ongoing process of exploration that is making our thinking clearer, freeing us from the debilitating delirium of hunger' (p. 60). In Rocha's formulation, hunger itself becomes the symbol of resistance and a basis for the demand for social justice.

Rejecting what he considered the 'reactionary' elements in the codes of dominant cinema, Julio Garcia Espinosa ([1983] 1997) promoted 'imperfect cinema': 'a new poetics for the cinema [which] will, above all, be a "partisan" and "committed" poetics, a "committed" art, a consciously and resolutely "committed" cinema – that is to say, an "imperfect" cinema' (Espinosa 1997, p. 79). Such manifestos for aesthetically and politically revolutionary cinematic and artistic practice emerged from the political situation of the time and was informed by the work of scholars such as Frantz Fanon who explored the notion of national consciousness and violence in the struggle for political independence in colonized countries.

The theory and practice of Third Cinema was seen in these manifestos as self-consciously and deliberately setting itself apart from First and Second Cinema, which, as Chanan (1997) puts it, 'correspond not to the First and Second Worlds but constitute a virtual geography of their own' (Chanan 1997, p. 375). For Solinas and Getino, dominant studio-based commercial cinema of Hollywood and its emphasis in film as spectacle was First Cinema, an industry which promoted the notion of the extraordinary individual – the hero – as the agent for narrative development, and retained its hegemony in defining film narratives and institutional structures. Second Cinema, which challenged dominant and accepted codes of film and narrative, comprised 'art cinema' or 'auteur cinema'. While these allowed film-makers the freedom to transgress prevailing styles of film and to experiment with dramatic devices, and were, therefore, potentially revolutionary, Second Cinema soon acquired the institutional practices of dominant cinema, according to Solinas and Getino.

> In the process . . . the vanguard was defused and became a cinema made by and for the limited social groups characteristic of what the Argentinians call the dilettante elite. These groups were politically reformist – for example in opposing censorship – but incapable of any profound change.
>
> (Chanan 1997, p. 376)

The genuine alternative to both the hegemony of First Cinema and the flawed or incomplete aesthetic experiments in Second Cinema was, for Solinas and Getino, a practice of film-making that radically reorganized the production process – ideally making it a collective project – as well as the content: 'Guerilla film-making proletarianizes the film worker and breaks down the intellectual aristocracy that the bourgeoisie grants to its followers. In a word, it democratises. The film-maker's tie with reality makes him more a part of his people' (Solinas and Getino 1997, p. 50). Two significant issues emerge from this: firstly, the idealistic or utopian logic that underscores the initial conceptions of Third Cinema contained in these manifestos, and secondly, its commitment to revolutionary practice against imperialism and neo-colonialism.

In terms of the overarching claims constituting formulations of Third Cinema regarding cinema's potential contribution to emancipatory politics, subsequent theorists and film activists have constantly attempted to reform and refine its political and artistic commitments. Reiterating Third Cinema's allegiance to theory development as well as to practice, later refinements (see for example, Burton 1985; Chanan 1997; Gabriel 1982; Wayne 2001, 2002; Willemen 1989) have tried to retain its critical edge while augmenting the conception of Third Cinema to include more diverse practice. Although Third Cinema resonates with the political and cultural concerns of the concept of the 'third world' and with the project of decolonization, and received its genesis and initial impetus in a complex formulation which combined the writings of Frantz Fanon with the notions of dependency and neo-colonialism, as a politically inflected cultural and artistic practice, it is not necessarily confined to film-making practice in a particular geographical region. Stam (1991) locates debates about Third Cinema alongside the conceptual re-evaluations of Eurocentrism, multiculturalism, Afro-centrism, and the 'third world'. 'In purely classificatory terms,' he claims,

> we might envision concentric circles of denotation for 'third cinema': (1) a core circle of films produced by and for third world people (no matter where those people happen to be physically located) and adhering to the principles of third cinema . . .; (2) a wider circle of the cinematic productions of third world peoples (whether or not the films adhere to the principles of third cinema, and irrespective of the period of their making); and (3) a final circle, somewhat anomalous in status, at once 'inside' and 'outside', consisting of those films made by first or second world people in support of third world peoples and adhering to the principles of third cinema.
>
> (Stam 1991, p. 219)

It is important to recognize that, since its inception in the 1960s, political cinema has expanded to include a range of practices and genres, as Shohat (1997/2000) points out, 'the resistant practices of such films are neither homogeneous nor static; they vary over time, from region to region, and, in genre, from epic costume drama to personal small-budget documentary. Their aesthetic strategies range from "progressive realist" to Brechtian deconstructivist to avant-gardist, tropicalist, and resistant postmodern' (Shohat 2000, p. 1997).

In accordance with the notion of cinema as transformative practice, Third Cinema, particularly in its initial conception by practitioners and scholars, conceived of the relationship between film and the viewer as dynamic and dialectical. The development of 'radical consciousness' that Gabriel (1982), for instance, insists on as the rationale for Third Cinema involved the attempt to 'decolonize the mind' – which finds echoes in the Kenyan writer Ngugi Wa Thiong'o's call for a similar process of the decolonization of the imagination – enabled by 'films with social relevance and innovative style and, above all, with political and ideological overtones' (cited in Guneratne 2003, p. 11).

In that polemical restatement of Third Cinema's self-conscious political project we have its essential characteristics as announced in the initial manifestos. Crucial among them is the audience's relationship with the text, which is conceived as active and participatory, thus anticipating the concept of the 'active' audience in media research in the 1990s. The film and the accompanying manifesto that is credited with being the progenitor of 'Third Cinema', Solinas and Getino's *The Hour of the Furnace* provides a classic instance of how this perception of the audience–text dialectic informed the stylistic and artistic innovations strived for by film-makers. As Chanan (1997) argues, the film included 'intertitles' which not only interrupted the flow of the documentary's narrative, but also posed questions about contemporary Argentina that audiences were encouraged to reflect on. In addition, Solinas and Getino's idea of it being more a 'film act' rather than a film in the customary sense, included stopping the screening at particular junctures in order to enable debate and discussion among the audience. The resulting film is an assemblage of styles and formats, explicitly organized to interfere with the normally passive experience of film viewing.

> The end product amounts to a militant poetic epic tapestry, weaving together disparate styles and materials ranging from didacticism to operatic stylisation, direct filming to the techniques of advertising, and incorporating photographs, newsreel, testimonial footage and film clips – from avant garde and mainstream, fiction and documentary.
>
> (Chanan 1997, p. 373)

In Stam's (1990) evaluation, the insistence on audience participation reveals an inherent paradox with regard to *Hour of the Furnaces*, namely, that its political content is explicit and unambiguous and consequently can be argued as not providing the viewer the opportunity for engagement, as would a more polysemic or equivocal text. On the other hand, however, as Chanan (1997) points out, 'the openness of the film lies elsewhere: in the *political* relationship between the film and the viewer – at least, in the clandestine circumstances in which the film was necessarily viewed in Argentina in the years before 1973' (p. 373, emphasis in the original). The critical point to note here is that the overt political critique that Third Cinema film-makers saw themselves as being involved in entailed a conception of the audience which was different from the First Cinema, or the cinema of spectacle, which assumed a passive audience.

Wayne (2002) makes a similar point in his discussion of the merits of the film *The Battle of Algiers* (1965):

> It is precisely *this question of the audience* and the nature of their engagement with the text which is central to Third Cinema. Indeed, Third Cinema has appropriated the theme of the active spectator from the avant-garde. . . . The transformation which Third Cinema effects on modern art/active spectator relationship is to relocate them both back into the broader social struggles from which they have been severed, so that the spectator is no longer engaged in a purely aesthetic activity. . . . Nevertheless, if we are interested in the *relationship* between text and audience, we must still ask what the text contributes to the production of meaning.
>
> (Wayne 2002, p. 215, emphasis added)

In his book *Political Film* (2001), Wayne invokes the term 'dialogic' as theorized by the Russian scholar Mikhail Bakhtin to describe the relation between film and audience that Third Cinema aspires to, namely to allow and encourage the audience to engage with the film's political statement. The Solanas and Getino film *The Hour of the Furnaces*, the progenitor of the theory and practice of Third Cinema, contains textual features such as division into chapters, that allowed the film to be stopped to allow political debates among the audience.

Renewing Third Cinema theory

Wayne (2001, 2002) presents perhaps the most consistent argument for a reassessment of the original theoretical underpinning of Third Cinema. For instance, the tripartite division of First Cinema as dominant commercial, Second Cinema as art and Third Cinema as political is to him an unsatisfactory distinction particularly in the context of recent developments which muddy such clear demarcations. Rescuing the logic of Third Cinema from its conventional blending with Third-World film practice is for him central to this reassessment. This involves acknowledging the complexity of the processes which constitute First and Second Cinema and the distinctions between them, and recognizing that, 'First, Second, and Third Cinema do not designate geographical areas, but institutional structures/working practices, associated aesthetic strategies and their attendant cultural politics. . . . [W]e can have First and Second Cinema in the Third World, and Third Cinema in the First World' (Wayne 2002, pp. 211–12). The first consideration in the reappraisal of Third Cinema theory and practice is, in other words, its production practices as well as its aesthetic-political aspects, both of which together constitute the cultural politics of social transformation inherent in Third Cinema.

Given the differences between the three cinemas in terms of working practices and textual strategies Wayne argues,

> it follows that all three cinemas take up their own distinctive *positionings* in relation to a shared referent: i.e. the historical, social world around them. Thus, each cinema also has relations of dialogue, interchange and transformation between them as each works over and on the same cultural/political material (for example, the anti-colonial struggle), but pulls and shapes that material into different, often radically different, meanings and possibilities.
>
> (Wayne 2002, p. 212)

This is an important distinction: even when First and Second Cinemas address similar issues, or have similar points of reference as Third Cinema, the ways in which they utilize textual and production possibilities are distinct. The transformative potential of Third Cinema rests precisely on this: its adoption of aesthetic strategies that not only involve audience participation in particular ways, but employ discursive practices markedly different from the other two cinemas. For Wayne, therefore, Third Cinema does not amount to a simple or straightforward rejection of First and Second Cinemas, but a critical engagement with and dialectical transformation of them. While a primary focus of Third Cinema is the political opposition to dominant and avant-garde cinema in terms of form and address, this nevertheless does not translate into an attempt to reinvent cinema or the arrogation of a position of formal opposition. That is,

> it seeks to *transform* rather than simply reject these cinemas; it seeks to bring out their stifled potentialities, those aspects of the social world they repress or

only obliquely acknowledge; Third Cinema seeks to detach what is positive, life-affirming and critical from Cinemas First and Second Cinema and give them a more expanded, socially connected articulation.

(Wayne 2002, p. 214)

But in order to understand and theorize the urgent need for Third Cinema and how it differs from the other two, we have to have a clear understanding of cinemas First and Second. The analysis of the dominant and avant-garde cinematic representations, however, needs to be carefully delineated, for intrinsic to the framework of analysis is the hegemony of dominant intellectual paradigms that simultaneously impose elitist and arcane perspectives while ignoring the core elements of Third Cinema theory and critique. From the standpoint of Third Cinema, such analysis ought to be construed, according to Wayne, as a challenge to existing dominant paradigms such as Lacanian psychoanalysis and the extremes of postmodernism, as they neglect the material aspects of cultural exchange and production. An engagement with First and Second Cinemas includes taking into consideration the complex ways in which the politics of the distribution of cultural resources that derive from social relations of production contribute to the politics of extremism, including fundamentalism and fanatical nationalism, in which representation assumes extremist forms. Instead of psychoanalyst or postmodernist analysis, therefore, Wayne recommends a 'genuinely socialist, indeed Marxist' analysis of First and Second Cinemas, a critique that is intrinsic to Third Cinema practice.

Chanan's (1997) and Guneratne's (2003) contributions to the development of Third Cinema theory likewise attempt to recuperate the critical edge of Third Cinema while acknowledging changes in global politics as well as aesthetic transformations in cinematic representation. Chanan, for instance, is concerned with the effacement of local differences in the initial formulations of Third Cinema that idealistically called for the transcendence of local and national differences in the name of a transnational politics. Mindful of the contributions to the critiques of social inequality addressed by Second Cinema auteurs, he seeks to enlarge the rubric of Third Cinema by tracing the modifications made to the original manifestos by their authors.

Guneratne (2003) is troubled by the sidelining of Third Cinema theory by mainstream academic work on cinema. While on the one hand its original idealistic formulation embraced what was referred to as the Third World and, therefore, covered a wide geographical region in which the majority of the world's films were produced, paradoxically it has come to stand as a generalized concept: 'an increasingly ephemeral Third World now teetering on the brink of being globalized away' (Guneratne 2003, p. 1). Neither its critique of commercial cinema in the developing world nor its foundational aspirations marrying revolutionary theory and practice in the interest of social transformation has been taken adequately into account, according to Guneratne – a state of affairs that has reflected the general neglect, until relatively recently, of cinemas from the developing world in the classrooms of metropolitan centres.

For him this relative neglect is doubly unfortunate as, despite Third Cinema theory being embodied in 'unforgettable films' from different continents, depicting its critical and political credentials and expressing calls for social justice inspired by activist-theorists such as Frantz Fanon, Che Guevara and Amilcar Cabral, such films are rarely discussed in relation to the theory. This is primarily because the 'discipline of Film Studies, no less than the medium from which it derives, has been shaped by social forces and intellectual currents of a turbulent century, and the marginality of the *petit histoire* of Third Cinema in its grander progress is less a tale of neglect than one of considered omission or deliberate exclusion' (Guneratne 2003, p. 2).

Despite the historical-cultural specificities and the political-ideological commitment that were integral to Third Cinema theory and practice, its critique included universal themes such as neo-colonialism. For Guneratne this involved a theoretically-informed political engagement with the universalist agendas of Western history (with which contemporary post-structuralist critiques are preoccupied) and the consequent erasure of other histories and experiences. The address of specific historical conjunctures in other words, is critical to Third Cinema, even while First Cinema largely continues to ignore these.

This defining characteristic of Third Cinema was evident even in its original assumptions and conceptualizations by Latin American film-makers:

> Latin American film-makers, more practiced than their still-colonized African and Asian brethren in standing at an analytical remove from the ideologies of Neocolonialism, understood well that the history of the West is also the erasure of the reality of the West's others. . . . Indeed, one could even argue that the contestation of the historical bedrock of Eurocentric imperialist self-justification was to become the foundational premise of post-revolutionary Cuban Third Cinema.
>
> (Guneratne 2003, p. 5)

Wayne (2001, 2002) similarly touches on neo-colonialism, but for him the specificities of Third Cinema theory is central to the critique of contemporary manifestations of global capitalism and the patterns of inequality that it entails:

> developing the theory of Third Cinema may be seen as something of a 'holding operation' in the dark times of neo-liberalism's hegemony. Revolutionary conjunctures are the womb from which Third Cinema emerges, and while Third Cinema can be made in conditions which are temporarily or spatially distant from revolutionary conjunctures . . . inspiration, political tradition and memory are the umbilical chord which nourishes Third Cinema in a time of reaction and barbarism.
>
> (Wayne 2002, p. 212)

The timeliness and contemporary relevance of Third Cinema theory and practice is underlined by 'the persistent failure of the western avant-garde', that is, Second

Cinema, to move from a self-conscious preoccupation with matters of form for its own sake to what Wayne, borrowing from Willemen, refers to as 'social mobility', by which he means making 'the ambition to make the social world intelligible or explicable. It yokes the question of artistic form to cognition and knowledge' (Wayne 2002, p. 367). Eschewing social comment and political commitment – the hallmarks of Third Cinema – the politics of form overrides content in the avant garde, with the result that aesthetic strategies are divorced from serious political concerns.

Guneratne (2003) identifies three main reasons for the neglect of Third Cinema theory in mainstream academic research and pedagogy. Firstly, the semantic confusion about the term 'Third World' – the 'perverse polymorphism of the Third World desig-nation' as he calls it (p. 7) – and the political ramifications stemming from it, contrib-uted to the second generation of Third Cinema theorists questioning the validity of the distinction between Third Cinema and Third-World Cinema, and the relative disregard of the particularities of specific historical and political conjunctures within the 'Third World' in favour of a more unvaried challenge to representational authority. Guneratne argues that despite this apparent schism among Third Cinema practitioners and theor-ists the main contributory factor to the marginalization of the theory is the Eurocen-trism of critical frames and the epistemologies that underpin them, which are to him not only Eurocentric but 'almost exclusively Anglo-Francophone in outlook and orien-tation' (p. 9). Given that its initial impetus came almost entirely from Latin America, this critical provincialism further removed Third Cinema theory from metropolitan academic discourse.

Secondly, the critical perspective of 'Third Worldism' has led to the exoticization and homogenization of cultural products from this 'imaginary terrain. . . . Ignoring audiences in "third world" societies, scholars working in developed countries have tended to project their own political agendas as moral and aesthetic requirements upon films from the "third world" without, however, insisting on similar requirement for First World Cinema' (p. 10). This 'critical imperialism' adds to the burden of represen-tation borne by artists from marginalized and minority communities, in the sense that a Third-World film-maker or a minority writer is assumed to be the spokesperson of an entire community or geographical zone.

Several contributors to *Questions of Third Cinema* (Gabriel, Taylor and Minh-ha in particular) raise pertinent and critical questions on various dimensions of critical practice and theory in dominant academic discourse. Minh-ha, for instance, queries the authorial licence afforded to First World representations of Third-World cultures and space, even while it is denied to the film-maker from one part of the Third World to speak about people from another part.

Guneratne locates the polemical stance of the foundational manifestos as a possible third reason, as they provided a 'disparate constellation' of committed and revolution-ary voices rather than a body of theory carefully argued and presented. The rigidity of the tripartite division of the three kinds of cinema, according to Guneratne, added to the misinterpretation of Third Cinema theory, as it allowed neither for critical elements to be present in First dominant cinema of entertainment or the Second cinema of the intellect, nor for possible influences across the three cinemas, that the radical elements of Third Cinema aesthetic practice could arguably spill over into the entertainment cinema, or that it could borrow narrative strategies and formal experiments from Second Cinema. Pontecorvo's response to charges that *The Battle of Algiers* had its critique of Algerian politics blunted by the elements of the thriller genre is noteworthy. His defence touched on the apparent contradiction in capitalist cultural production, namely, that the profit motive drove its logic and therefore towards innovation, while its long-term interests were served by not challenging its own hegemony through the creation and circulation of novel critical ideas.

Despite the exploration of political and social issues in such films as Costa Gavras's *Missing* (1981) and John Boorman's *The Emerald Forest* (1985) – films that deal with political issues that potentially offer alternatives to the status quo or challenge historical accounts – Wayne is sceptical about what such films can achieve in terms of social and political change, and considers their critical engagement with wider social and cultural forces to be of limited value. The main contributor to this limitation is the way in which the narrative structure of, and aesthetic strategies adopted by, such films circumscribe their potential to articulate political and social meanings, and thereby to offer alternatives to what is. Third Cinema's declared intent of expanding the political and cultural horizons of the audiences consequently sets it apart from Second and First Cinema, and underscores it as a committed and utopian cinema aimed at achieving radical change. Inherent in this is Third Cinema's constant search for alternative aesthetic strategies:

> This expansion of our horizons is as much about what cinema can and cannot do as it is about calling for change in the wider social world. So, while there are contradictions within capitalism, while there is some latitude for progressive cultural workers, we must not block up our capacity to imagine radically different cinemas and visions of radically different social and political relations.
>
> (Wayne 2002, p. 215)

He identifies three broad elements that characterize the dialectics of Third Cinema vis-à-vis First and Second Cinema, namely the context of production, aesthetic strategies including four key markers of films that fall under the rubric of Third Cinema, and which distinguish them from other films that engage with serious political issues: 'historicity, politicisation, critical commitment, and cultural specificity' (Wayne 2002, p. 217), and the films' dialogic relationship with their audiences – a feature that we encountered earlier.

Using the example of a British based non-profit collective, Amber Films, Wayne (2001) argues that the question of production infrastructure is part of the critique of First Cinema by Third Cinema. Contrasting John Boorman's film *The Emerald Forest* (1985) to Jorge Sanjines's work with the Ukamau group in Bolivia, in particular their use of filming techniques such as long shots to facilitate the representation of the collective, Wayne tries to demonstrate the differences in the conception of their role by the film-makers. Whereas Boorman's self-perception as an artist informs both the mode of production as well as the narrative of *The Emerald Forest* and compromises its political message, Wayne applauds Sanjines's conscious effort to provide agency to his peasant actors in the Ukamau group's early film *Blood of the Condor* (1969). More specifically, 'Sanjines bothers to think about the relationship between form and content, whereas Boorman, an aspirant Second Cinema director working with little room for manoeuvre within First Cinema, must simply impose the classic model onto the subject matter' (Wayne 2001, p. 56).

While his chosen examples illustrate what he refers to as the 'democratic modes of production' (p. 47) pioneered and maintained by Third Cinema in its efforts to break down the hierarchies inherent in the creative process of film-making, this aspect of his argument appears the weakest, perhaps because it reflects the idealism that continues to remain close to the heart of 'pure' Third Cinema. This is not to quibble with the radical intent that informs such attempts at collective production, nor to undermine the challenge to capitalist modes of production epitomized in studio-based film-making. As Wayne himself concedes, the Third Cinema mode of production does not necessarily guarantee the production of Third Cinema films, particularly since those documentaries and films made in such collectives have to still contend with the realities of projection and distribution. Moreover, the films that he identifies as depicting the aesthetic strategies and political commitment specific to Third Cinema are not always the result of democratic and collective production techniques.

His discussion of the thematic and aesthetic elements of a typical Third Cinema text, however, is much more convincing and useful, in particular his discussion of individual films to illustrate the importance of the four 'marker's of Third Cinema film. Building on Walter Benjamin's observation about the 'image-creating medium' being used to closely examine and depict history, Wayne (2002) attempts to establish one task of Third Cinema to be *historicity*, that is, the examination of the contradictions, changes and conflicts that constitute the process of history.

This is developed further in Wayne (2001), in which he uses the example of Steven Spielberg's *Amistad* (1997), he argues that Third Cinema offers a critique of the 'eternalisation of the present' in capitalist societies in which 'a historically determined society (dominated by capital) is simply projecting itself back into the past. By finding itself in the past, the present reassures itself that it was always meant to be and that there will be no other alternatives or paths for humankind' (Wayne 2001, p. 60). Third Cinema, through the exploration of the complexities of historical change, as well as the undermining of the capitalist conception of the individual as the agent of change (and the conception of the individual artist), seeks to reassert the social and political dimensions of history. As he points out, the intricate historical and social aspects of slavery in the USA is left out of *Amistad*'s storyline which promotes instead individuals as agents of change without an adequate examination of the social context of their actions. Tomas Alea's Cuban film *The Last Supper* (1976), and Ousmane Sembene's

Camp de Thiaroye (1987) on the other hand, by portraying the actions of the protagonists within the context of the contradiction between the Church and capital, and of the
response of African soldiers of the Second World War against French racism respectively, explore, according to Wayne, the prematurity of subaltern revolt in the history of
political transformation in Cuba and Africa.

Our critique of *Hotel Rwanda* too, can be made along these lines, that while it
shows the brutality of the conflict, it nevertheless is an ahistoric depiction of the civil
war in Rwanda. The narrative strategies that it adopts, which approximate the thriller
genre, elevate the actions of the central character above that of the political context of
the conflict. Despite allusions to the relative powerlessness of the United Nations
peacekeeping force stationed in Kigali and the apparent neglect of the situation by
Western powers, the film ends on a happy note, thereby highlighting its preoccupation
with the heroic individual and his family. The conflict is, therefore, presented as an
impediment to the family's well-being, rather than a complex situation with specific
historical dimensions. Wayne's second marker for Third Cinema – *politicization* – the
idea of that revolutionary cinema contributes to the political awareness of the marginalized groups within a global or local community through critical commentary on the
processes that contribute to their oppression and exploitation, is consequently absent
in *Hotel Rwanda*.

Pontecorvo's *The Battle of Algiers* is often regarded by scholars as quintessential
Third Cinema as it portrays the role of a handful of revolutionaries in the political
awakening of Algerian populace in the struggle for national independence, and the
French colonial power's clinical and brutally effective efforts at suppressing it. Its
contemporary relevance in the context of the 'war on terror' was underlined at its re-
release in 2004. Wayne, however, is doubtful of its *critical commitment*, his third
characteristic of Third Cinema, believing that the film fails to engage sufficiently with
the class dimensions of the nationalist struggle. By 'critical commitment' Wayne refers
to Third Cinema's critique of First Cinema's attempt to engage the audience emotion-
ally; Third Cinema in contrast is interested in encouraging the audience's critical and
cognitive engagement, and thereby presenting an alternative to 'the cultural industry
[which] has become extremely adept at orchestrating emotionality while deliberately
atrophying the desire for understanding' (Willemen 1989, p. 13).

By ignoring the facets of class and gender in the struggle for national liberation the
film, according to Wayne, disregards Fanon's ([1961] 1970) argument about class differences within such struggles, that 'exploitation can wear a black face, or an Arab
one. . . . The people must be taught to cry "Stop thief!" In their weary road towards
rational knowledge the people must also give up their too-simple conception of their
overlords' (Fanon 1970, p. 116). Fanon emphasizes the gravity of this consciousness
post-independence, when the exploited need to stringently oppose privilege. As Wayne
points out, 'Today, in the wake of the disappointments of a post-apartheid South
Africa, Fanon's concerns about how the masses are shut out of power by the elites
continues to resonate' (Wayne 2002, pp. 222–3). Consequently, the fact that *The Battle*

of Algiers fails to address the class difference within the struggle weakens its stature as a Third Cinema film.

Wayne is also critical of praise for *The Battle* for its apparent neutrality, which to him detracts from its political commitment, as Third Cinema 'would want to point the finger . . . But to do that requires taking a position, making a commitment' (p. 217). His scepticism of the value of the film's neutrality stems from his understanding that the ideas of 'neutrality', or 'balance' raise the question of valorizing a film on the basis of the distinction between politics and propaganda. A 'typical' Third Cinema text would, for him, be impervious to such distinctions, preferring instead to be unequivocally, and critically, dedicated to a cause.

This recalls Espinosa's ([1983] 1997) pronouncement on the political aspect of Third Cinema, 'A new poetics for the cinema will, above all, be a "partisan" and "committed" poetics, a "committed" art, a consciously and resolutely "committed" cinema – that is to say, an "imperfect" cinema' (Espinosa 1997, p. 79). Consequently Wayne finds the textual formation of *The Battle* 'compromised', as it 'never quite manages to transform its First and Second elements and influences fully into the service of Third Cinema, even though it has one foot in the latter category' (Wayne 2002, p. 217).

It is possible to argue the case that Shaji Karun's *Piravi* (1988), which depicts the pain an aged father experiences at the disappearance of his son and his growing frustration at the faceless and implacable bureaucracy, presents a fictional account of a real-life incident of the alleged arrest and disappearance of an engineering student, a suspected Naxalite revolutionary in the southern Indian state of Kerala. Shaji uses the tragedy of the incident and its repercussions on the student's family to explore the ways in which the Emergency declared by Prime Minister Indira Gandhi affected ordinary life, particularly among the lower classes. Not so much a critique of capitalism as of the dangers attendant on the undermining of democracy, *Piravi* affirms Wayne's point about political commitment and historicity. Located as it is in the immediate political and socio-cultural milieu of Kerala, it reinforces the final characteristic of Third Cinema that he identifies, namely, *cultural specificity*. As he argues,

> a grounding in the cultural dynamics of the milieu deserves a special category, because cinema is part of culture and its greatest contribution can be in the realm of culture. Third Cinema is characterised by its intimacy and familiarity with culture . . . Further, Third Cinema explores how culture is a site of political struggle.
>
> (Wayne 2002, p. 224)

Intervening in the site of culture, Third Cinema attempts to reverse the attempts by the power elite to control culture. Nevertheless, Third Cinema is not a simple gainsaying of imperialism through the uncritical defence of 'native' culture. Its treatment of 'national' culture or 'tradition' anticipates and colludes to a certain extent with the critique of nationalism by postcolonial theory, but unlike the latter, Third Cinema theory informs practice.

National and gender politics

Adjudications of a film's political commitment and historicity clearly involve considering it within the parameters of what Ginsburg has referred to in the context of indigenous cultural production as 'embedded aesthetics'. The category of 'cultural specificity' further underlines the significance of critical assessments having to take into account the local cultural and historical formations. Wayne's (2002) approval of Pontecorvo's defence of *The Battle of Algiers* in terms of its favourable reception by those involved in revolutionary politics is a clear case in point, as it acknowledges the film's audiences as socially and politically situated in particular times and locations. Films such as *Piravi* that engage critically with local and national politics are at the least poised between the intersections of First, Second and Third Cinemas, poised between commercial constraints, aesthetic originality and political commitment. National culture will be discussed in greater detail in Chapter 7, but it is worth noting here a few relevant issues in relation to Third Cinema.

In his commentary on commercial cinema, Nandy (1995) argues that its economic imperative drives such cinema towards taking an 'instrumental view of cultural traditions and worldviews and present them theatrically and spectacularly' (Nandy 1995, p. 204). To the extent that this requires generalizing issues and 'exteriorizing' their psychological problems, Nandy maintains, these films are 'anti-psychological'. In other words, they represent psychological conflicts in terms of inter-group conflict or as arising from specific conjunctions of outside circumstances. In the context of mainstream Indian cinema, for instance, 'the grandiloquent stylisation of the Muslim aristocratic traditions of North India, Goan Christian simplicity and love of a good life, Rajput valour, Bengali romanticism; they are all essential to the basic style of the commercial cinema' (Nandy 1995, p. 205). Thus their narrative logic is driven by such generalizations of group or community traits, and by their responses to external events. 'Together they allow commercial cinema to "spectacularize" and de-psychologize everything that it touches . . . and subject every sentiment and value to the judgement of the market' (*ibid.*). It is possible to add to Nandy's argument that, along with the loss of the psychological aspects of character development is also lost their political motivations and, therefore, the absence of political commitment in such films.

With regard to Third-World national cinemas, two considerations are pertinent here. Firstly, the instability of the constitution of a putative national culture, as it inevitably subsumes within it a diversity that it attempts to overcome and, to a certain extent, conceal. It, therefore, raises the questions of the role of the national cultural and political elite in the construction of unitary national imaginaries, and the hegemonic discourses that they employ. Shohat ([1997] 2000) for instance has argued that 'Third-Worldist films are often produced within the legal codes of the nation-states, often in (hegemonic) national languages, recycling national intertexts (literatures, oral narratives, music), projecting national imaginaries' (p. 1996), a consequence of which is that 'the topos of a unitary nation often camouflages the possible contradictions among different sectors of Third-World society. The nation states of the Americas, of Africa and Asia often "cover" the existence, not only of women, but also of indigenous nations (Fourth World) within them' (p. 1999). This will be explored in greater detail in a later chapter, but in terms of political film-making, national cinemas have included traditions and auteurs who have consistently critiqued the hegemony of national culture and nationalist politics.

Secondly, as Aijaz Ahmad (1987) has argued, the notion of 'three worlds' obscures differences within both the First and the Third Worlds, and the commonalities between them, prompting his assertion that 'we do not live in three worlds, but one'. What is significant for our present purposes is that both these points highlight differences within the national context in the developing world, and complicate the relations within and between the nation-states. In terms of cinema too, it is important to recognize that the commercial cinema that Nandy is rightly critical of is one of the assorted cinematic traditions in the developing world. It is the recognition of this issue that prompts Guneratne (2003) to record the challenge posed to Third Cinema theorists by 'the teeming sub-national cinemas of such extended "nations" as Indonesia' (p. 20), where the presence of diverse, culturally- and geographically-distinct nationalities problematizes the notion of the nation. Sen's essay, 'What's "oppositional" in Indonesian cinema?' is an engagement precisely with that issue of 'the "nation" in Third Cinema' (Sen 2003, p. 154).

Guneratne refers to the recuperations of African collective and mythic memory in Sembene's films such as *Xala* (1974), *Ceddo* (1976), *Le Camp de Thoraye* (1989) and *Guelwaar* (1992) by way of illustrating the film-maker's commitment to the examination of the patriarchal and corrupt systems in Senegal. Likewise, he alludes to the socialist credentials of the Indian director Ritwik Ghatak, a source of inspiration for other Indian and Latin American film-makers.

Armes (1987), despite the validity of the criticism of him by Stam (1991) as being Eurocentric, offers a comprehensive overview of Third-World cinema considered alongside or in the context of local political economy and history, and the complex relations between the developed and developing worlds. His brief but noteworthy examination of 'new' or 'alternative' Indian cinema is a case in point. As noted by Guneratne (2003), India's multiple traditions of film-making, that combines elements of First, Second and Third Cinemas, is 'the most maddeningly intricate because of its polymorphous, seemingly incommensurable diversities' (p. 20). Armes's careful delineation of the main features and auteurs from the Indian 'new wave' tradition and its regional variations, however, provides a way of negotiating this complex terrain. The regional cinemas from the various linguistically diversified states, constitute a politically important and lucrative industry in various languages like Marathi, Bengali, Oriya, Tamil, Telugu and Malayalam.

Superimposed onto this regional variation to the Bombay film industry, however, is the 'new wave' Indian Cinema, funded by the government and engaging with serious social and political issues of post-independence India. Inaugurated by Satyajit Ray's

Pather Panchali, the films provide artistic and political alternatives to mainstream narratives and traditions. While as Armes concedes, most of these have been commercially unsuccessful, relative to the mainstream industry, they have produced critically challenging cinema, both experimental in terms of film aesthetics (for example, Mani Kaul's *Uski Roti* (1970) and *Dhrupad* (1982)) and political in terms of dealing with subjects like caste prejudice (Shyam Benegal's *Samar* (1998)), state corruption (Saeed Mirza's *Albert Pinto ko gussa kyon atha hai* (1980)), religious persecution (Sathyu's *Garam Hawa* (1975), and female bonded labour (Narsing Rao's *Daasi* (1988)).

In his study of the complex negotiations with history and historiography in African cinema, Bartlet (1996) explores the attempts by film-makers from different African countries to 'decolonize the gaze', a self-avowedly political project which conceives of cinema as 'a tool for revolution, means of political education to be used for transforming consciousness', which placed African cinema alongside other emergent and nascent Third-World cinema's aim to promote radical change in their societies. As Gaston Kabore, the film-maker from Burkina Faso, declared, 'My ambition is for my cinema to reflect a reality in which I participate and which I contribute to shaping' (quoted in Bartlet 1996, p. 17). In a climate of continuing political, economic and cultural dependence, Bartlet argues, 'such a cinema could exist only as a result of the determination of a number of individuals with strong personalities who did not hesitate to attack the established regimes' (p. 35).

This professed political objective included critiques of governance in newly independent states, as for example in Niger film-maker Oumarou Ganda's *L'Exile* (1980) that begins its narrative with images of protest movements including Paris May 1968 and riots in Salisbury (Harare), and Sembene's novels and films that consistently promote a cultural and political delinking from the West, even while they took a critical look at emerging new state of Senegal. Similarly, Ethiopian film-maker Haile Gerima's *Harvest 3000 Years* (1975) combines aesthetic innovation and experimentation with an impassioned political critique.

Cinematic representations of national identity

In an essay that subsequently launched a heated debate on nationalism and literature, Jameson (1986) presented his argument that, in the context of multinational capitalist globalization distinguished between the 'private and the public' and 'the poetic and the political' that marked, respectively, the difference between the culture of the Western modernist novel and Third-World literature, the latter is 'necessarily' allegorical in its attempt to go beyond the individual story and experience, whose narrative 'cannot but ultimately involve the whole laborious telling of the experience of the collectivity itself' (quoted in Zhang 1994). All Third-World cultural production was for him heavily imbricated with the national problematic, the politics of which was negotiated and explored in an allegoric form. Third-World texts, 'even those narratives which are seemingly private and invested with a properly libidinal dynamic, necessarily project a political dimension in the form of national allegory: the story of the private individual destiny is always an allegory of the embattled situation of the public Third World culture and society' (*ibid.*). While the wide generalizations in Jameson's argument have been interrogated and critiqued (the most famous example is Ahmad 1987), it is possible to use it, as Zhang (1994) does, to analyse the narratives of national imaginary in cinemas and literatures of the developing world.

This is particularly relevant to the analysis of the ways in which cinemas narrate the nation. If nations are construed as consisting of the fields of narrative and discursive enactments of a culture, cinema as a medium presents an exemplary site for such sanctioning, as noted by Rosen (1991), and Dissanayake (1994a), among others. For Dissanayake, moreover, cinema as practice and institution presents a powerful way of engaging with the complex and overlapping discursive spaces of the global, the regional, the national and the local, specifically in states such as India, in which the idea of a collective national identity subsumes within it a multitude of differences – linguistic, ethnic, caste, religious. Cinema, therefore, plays a crucial role in its national form, which is involved in constructions of national myths and histories, privileging 'ideas of coherence and unity and stable cultural meanings associated with the uniqueness of a given nation' (Dissanayake 1994a, p. xiii).

On the other hand, the many facets of national cinema also provides the opportunity for cultural producers to engage critically with the idea of cultural unity and uniqueness of the nation, and with the hegemonic discourse that is part of it. Once again, Indian cinema, with its regional and linguistic variations and multiple production sites, presents a telling example.

> The homogeneity of the nation-state and its legitimising metanarratives begin to be fissured when film-makers seek to give expression to the hopes and experiences and lifeworlds of the minorities whether they be ethnic, linguistic, or religious. . . . Indeed one discerns a tension between nationhood and cultural identity in almost all Asian countries, and cinema enables us to understand the contours of this phenomenon more clearly. . . . Questions of cultural difference, assertion of agency, and subjectivity lie at the heart of the more interesting Asian films dealing with minority experiences.
>
> (p. xvii)

National cinema clearly performs an ideological role in the construction of a national imaginary, as Bhabha (1990) notes: 'The scraps, patches, and rags of daily life must be repeatedly turned into the signs of national cinema culture while the very act of narrative performance interpellates a growing circle of national subjects' (Bhabha 1990, p. 297). In postcolonial contexts this assumes a critical importance as formations of national culture have had to deal with ambivalent identities intrinsic to the formations of states. Apart from instances like India, as mentioned above, this is most evident in sub-Saharan Africa, where, as Rosen notes, postcolonial states were often 'defined as a result of colonial histories and political configurations, with less relation to cultural and linguistic groupings and indigenous histories rather than other colonized areas such as southeast Asia' (p. 147). As a consequence of this representations of national history become critical, as national identity presumes a collective past and a common heritage that together contribute to a unified culture.

As exemplified in the cinema of Ousmane Sembene, the Senegalese writer and film-maker, considered to be the 'Father of African cinema', films made in that region often engaged with and constructed particular narratives of national history that subsumed ambivalences and diversity. Senegal, for example, in its efforts at self-definition had to contend with at least six indigenous languages as well as the colonial language, French. Sembene's films, such as *Xala* (1974) and *Ceddo* (1976) engage critically with the irony of using French as an official language in post-independent Senegal and the ambiguities, contradictions and struggles that characterize postcolonial African state formation. For Rosen, Sembene's films 'as a medium that addresses a mass African audience has consistently centered on issues deriving from the heritage of colonialism and liberation, on African identity, and consequently on history' (Rosen 1991, p. 148). He demonstrates how Sembene explores the complexities of Senegalese identity and nationhood in *Ceddo*, in which the film-maker uses a key moment in the nation's history to delineate the interplay between collective groups and socio-political forces. One of the central characters is the griot, 'a public story teller, rhetorician, musician, hired praise-singer, poet. . . . The griot is possessor of verbal and narrative expertise, a repository of the power of the word and of social memory' (p. 154), a symbol of the African oral tradition, to whom Sembene has often related himself.

Rosen's point regarding the opposing forces of tradition and modernity as invoked by constructions of African history is important here. This is explored in greater detail by Mudimbe (1994), and is related to other oppositions, as Rosen observes, including rural versus urban, and oral culture versus print cultures, and reproduces the colonial self–other dichotomy in contemporary formations of African identity. 'When it infiltrates historiography, the only movement possible to validate is along a uni-directional path *out from* traditional forms of culture and social organization *towards* modern, written cultures, and inescapable journey *from* the tribal nation *to* the centralized nation-state' (Rosen 1991, p. 163). However, this opposition offers the opportunity to productively and critically engage with important socio-cultural issues too, as demonstrated in Sembene's latest film, *Moolaade* (2004), which through the allegory of opposition to female genital mutilation by a group of rural women, examines and critiques the patriarchal aspects of traditional Senegalese society.

With regard to Asian cinema, Dissanayake (1994) offers a useful collection of essays that explore the narrative contours of different Asian national cinemas. For instance, Zhang (1994) examines the construction of significant aspects of Chinese history and culture in Zhang Yimou's *Red Sorghum* (1988). Despite the depoliticized narration that places it at odds with the strictures of the Communist Party regarding the political relevance of cultural production, Zhang interprets the film as providing an opportunity for audiences to reflect critically on the wider social and cultural issues of contemporary China. In fact, the film's positioning itself in opposition to the dictates of the Communist Party lends it a subversive marginality.

While conceding that *Red Sorghum* cannot be considered Third Cinema text, Zhang nevertheless concludes that its poetic eulogy of the life of a nameless couple allegorically recuperates the concept of liberation at the national and individual levels. Its poetic narration is, to Zhang, 'ultimately political in nature. The aspiration to liberate people's thoughts from political indoctrination, to subvert the seemingly insurmountable authority of dominant ideologies, and in short, to advocate a new ideology of the body in contemporary China, is, and must be, a political aspiration' (Zhang 1994, p. 39).

Similarly, Yue's (1998) examination of the ideological fantasy in Zhang Yimou's films comments on the attention to 'so-called women's issues' that Yimou's characteristic visual style encompasses. The films 'typically construct a sensory experience of China that is at once beautiful and cruel: beautiful because of Zhang Yimou's superbly choreographed cinematography, and cruel because of the profound sense of emotional entrapment the filmic characters, generally the female lead, experience' (Yue 1998, p. 57).

Wilson's (1994) analysis of narratives of national identity in two Korean films, *Mandala* and *Black Republic* is based on the assumption that Korean films after the 1980s offer a way of engaging with contemporary transformations in Korean urban and rural society and culture, and their impact on notions of a collective cultural identity. He too finds in Jameson's argument on the necessarily allegorical nature of Third-World cultural production a useful framework with which to examine national cinema.

The traditional–modern dichotomy is explored by Dwyer and Patel (2002) in their analysis of the depiction of Indian women in film posters. The visual diacritics of the 'traditional' Indian woman draw on symbolic markers, including conventions of clothing, hairstyles and bodily postures, and are presented in opposition to 'Western' Indian women, depicted as wearing 'modern' Western style clothes and hairstyles, adopting poses that are at variance with the demure traditional woman. The filmic narratives too, often use this duality to represent different moral universes that the traditional and modern Indian women purportedly inhabit. Drawing on Thomas (1989), Dwyer and Patel link this textual opposition to nineteenth-century India, that is, during the colonial period, when this dual structure

> was a product of both nineteenth century orientalist thought and the Independence Movement. For Nationalists, this glorification of Indian womanhood located in the ancient past fitted with their search for an 'authentic Indian' identity; and as a nationalist construct this identity existed in opposition to Western culture and therefore modernity, which was seen to be inherent to it. Hence the 'traditional'

was set against the 'modern' and it was this oppositional structure that was translated into film.

(Dwyer and Patel 2002, p. 198)

The image of the 'traditional' Indian woman is also associated with Hinduism, and forms part of the discourse on Hindu nationalism in many contemporary Indian films, which promote a Muslim 'other' as a symbolic opposition to the constitution of the Hindu nation. The use of cinematic codes and narratives to promote a national culture in India has had a long history. As far back as India's first feature film, *Raja Harish-chandra* (1913), the first cinematic reworking of Hindu mythology was, according to its film-maker Phalke, an entirely *Swadeshi* or home-grown product (Rajadhyaksha 1996). As Cubitt (2005) notes, Phalke's films were imbricated in the formation of a Hindu nationalism, invoking 'authentically' traditional Indian beliefs in their reworking of Hindu epics.

With regard to the persistent 'othering' of Muslim communities in India, Mishra (2002) finds the history of their depiction in Indian cinema analogous to the treatment of African-Americans in Hollywood narratives. The trend, he believes, continues to the present day, even though ironically, many of the current leading actors are Muslims. This leads to

a number of uneasy consequences. First, their marginalisation may imply that they are not legitimate objects in the domain of the popular, or more dangerously . . . they are defined totally by a prior Hindu discourse of the atavism of 'Muslim lust'. Second, their stereotypification means that their emotional range is limited. . . . Muslims are excluded from situations in which they may come into complex emotional or physical conflict with the Hindu. . . . With rare exceptions, in Bombay Cinema the Muslim as a character is simply written out of consider-able chunks of cinematic history.

(Mishra 2002, p. 217)

To Mishra this is indicative of a largely unacknowledged 'silence or repression located at the very heart of national culture' of which Hindu nationalism is a symptom.

Contemporary Indian cinema has had to negotiate the complex political ramifica-tions of the rise of Hindu nationalism, that includes, as Cubitt (2005) claims, a narra-tive form and a political content both of which remain faithful to the construction of popular cinematic codes and themes. While *Roja* has as its narrative locus the con-temporary conflict in Kashmir, and *Bombayi* deals with a romantic relationship between a Hindu and a Muslim against the backdrop of the Hindu–Muslim riots in Bombay, *1942: A Love Story* re-enacts an event in the history of colonial India, present-ing it as a key moment in the Indian struggle for independence. The latter 'is one in search of an adequate form in which to resolve a critical question in the experience of Indian nationhood in the 1990s' (Cubitt 2005, p. 310). The lead characters' sacrifices for the cause of national struggle are, Cubbitt argues, to be understood as representing the heroism of the ordinary Indian, the representative of the Indian masses. 'Through such characters the anonymous crowd is imbued with narrative depth, and we are allowed to feel, in the style of the Odessa Steps sequence in *Potemkin*, that each face stores some tale of brutality and bereavement' (Cubitt 2005, p. 313). Mishra is right in insisting that *1942*, as a film made at the time of Hindu fundamentalist politics should be seen as an attempt by contemporary Bombay cinema to reassert its commitment to Indian national culture.

One final point: it is important to recognize that, while a majority of film-makers willingly collude with the hegemonic homogenization of a national culture for ideological and financial reasons, there are others who in their films, offer comprehensive critiques of nationalism from the perspective of ethnic, religious or linguistic minorities. Films made at various regional production centres in India are an obvious example, presenting in cinematic form yet another chapter in the constant contestation between sameness and difference, and between the various spheres of cultural production at the global, national and local levels. As Ania Loomba has noted, 'In "metropolitan" nations as well as third world ones, the difficulty of creating national cultures that might preserve, indeed nourish internal differences has emerged as a major issue in our time' (Loomba 1998, p. 61).

Examples of revolutionary, critical and political Third-World cinema abound. Other regions such as Latin America, the Middle East, Iran, Turkey and East Asia too have strong and emerging film traditions that employ new and distinct cinematic idioms with which to explore the socio-cultural formations of their societies (see Armes 1987 and Downing 1987).

Shohat (1997) focuses on another specific aspect of Third World Cinema: feminist film and video work, and raises complex theoretical and political issues that emerge from such work and touch on the Eurocentric nature of academic feminist politics. Refusing to be subsumed into the Eurocentric universalization of 'womanhood', and conscious of the white woman's privileged position in relation to neo-colonialist and racist systems that underwrite aspects of global economics and politics, Third-World (or, to use Shohat's terminology, 'post-Third-World') feminist works promote a situated and location-specific form of resistance to oppression. Crucially, such works are 'embedded in the intersection between gender/sexuality and nation/race' (Shohat 1997, p. 1996), engaging with masculinist constructions of the nation and the patriarchal practices that inhabit them, and attempting to enunciate a situated history for women in specific locations.

Feminist cultural production in 'post-Third-Worldist' locations then, by being rooted in specific locales and forming a resistance against local expressions of patriarchy, offers a critique of Eurocentric feminism and its universalizing tendency. As a result, '[e]xamining recent Third-World feminist cultural practices only in relation to theories developed by what has been known as "feminist film theory" reproduces a Eurocentric logic' which sees Third-World feminist practice 'as "burdened" by national and ethnic hyphenated identities' (Shohat 1997, p. 1995). What is required in order to counter such patronizing attitudes to Third-World feminist film-makers, 'the dark women who now also do the "feminist thing" ', is a contextualization of their work in 'national/racial discourses locally and globally inscribed within multiple oppressions and resistances'. By way of example, Shohat examines films such as the Tunisian *Samt al Qusur* (1994) that locates the national struggle in the domestic sphere, and explores the daily struggles of working-class women employed as servants in the palace.

The collection of essays in *Rethinking Third Cinema* (2003) explore a range of issues that explore the links between 'Third Cinema' and 'Third World Cinema', among them the provenance of Third Cinema theory and its appropriateness to Third-World polit-ical film and other cultural practice. Such queries are both a part of an ongoing refinement of Third Cinema theory as well as an appreciation of the situated politics of cultural practice in the developing world. Shohat's interventions on feminist and feminist film theory are instructive here, as they offer a possibly analogous way of engaging with Third Cinema theory: 'Discourses about gender and race still tend *not* to be understood within an anticolonial history, however, while the diverse recent post-Third-Worldist feminist film and video practices tend to be comfortably subsumed as a mere "extension" of a "universal" feminist theory and practice' (Shohat 1997, p. 1995). In order to rectify this situation she proposes the examination of such work 'in the light of the ongoing critique of the racialised inequality of the geopolitical distribution of resources and power' (p. 1996). A complementary move that relates film practice, history and politics in various regions of the developing world to the refinement of Third Cinema theory seems crucial, both as a way of developing an alternative to existing film theory, and as a way of understanding the material, situated local histor-ies of these regions. Exploring the counter-hegemonic articulations of the local requires the acknowledgement of the cultural practice of political film-making alongside attempts to reassess the theory of Third Cinema.

Further reading

Downing, J. (ed.) (1987) *Film & Politics in the Third World*. New York: Praeger.
Gabriel, T. (1982) *Third Cinema in the Third World: the Aesthetics of Liberation*. Ann Arbor, MI: UMI Research Press.
Guneratne, A. and W. Dissanayake (eds) (2003) *Rethinking Third Cinema*. NY: Routledge.
Pines, J. and P. Willemen (eds) (1989) *Questions of Third Cinema*. London: BFI.
Wayne, M. (2001) *Political Film: The Dialectics of Third Cinema*. London: Pluto.

6 | INDIGENOUS POLITICS AND REPRESENTATION

At the very end of her book, Rigoberta Menchu (1984), the Guatemalan activist and winner of the Nobel Peace Prize declares

> My life does not belong to me. I've decided to offer it to a cause. . . . The world I live in is so evil, so bloodthirsty, that it can take my life away from one moment to the next. So the only road open to me is our struggle, the just war. . . . And this is what I have to teach my people: that together we can build the people's church, a true church. Not just a hierarchy, or a building, but a real change inside people. I chose this as my contribution to the people's war. I am convinced that the people, the masses, are the only ones capable of transforming society.
>
> (p. 246)

Menchu's 'testimony' is emblematic of the politics of indigenous representation in multiple ways as it represents a multicentred politics of opposition and eloquently portrays the marginalization and subjugation of indigenous communities in Guatemala, and by extension Latin America as well as the rest of the world. It also contributes to arguments about subalternity and representation, and the complex ways in which it engages with the politics of liberation. It illustrates the instability of nationalism and identity and the possibility of forming coalitions across borders; and it invokes agency in a specific way that, even as it expresses the plight of the indigenous communities in Guatemala and reveals the murder of Menchu's own family, remains self-confessedly silent about other aspects of their identity.

> My commitment to our struggle knows no boundaries nor limits. That is why I've travelled to many places where I've had the opportunity to talk about my people. Of course, I'd need a lot of time to tell you all about my people, because it's not easy to understand just like that. . . . Nevertheless, I'm still keeping my Indian

identity a secret. I'm still keeping secret what I think no one should know. Not even anthropologists, or intellectuals, no matter how many books they have, can find out all our secrets.

(Menchu 1984, p. 247)

Reflecting on this testimony that not only insisted on keeping secrets but also proclaimed that intention, Sommer suggests that it is a rhetorical and performative device that Menchu adopts to maintain a political distance between herself and the reader: 'to close in on Rigoberta would threaten her authority and leadership' (Sommer 2001, p. 176). In effect, this Quiche Indian peasant woman, 'still illiterate, in newly learned, occasionally incorrect Spanish, a young woman managed to turn a possibly condescending interrogation into a platform for her own leadership' (*ibid.*).

The controversy following Stoll's (1998) assessment of the veracity of Rigoberta Menchu's testimonial narrative is strongly indicative of the problems that continue to plague subaltern forms of representation that do not follow the strictures of scholarly or dominant norms of discursive presentation. Even more significantly, particularly in the case of indigenous communities and their struggle over land claims and other rights when conventions of legal representation are invoked, the process of Othering moves beyond the cultural issues of representation to ethico-legal procedures. As in the case of Australian Aboriginal communities, testimonies not bound to documented, written evidence, and accepted as such by legal authorities are often ruled as inadmissible. This not only reveals the emphasis placed on the notion of private property in capitalist societies where private ownership forms one of the bases of law, but also, as we see during the course of this chapter, is implicated in diverse situations and discourses such as history, and national memory and identity.

In reply to Stoll's questioning of the accuracy of Menchu's testimony on the grounds of its inconsistencies, doubt about whether she actually could have witnessed the events she describes, and on whether Menchu's Spanish was sufficiently advanced for her to be able to express herself adequately, Gugelberger (1999), argues that Stoll misunderstood the fundamental aspect of testimonial literature, that it 'is a complex genre on the threshold of other genres that continues to defy definition. One would expect an anthropologist not to confuse it with autobiography, life history, or documentary' (Gugelberger 1999, p. 48). He, therefore, charges Stoll of 'hairsplitting of the worst kind' (p. 49).

In an essay on the political significance of the *testimonio*, Yudice (1991) points to the contribution of the genre in weakening the role of the intellectual or artist traditionally conceived as being the spokesperson of the voiceless as the subaltern, as the poet Pablo Neruda suggested:

From across the earth bring together
all the silenced scattered lips
and from the depths speak to me . . .
Speak through my words and my blood.

(cited in Yudice 1991, p. 15)

Through the act of testimony the individual articulates collective concerns and experiences, not as a spokesperson burdened with the responsibility of representing the community, nor as a mere conduit.

> In contrast, the *testimonialista* gives her personal testimony 'directly', addressing a specific interlocutor. . . . [T]hat personal story is a shared one with the community to which the testimonialista belongs. The speaker does not speak for or represent a community but rather performs an act of identity-formation which is simultaneously personal and collective.
>
> (Yudice 1991, p. 15)

The issue of indigenous representation, its difference from the norm and its relation with indigenous world-views and cosmologies, informs debates on contemporary politics of landless peoples and the condition of subalternity. In San Juan's (1998) terms, 'Menchu is both a singular person and an allegorical figure. Her testimony is less an auto-biography in the conventional sense than a history of lived experience, a cosmography of the indigenous peoples of Central America and by extension of the Fourth World' (San Juan 1998, p. 37). Her testimony presents an ethnographic account of the life of Quiche Indians, culminating in the delineation of the horrific torture and murder of her family members, an assertion of the suffering of indigenous communities in Central America.

Sommer (1991) similarly argues the case for the value of Menchu's testimony, on the basis of its transcending agency claimed by the state, a political party, or a particular class. Contained in the testimony is the kind of coalition politics that provides the possibility for opposing the social complexities in Latin America. Such first-person testimonies, Sommer argues, have the benefit of demonstrating that these struggles 'are as multiple and flexible as any in the so called First World, often combining feminist, class, ethnic, and national desiderata' (Sommer 1991, p. 48).

This is a point made in Harindranath (2000), that social movements organized by peasant and tribal women in rural India combine what are normally assumed to be distinct areas of academic and political intervention, namely, environmental activism and feminism. The logic of these protests stems from the way that development programmes affect the lives of these women. Nevertheless, they destabilize the normative universality of epistemological boundaries carefully guarded by metropolitan theories and debates. This is, as Sommer suggests, an instance of looking at the First World from the Third World.

Contextualizing Menchu's testimony in the debate on the relative merits of non-Western literature and art, Beverley (2004) declares that to him,

> I, Rigoberta Menchu is one of the most interesting works of *literature* produced in Latin America in the last fifteen years; but I would rather have it be a provocation in the academy, a radical otherness . . . than something smoothly integrated into the curriculum for 'multicultural' citizenship in an elite university.
>
> (Beverley 2004, p. 68, emphasis in the original)

Beverley's intervention here is not a reflection of his doubt over the veracity of Menchu's testimony. Rather, it is a response to pronouncements of what constitutes literature. Further, it is an acknowledgement of the testimony as a case of the strategy of 'writing in reverse', in Guha's terms (1983), an instance of subaltern agency. For him, therefore, it is important 'to worry less about how *we* appropriate Menchu, and to understand and appreciate more how she appropriates *us* for her purposes' (Beverley 2004, p. 69).

The 'indigenous' in nationalist discourse

Seed (2001) claims that

> indigenous communities remain the world's most subaltern despite the major advances in health, living standards, and political rights over the last five hundred years. Initially decimated by diseases from foreign invaders, natives died off in record numbers during successive waves of European colonisation . . . [I]n newly independent states, aboriginal peoples usually continued to reside in isolated communities or in labor reservoirs as basic economic rules instituted by European colonisers remained in place.
>
> (Seed 2001, p. 129)

At the end of the twentieth century, 'aboriginal peoples remained impoverished, dwelling on the margins of sleek new nation-states'. Processes of marginalizing the indigenous, or 'Fourth World' communities can be traced back, as Gupta (1999) claims, to the discourses and policies of colonial powers. Equally implicated in the marginalization, however, are national discourse and the practices and theories of development. The complex relations indigenous communities have had with colonial, national and developmental discourse, in both historical and contemporary terms, is worth examining as it exemplifies their disenfranchisement from nation building and development, as well as from the processes of state planning.

Gupta (1999) notes the paradox of the increasing interest in indigenous communities among environmentalists, entrepreneurs, multinationals and new-age philosophers happening simultaneously with the restructuring of capitalist production in the age of late capitalism. The latter is a process whereby, through diverse ways such as eco-tourism, research on indigenous medicine and exploitation of habitats, indigenous groups are progressively drawn into the circuits of capital. The anomalous situation which finds indigenous communities exploited even as they are being celebrated and romanticized as the true guardians of the environment and for their apparent non-materialistic lifestyle also provides the opportunity for resistance on both the discursive and the political levels. Arguing that 'supposedly archaic attitudes to "the indigenous" suffuse present development practice' (p. 168), Gupta explores the constituents of colonial and nationalist discourse in relation to the indigenous in India, its utilization as a notion in the complex discursive terrain that simultaneously overlapped at some points and were antagonistic in others. Both the colonial power and the nationalists shared the idea of 'progress', to be achieved through scientific and rational planning and development. Caught in this tug of war, indigenous peoples became signifiers of 'tradition' or 'backwardness' in multiple ways as they were discursively recuperated in colonial and national rhetoric.

The complexity of the place of the indigenous in this discursive construction is revealed when we consider the contradictory positions in which they were placed in colonial scholarly and bureaucratic enterprise. On the one hand were the Orientalists who, as Gupta argues, saw in the indigenous the originary traditions untrammelled by the traps of progress, in whom it was possible to locate the values that had constituted India's grand past civilizations. This reification and romantic recuperation of a putative glorious past in the indigenous 'native' is thus similar to the contemporary moves adopted by certain environmental groups for whom protecting the alleged 'purity' of such communities override issues of their exploitation by mainstream society and their economic survival. 'In short, indigenous culture was worthwhile only to the extent that it was a museum artifact. The greatness of the Indian past had to be resurrected, but only in the manner one reconstructs a civilization in a cultural museum' (Gupta 1999, p. 169).

This attitude to the indigenous is not restricted to the Orientalists among the colonizers, as shown in the pro-independent nationalist discourse as well as in the more recent retelling of the history of India as an allegedly Hindu nation. Here the 'native' is once again imbued with discursive significance as the embodiment of certain 'authentic' values, this time as bearing traces of ancient Indian civilization as depicted in Hindu mythologies. They were thus invested with the 'greatness' of the Indian past which had been devastated through colonial exploitation. In indigenous or, in the case of India, 'tribal' cultures, aesthetic forms were the markers of this 'glorious' past, which needed to be resurrected in order to recapture what was quintessentially Indian, and 'glorious'.

In the case of both the colonial Orientalists and the nationalists (and the Hindu fundamentalists in the 1980s and 1990s), however, the indigenous is emblematic of a primordial culture, which was closer to the state of nature and was to be recovered and retained in that state, respectively, for anthropological interest and as a symbol for a once-great civilization to which to return after independence.

As pointed out by Gupta, the Orientalists were the most sympathetic group among the colonizers: 'they actually constituted the liberal group' (Gupta 1999, p. 170). For other sections of the colonizing powers indigenous communities represented the 'savage', the pre-scientific, the superstitious and the uncivilized whose redemption through a combination of Christianity and science that marked the process of modernization was the 'white man's burden'. Part of nationalist discourse too, invoked his attitude to the indigenous, displaying anxiety among the predominantly middle-class leaders of the liberation movements. 'The contrast between orientalist and modernizing positions was incorporated as an agonistic splitting *within* nationalist discourses, so that diametrically opposed positions were found to cohabit uneasily within them' (Gupta, p. 171, emphasis in the original). Gupta uses as an example Gandhi's ambivalent take on rural India which on the one hand appropriated Orientalist notions of authentic Indian cultures while simultaneously promoting the urge to reform what he considered were signs of 'backwardness' or superstitious traditions, such as his attempt to improve the treatment of Harijans or 'untouchables'. Relating this to Chatterjee's (1986) exploration of nationalism as derivative discourse, Gupta points out that nationalist discourse included

> the positioning of a utopian past in contradistinction to a savage slot. Tribal peoples occupied the 'savage slot' of nationalist thought, simultaneously as noble savages, simple and primitive, and as 'scheduled tribes' [in the Indian Constitution] most in need of 'upliftment' because of their lack of agricultural, financial, and educational resources.
>
> (Gupta 1999, p. 171)

Crucially for our purposes, what the instability of discourses on indigeneity underline is the lack of agency: the indigene, the tribal, the 'scheduled tribe' were spoken for by Orientalists, nationalists, or modernizers in the sense that the indigenous communities were located in specific subject spaces by those who were speaking for them. This, along with the corollary denial of agency marks the indigenous as arguably the most subaltern of communities both historically and in the contemporary global culture and society in which their marginalization continues, punctuated occasionally by recognition of the legitimacy of their land claims, or the aesthetic attributes of their cultural production. The subalternization of the indigene persists in various ways, as for instance in development literature, or in the debates among contemporary historians about the validity of the claims of massacres of Aboriginal populations in Australia.

This is not to deny the increasing awareness and acknowledgement of indigenous issues around the world. The United Nations (UN) declaration in 1994 on behalf of Indigenous Nations, for example, noting the 'urgent need to respect and promote the inherent rights and characteristics of Indigenous Nations, especially the right to lands, territories and resources, which derive from each Nation's culture', asserts the rights of indigenous communities 'to exist in peace and security as a distinct people and to be protected against any type of genocide' (UN 1994, p. 1).

Gupta (1999) notes the elevation of 'indigenous knowledge', with its own acronym IK, as part of development discourse. As evidence of this elevation is the increasing interest in indigenous practice among non-governmental agencies, university researchers and international development agencies all of which have sought to investigate and include indigenous knowledge and knowledge systems in their deliberations on, for instance, sustainable development. Nevertheless, there are still concerns about the exploitation of indigenous expertise, and about the ways in which the recuperation of this knowledge involves what Gupta calls 'defining by negation', which to him is symptomatic of its status as a residual category, where everything that is not part of the Western, international knowledge system is inserted. In fact, an effort to describe what 'indigenous knowledges' are, rather than what they are not, throws together elements from different epistemological and ideological orientations into a haphazard mixture.

(Gupta 1999, p. 173)

History and the construction of collective national memory are implicated centrally in indigenous politics. Stephen Muecke (1992) notes that the struggle for space that informs much of contemporary politics comprises 'real space', as in land rights, as well as a more 'metaphorical space', which is the struggle of representational legitimacy, including that of history. A case in point is Australia, where various debates on the history of colonial conquest and settlement and its impact on Aboriginal nations and communities has been a topic of, sometimes vitriolic, debate in recent years.

Banerjee and Osuri (2000) point to the journalistic framing of a massacre of 40 people in Tasmania in 1996 as 'Australia's worst mass murder' (*Sydney Morning Herald*, 29 April 1996) as symptomatic of a consistent disregard of the deaths of Aboriginal populations at the hands of the settlers. As Banerjee and Osuri ask, 'Why, for instance, was this event termed the worst massacre in Australian history, when the Australian nation seemed to have been founded on a history of massacres? Why did both print and television media limit themselves to a 10–40 year history of massacres in Australia?' (Banerjee and Osuri 2000, p. 264).

Most significantly, they are interested in the regimes of discourse (Foucault 1980; Hall 1997a) that underpin and legitimize such representations by the media and political leaders. Pointing out that 'massacres of Aboriginal people took place as late as the early 20th century' (p. 269), Banerjee and Osuri emphasize the need to examine the 'discursive unity' that characterizes the erasure of Aboriginal massacres from the public imagination or the silences on the issue in the public sphere. For them, the construction of historical narratives as knowledge is part of the struggle over collective memory, a claim that is illustrated, as we saw earlier, in the case of a deliberate retelling by Hindu nationalists of Indian history as Hindu history.

Far from being an 'objective' recuperation of past events, historical research, or historiography, has increasingly come to be seen as imbued with issues of power and the construction of knowledge. Said's (1978) seminal work on constructions of Orientalism explores the mechanisms and discursive strategies that contributed to the establishment of colonial knowledge and how that informed its bureaucratic practices of colonial rule. As we saw in Chapter 3 on the subaltern, the revisionist history that the Subaltern Studies Group has been involved in is inspired by such critiques of colonial and national historiography. As Banerjee and Osuri point out, the role of historical knowledge and research into the subjugation and marginalization of communities has been argued by theorists such as de Certeau (1986), who have asserted the ways in which the assemblage and presentation of historical data tie in with the construction of memory through certain disciplinary procedures that purport to guarantee its disinterested objectivity.

Given the centrality of land claims in indigenous politics, particularly in settler colonies, the production of historical knowledge and its alliance with legal strictures bears scrutiny. For instance, the ruling by the Australian Federal Court overturning the claims of the Yorta Yorta community for their ancestral land on the grounds that they had not occupied it in conformity with their traditions overlooks the history of the community's displacement from their land by white settlers. Implicit in this ruling is the collusion of historical knowledge and its links to selective memory on the one hand, and on the other the violence of the legal system, which disregards alternative histories and their genres. Apart from the actual dispossession of their land, however, is the ruling's undermining of their Aboriginal identity, as its reference to 'traditional laws and customs' invokes particular imaginings of Aboriginal life. As Des Morgan, a Yorta Yorta activist, demanded,

> Do you have to be naked and dancing for them to recognize you as Aboriginal? My ancestors' spirits walk that land, the same as my spirit will walk the land when I die and my children's spirits will follow me. How can they deny our existence? I don't need a white judge to tell me who I am. I am Yorta Yorta.
>
> (cited in Banerjee and Osuri, p. 274)

Ghassan Hage (2003) in his examination of the role of the construction of historical knowledge and memory in Australian identity identifies the centrality of debates surrounding the recognition of past atrocities against the Aboriginal populations and the question of reparation. According to Hage, a turning point in the public discourse on Aboriginal issues originated from the famous 'Mabo decision' in 1992, when the Australian High Court ruled in favour of an indigenous group led by Eddie Mabo, and restored their land which had been under the control of the Queensland parliament. The watershed ruling overturned the claim by the original European settlers that Australia was *terra nullius*, by which they could legally own the land they had settled in. However, a few of the judges involved in the landmark ruling went further, referring to the ethical questions underlying practices of systematic dispossession that marked Australia's past: 'the nation as a whole must remain diminished unless and until there is an acknowledgement of, and a retreat from, those past injustices' (cited in Hage, p. 80).

The Mabo decision, together with more visible indigenous struggles, have been conducive to what Hage refers to as 'an important cultural transformation in Australia. For the first time, talking about the "British invasion of Australia" no longer positioned the speaker on the radical fringe' (Hage 2003, p. 81), as the historical aspects of the invasion are gradually becoming part of the public culture. As noted by Muecke (1992), struggles over issues such as land rights, access to housing, medical and legal facilities, and alternative education have forced white Australians to confront the reality of Aboriginal life more than before. Despite this, however, Hage sees an irreconcilable contradiction between the social imaginaries of the settlers and the indigenous Australians, riding as they do on different historical imaginations.

> It is not an exaggeration to say that the possibility of a non-contradictory set of national memories of Australia's history is still very remote. We are far from reaching a stage where 'we', Indigenous and non-Indigenous people, can remember the acts of dispossession and murder within that history without partisan affective history.
>
> (Hage 2003, p. 93)

The recent 'history wars' that have erupted around the topic of the genocide of Australian Aboriginal communities appear to support Hage's argument. Challenged by Keith Windschuttle in *The Fabrication of Aboriginal History* (2002) and the media coverage that followed its publication and the subsequent debates, historical accounts of white settlement in Australia, particularly those researching the deaths among Aboriginal groups during the violence that was inaugurated by the early European settlements, have come under close scrutiny not only by other researchers but also by the media. What is at stake here, apart from the veracity of historical research and its methodologies, is the contest over national memory, and what is beyond doubt is that the 'history wars' have contributed to a further cleaving of indigenous and settler accounts of history.

'One of the main problems for Aboriginal history,' argues Muecke (1992), 'is to authenticate the appropriate discourse for its transmission' (1992, p. 60), part of which is to challenge the links between history and the language of history. In the words of Marcia Langton, cited in Muecke, 'When the cues, the repetitions, the language, the distinctively Aboriginal evocations of our experience are removed from the recitals of our people, the truth is lost to us' (quoted on p. 60). It is thus possible to agree with Muecke's argument that events exist only so far as they are represented, 'that is, while things do happen by themselves, as it were, they are only "knowable" when they are articulated in discourses' (Muecke 1992, p. 61). It is worth noting here that racial discourses contributed to, and legitimized, the killing of indigenous peoples in most areas of the world. As a report for the Independent Commission on International Humanitarian Issues (ICIHI) avers, 'At the heart of the indigenous issue is the racist attitude of dominant societies dating back to the invasion by the Spanish Conquistadores who excused the murder of native inhabitants because they were "less than human" (ICIHI 1987, p. 13).

Indigeneity, land and representation

In a recent book, Muecke (2004) narrates an incident involving the then Australian Minister for Immigration and Multicultural and Indigenous Affairs, Philip Ruddock, who was quoted in *The Washington Post* in 2000 as saying of the Aboriginal communities, 'we're dealing with people who were essentially hunter-gatherers. They didn't have chariots. I don't think they invented the wheel' (quoted in Muecke 2004, p. 142). The debate that followed missed the point, Muecke feels, as it overlooked the racialization underlying the civilizational hierarchization implicit in Ruddock's statement, which displaces the focus from the issue of land rights and access to resources to one of race. One result is the undermining of the validity of Aboriginal claims:

> if it is publicly accepted that the 'real' problem is not one of historical injustice but rather of the inherent nature of the Aborigines as 'racially' inferior, then acts of injustice against Aboriginal people need not be judged by the standards of civil society; in this horrible logic, they cease to be amenable to moral or juridical consideration.
>
> (Bruno David, quoted in Muecke 2004, p. 143)

By evoking the alleged absences in Aboriginal society Ruddock's statement places it lower in civilizational rankings than a putatively 'developed' culture that makes up the rest of Australia, effectively altering the emphasis on indigenous cultural practices and their connections with land and space.

Space is deeply implicated in Aboriginal artistic representation, underlining the importance of land to indigenous cultures. The struggle for justice that unites indigenous communities around the world includes the use of their land. 'Indigenous peoples seek recognition, by governments and the international community, of their existence, of their problems and perspectives. They want recognition that their land is essential for their economic, political and spiritual needs' (ICIHI, p. 40). Tony Bennett's (1998) discussion of the role of hunting in Australia at the time of early European settlement presents a useful metaphor for the differences in the perception of land and territory between the settlers and the indigenous populations, and how this illuminates the relations between the two communities. Using Tom Griffith's research (1996), Bennett argues the case for hunting as marking the distinction between indigenous and European cultures. Intrinsic to this is the anthropological discourse that emphasized this difference in terms of a hierarchy of civilizations, echoed in Ruddock's statement discussed earlier. As Griffiths points out,

> Europeans perceived the indigenous culture as preoccupied with subsistence hunting, an activity that was seen as desperate and dependent. In the imperial culture, hunting was an elite sporting and intellectual pursuit, class-conscious and recreational: it was a quest for sport, science and trophies, a 'refined' hunting and gathering.
>
> (quoted in Bennett 1998, p. 185)

This alleged distinction in the role of hunting in the two cultures not only served to reinforce the settlers' perception of the Aboriginal peoples as 'closer to nature' and 'less civilized' than Europeans, but also, as Bennett reminds us, 'as an accentuation of this difference ... Aborigines were also translated from hunters into hunted in the early collecting practices of Australian natural history and ethnology' (Bennett 1998, p. 185).

Gupta's argument about the liberal Orientalist attitude to 'native' Indian culture as repositories of particular value systems and civilization gets reinforced in this context as 'Australia's hunter-gatherers made the transition to the other side of the hunting equation in becoming, precisely, the hunted and the gathered to be displayed, alongside Australia's flora and fauna, as the trophies of a conquering and dispossessing power. (Bennett 1998, p. 185). The conqueror's prerogative contributes thus to the production of knowledge about native populations, uniting the colonized under the banner of a collective 'Other', culturally 'different' and purportedly 'inferior' to European culture. This had the double effect of, on the one hand, providing a convenient rationale for the conquest and dispossession of native cultures and their territories, and on the other, undermining the legitimacy of claims for independence and self-rule. Even more crucially, it contributed, and in some cases continues to contribute, to the silencing of native voices and the denial of their histories. The consequences of this has been manifold, including, as we saw earlier, in the arena of legal claims for land rights.

The continuing resonance of Myers's (1988) argument about the fascination of non-Aboriginal Australians for the Outback, where they might encounter 'stone age' hunter-gatherer communities is felt in the way the Outback performs the function of 'difference' in the Australian tourism industry. This reveals both the more recent 'discovery' of Aboriginal art and culture, and its commodification, as well as the complex dialectic that constitutes Australian national identity, comprising both an inside and an outside, both temporal and spatial, in which indigenous communities are assigned specific places and performative roles. In the words of Ginsburg (1995)

> Commodified images of Aboriginal producers along with Aboriginal acrylic paintings and popular music groups such as Yothu Yindi are part of the cultural capital on which contemporary Australia builds its national image for consumption and circulation in the arenas of tourism, political affairs, and the marketing of culture overseas.
>
> (Ginsburg 1995, p. 125)

Locating the significance of land to Aboriginal culture and its constant negotiation and renewal, Bennett points to the centrality of 'a strategy of place' to indigenous cultural and political resistance. Inherent in this resistance is time and the recuperation of Aboriginal history whose erasure has been part of the palimpsest of imperial culture and society. Time and space mingle in Aboriginal political culture and resistance, as it is 'committed to the extension of time, to stretching indigenous time as deep and as far back into the past as possible, anchored always in the land, in order to project an equivalently lengthy future into which a distinctive indigenous culture will survive' (Ginsburg 1995, p. 186).

In a recent essay on the problematic of identities, Martin-Barbero (2002) makes a similar argument about the role of history in indigenous identity. Pointing to the insufficiency of the developmentalist approach that contrasts modernity to tradition as irreconcilably different, and to the problems with the postmodernist idealization of indigenous difference or a celebration of hybridity that overlooks conflicts and cultural resistance, Martin-Barbero asserts that

> it is only within an historic dynamic that the indigenous can be understood in all its cultural complexity, in all its temporal diversity, living on in certain nomadic ethnic groups of the Amazonian forests, in the conquered, colonized indigeneity, the diverse modes and entry-points of their modernization, and also in the forms and movements of miscegenation and hybridisation.
>
> (Martin-Barbero 2002, pp. 631–2)

The spatial and temporal dimensions of indigenous experience and politics, and the role of territory, place and aboriginal alternative history in resistance struggles, are important for our present purposes in two ways. Firstly, they highlight the inadequacies of theoretical generalizations that inform the orthodoxy of academic literature on globalization, as discussed in Chapter 1. In contrast to Giddens's claim of the 'phantasmagoric' aspects that constitute our phenomenological experience of place, and of the 'time–space distanciation' that characterizes globalization, in the context of indigenous peoples, space and time (history) are located and grounded in the land they inhabit. For such cultures and knowledge systems territories are distinguished by particular topographical dimensions. The other is the aesthetic dimension of Aboriginal culture and politics, the engagement with space in artistic practice and how that engages with expressions of political resistance. The centrality of the land and the fundamental differences between Western and Aboriginal forms of representing it are captured in a statement by Australian Aboriginal artist Galarrwuy Yunipingu:

> most great paintings talk about the land and the significance of the land. Aboriginal people use other forms of art to talk about the land, for example bark paintings and dance. When I get out and paint myself and go bush, whether I am performing a sacred ceremony, or corroboree, I am performing an art that talks about the land ... When aboriginal people get together we put the land into action. When I perform, the land is within me, and I am the only one who can move, land doesn't, so I represent the land when I dance. I pretend to be the land, because the land is part of me. So I perform whatever I do on behalf of the land.
>
> (quoted in Ashcroft 2001, pp. 139–40)

This is revealing of the Aboriginal participation in space which, as Ashcroft (2001) points out, overturns the perspectival conception of space in which the viewer or artist stands removed from the scene, a stance that facilitates the depiction of landscapes and other spaces from a particular perspective. The development of portrayals of three-dimensional space, including methods of depicting depth and perspective, on a two-dimensional canvas is characteristic of the rules of pictorial engagement that inform Western art. In the context of Australia and other colonial spaces, Ashcroft argues, painters were able to utilize this strategy to cover apparently 'uninhabited' land, thus contributing to the colonial imagination regarding colonized spaces, 'which provides a ready opportunity to impose the priority of perspective, indeed the priority of visual space itself over any other indigenous modes of spatial perception' (Ashcroft 2001, p. 138). The differences in the representation of place, therefore, becomes a marker of distinction, separating the colonized from the 'native', and continues to inform contemporary politics of representation.

Significantly, the importance of place in Aboriginal societies and its cultural reson-ance, are based not on the Western perspectival tradition and its separation of subject and object, but on 'tangible locations' with which one's existence is closely and unalterably linked. In the place of a topographical space, therefore, is a system in which landmarks carry a particular significance and meaning for one's identity. 'A particular formation, like a stream or hill, for instance, may embody a particular Dreaming figure, whose location on the Dreaming track has a particular significance to a person's own life, "totem", clan relationship and identity because that person may have been conceived near it' (Ashcroft 2001, p. 139). The relations between representation and what is being represented is consequently different from Western traditions. Ashcroft insightfully observes that 'Aboriginal art is metonymic and symbolic rather than representational in function, and deeply implicated in the performance of religious obligations. Animal and abstract forms are drawn for their sacred significance because, like language, they *embody* rather than represent the power of the things they signify' (*ibid.*, emphasis in the original).

While the art of the colonial settlers explores ways of capturing and representing the landscape and 'indigenising place', he argues, Aboriginal art, an expression of a collective participation in the land and of the cosmology of community existence, attempts to embody the land. The differences in the conception of the communities' relationship with land, in other words, underlies the different artistic traditions: Aboriginal art,

> which includes the very important elements of song and dance, embodies the land. The idea of not owning the land but in some sense being 'owned by it' is a way of seeing the world that is so different from the materiality and commodifica-tion of imperial discourse that effective protection of one's own place is radically disabled when the new system – perspectival vision – becomes the dominant one as European spatial representations are 'inscribed' upon the palimpsest of place.
>
> (Ashcroft 2001, p. 140)

The entry of Aboriginal paintings in the international market has been noted and examined by ethnographers and theorists interested in what this development signifies in terms of Aboriginal politics (see for example, Myers 1991). Willis and Fry (2003) warn against interpreting this as an indication of 'progress', or a fundamental change in the lives of indigenous populations. What is required, they claim, is a reversal of the orthodox view, approaching Aboriginal art not from conventional discourses of art criticism, but from the perspective of mainstream aesthetic, critical and marketing norms and strategies and of what impact they have had on Aboriginal practice. Moreover, we should 'refuse to disarticulate Aboriginal culture from the crucial political agenda of social justice, including land rights, health, housing and employment. In doing this it becomes impossible to view the claimed artistic "achievement" (viewed in white terms) of a few as a marker of progress of the position of Aboriginal people in Australian society' (Willis and Fry 2002, p. 124). The categorization of indigenous art – and one can extend this to include musical forms, which are sold as belonging to the rather amorphous genre of 'world music – that accompanies its exhibition in galleries and museums, as well as in its critical reception, is often inserted into a putative history of art. This is an instance of 'visual discrimination', even as it is labelled 'a genre within a remade, contemporary primitivism' (p. 125).

The main reason for this, according to Willis and Fry, is because the Aboriginal artist and the 'cultured' non-Aboriginal Australian approach the art object from different perspectives, informed by the social, political and aesthetic space they occupy. Moreover, the international art market inscribes Aboriginal practice in particular ways, from the label of 'Aboriginal art' – which, Willis and Fry claim, is a product of Western culture – to the appropriation of indigenous visual culture. 'Commodification is the *motor* which drives the revival of Aboriginal arts and it ushers irreversible changes. What we are witnessing is the partially comprehended induction of often fringe-dwelling Aboriginals into the political economy of art' (pp. 125–6, emphasis in the original).

Most damagingly, what is normally presented as 'progressive' art is merely a change in definition of genres, and through their use of acrylic on canvas for instance, Aboriginal aesthetic practice enters the realm of 'high art'. For Willis and Fry, this does not constitute a change in the status of Aboriginal populations in Australia, and should not, therefore, be conflated with resistance and agency, for even while it succeeded in appealing to the taste of the international art market, it lost its political significance. Approached without this dubious ascription of authenticity and value, and

> viewing it instead through the discourses of race politics, it can be concluded that what has been achieved is not cultural intervention or resistance, or a place from which to speak 'their' cause, but rather, moderately successful assimilation. A shift has taken place from overt racism to cultural ethnocide. And control still rests ultimately with 'white' institutions.
>
> (Willis and Fry 2002, p. 128)

Mediations of Aboriginal experience and politics

In one of those not infrequent exchanges in journals, Childs and Guillermo-Delgado (1999) take exception to Beteille's definition of 'indigenous' in such a way as to not promote 'moral excitation' among certain anthropologists. For Beteille, the term 'indigenous people' is analogous to what 'native' meant in colonial times, with 'the moral signification reversed to a certain extent' (Beteille 1998, p. 190). In nineteenth- and early twentieth-century London, ironically the term 'native' meant the Indian or the African, and not the Briton. Beteille argues that persons of colour carried with them the identity as a native, and wonders if that has been replaced in postcolonial times by a similar essentialist view of indigenous persons. 'Has the crude anthropological association of race and culture acquired a more refined form in the concept of the indigenous people?'

For Childs and Guillermo-Delgado, on the contrary, the concept of 'indigenous' is 'being forged by numerous communities of indigenous peoples themselves, both in the Americas and around the world' (Childs and Guillermo-Delgado 1999, p. 211). Through this self-definition, it is possible to add, indigenous communities around the world are forming mutually beneficial alliances and common political platforms in the struggle for self-determination.

Apart from revealing quarrels within the anthropological community over terminological niceties, this exchange is indicative of a range of political questions that are currently being raised among indigenous communities themselves, and in academic discourses. Of these, the issue of indigenous agency and the politics of indigenous media are most relevant to us. Martin-Barbero (2002) makes the valid point about the continual process of affirmation and renewal that indigenous communities around the world are currently involved in, and 'it is only the prejudice of a covert ethnocentrism, which often even permeates anthropological discourse, that prevents us from perceiving the diverse meanings of development in these ethnic communities' (Martin-Barbero 2002, p. 632). Some of the spheres in which this transformation is manifested include, for Martin-Barbero, the variety and expansion of 'artesanal production in open interaction with modern design, even taking on certain logics of cultural industries', the establishment of indigenous common law, and 'the growing presence of television and radio stations scheduled and directed by the communities themselves' (ibid.).

For Ginsburg,

> The term 'indigenous media' respects the understandings of those Aboriginal producers who identify themselves as 'First Nations' and indexes the political circumstances they share with other indigenous people around the globe. Whatever their cultural differences, these groups all struggle against a legacy of disenfranchisement of their lands, societies, and cultures by colonizing European societies.
>
> (Ginsburg 1995, p. 136, footnote 6)

In terms of the constitution of indigenous media it is possible to identify two main areas of focus: the aesthetics of production, and affirmation of community identities and politics, that is, narratives of self-making. In the Australian context for instance, as Ginsburg (2005) argues, Aboriginal media can be seen as being forged by a combination of changing local situations and government policies, as well as transformations in

Aboriginal and Euro-Australian inter-relations. Ginsburg is interested in locating the diverse ways in which ideas of selfhood, including concepts of community ownership of property and expression as well as the politics of self-determination and land rights are negotiated in media discourses. Despite the Labour government's 'liberal left policy toward Aboriginal self-determination' in the early 1970s, that contributed to the emergence of diverse television, she finds that 'in practice Aboriginal culture is flattened, reified, and assumed to be homogeneous' (p. 122). Nevertheless, the increasing control by Aboriginal communities over their cultural output and images, and the resulting, corresponding increase in their visibility in the Australian public imagination have together contributed to such communities being positioned differently in the Australian national imaginary (Hamilton 1990).

In his account of the development of Aboriginal media practice and aesthetics (originally published in 1986), Eric Michaels (1994) explores their theoretical and political dimensions. Economic constraints, lack of production facilities, and Aboriginal notions of community ownership together contribute to a particular aesthetic, according to Michaels. Arguing that the simple act of holding a camera does not necessarily result in 'the transparent act of auto-inscription', Michaels problematizes the modes of address in these media and the relationship of the viewer to the text. Crucially, the narrative strategies, which the communities themselves deem to be successful representations in their discourse, can be difficult for the non-Aboriginal viewer who is used to a different style. In terms of Aboriginal self-representation in the Australian context, therefore, how is the success or failure of such texts as acts of self-determination to be judged? Michaels' descriptions of production practices adopted by Aboriginal producers provides a good insight into both their economics and their aesthetics:

> Quite early on, the Walpiri looked at the production system and decided that it really wasn't necessary to have several people in the studio to go to air. One person could turn on and focus the camera, do the announcements, and switch over the tapes. The . . . problem was finding a way to let people know when the station was broadcasting. The solution was to turn on some music (the signal is also received over AM radio), focus on a graphic, and let that play for perhaps a half hour before beginning programming. Then, word of mouth would circulate through the camps and let people know to turn on their TVs.
>
> Jupurrurla, one of the Walpiri TV producers with whom I was closely associated, is a big reggae fan, so for his schedule he begins with reggae music and focuses the camera on his Bob Marley T-shirt draped over a chair. After a while he refocuses on the compere's desk, walks around and into the shot, announces the schedule and any news, then walks out of the shot, turns off the camera and switches on the VCR. This procedure is repeated for each tape.
>
> For me, the effect is almost an essay in Brechtian – or more precisely, Beckettian – dramaturgy.
>
> (Michaels 1994, pp. 36–7)

As Ginsburg (1995) notes, however, Aboriginal work in film and video constitutes a wider variety of formats and styles. It is as diverse as the Aboriginal producers and subjects who contribute it, whether they are traditional inhabitants of the Australian bush, or city dwellers with access to the latest video and editing technologies, training facilities and a longer history of contact with Euro-Australians.

Apart from the different styles that the various communities adopt in their use of technology in narratives of self-representation, variations in the concept of ownership too are immanent in the works. At one end, for instance, are the urban Aboriginal film and video artists such as Tracey Moffat, who are comfortable with avant-garde styles and with the notion of individual authorship and who, while continuing to engage with Aboriginal issues and politics, are equally at ease with the global world of art and film. At the other end are the communities living in remote areas of Australia, for whom ownership of cultural production is collectively held. For instance, as Langton (1994) observes,

> Walpiri artists earn rights to paint certain preexisting designs, not to introduce new ones. Rights to a body of work are inherited, so that one's son, daughter-in-law, or some other individual continues producing the same designs. Therefore, 'a forgery, adequately executed, when circulated, may be no forgery'. Plagiarism is not a possibility in this tradition. What is feared instead is thievery – the unauthorized appropriation of a design, as well as the potential for such stolen designs to convey rights and authority to the thief.
>
> (Langton 1994, p. xxxii)

The complex financial, historic, cultural aspects of Aboriginal media aesthetics prompts Ginsburg (2003) to recommend, for the understanding of such forms in their own terms, and for their reception with the respect that they deserve, an 'embedded aesthetics' that takes into account the complex entanglements of their production. This is her response to Langton's view that it is necessary to 'develop a body of knowledge on representation of Aboriginal people and their concerns in art, film, television and other media and a critical perspective to do with aesthetics and politics, drawing from Aboriginal world views, from Western traditions and from history' (Langton 1993, p. 24). Ginsburg's 'embedded aesthetics' goes a long way towards addressing these concerns, as it promotes a response that accommodates the social relations of textual production and circulation.

The political potential of indigenous media production and representation is underlined in two other instances. Turner (1990, 1992) has recorded the appropriation of video technology and know-how by the Kayapo Indians, indigenous groups in central Brazil, who successfully deployed video technology to not only record and preserve their traditional ceremonies and knowledge of their environment, but also to document, with an eye to legal record, their encounters with government officials. In an extraordinary expression of media savvy, Chief Raoni had his appearance with the rock star Sting recorded as part of his attempt to bring their struggle to international attention.

Similarly, Valaskakis (2002) discusses the contribution of indigenous media to Inuit participatory development in Canada and the circumpolar regions, claiming that media technologies have 'played significant roles in forming Aboriginal political institutions and civic roles, increasing local and regional participatory development, and establishing circumpolar collaboration in an emerging Far Northern community that spans 24 time zones' (Valaskakis 2002, p. 401).

If indigenous media representations, like Aboriginal testimonies, can be seen as sub-altern agency, as indeed they should, the issue of essentialist articulations of collective or cultural identity has to be negotiated. Spivak's question, 'Can the subaltern speak?' is pertinent here, demonstrating the various strategies, however debated and debatable, being adopted by formerly marginalized and disempowered communities. Shohat and Stam (1994) forcefully argue the case for self-expression and self-determination in a theoretical context in which the idea of a 'coherent subject identity, let alone a community identity, seems epistemologically suspect'. For them, the concurrent denial of process of marginalization is a luxury that only the empowered can afford. Spivak's notion of 'strategic essentialism', and Hall's call for a 'fictional necessity of arbitrary closure' are a necessary tactic for the expression of collective identities that underpin struggles for recognition in multicultural societies. 'At least provisionally, identities can be formulated as situated in geographical space and "riding" historical momentum. . . . That identity and experience are mediated, narrated, constructed, caught up in the spiral of representation and intertextuality does not mean that all struggle has come to an end' (Shohat and Stam 1994, p. 346).

With regard to indigenous communities in particular, as Martin-Barbero (2002) has eloquently asserted, the understanding of such groups united around the world in their conquered and marginalized indigeneity, and their complex cultures can only be understood within an historical dynamic, to which polyvocal and diverse Aboriginal representations as subaltern agency remain critical. Shohat and Stam argue that

> [s]ome of the paradoxes of the global/local become manifest in the recent practices of 'indigenous media', that is, the use of audio-visual technology (camcorders, VCRs) for the cultural and political purposes of indigenous or 'fourth world' peoples. The phrase itself, as Faye Ginsburg points out, is oxymoronic, evoking both the self-understanding of aboriginal groups and the vast institutional structures of TV and cinema.
>
> (Shohat and Stam 1994, p. 150)

Significantly, '[w]ithin "indigenous media", the producers are themselves the receivers, along with neighbouring communities, and, occasionally, distant cultural institutions or festivals' (*ibid.*). Confronting the urgent indigenous issues involves having to transcend this imaginary boundary, allowing indigenous media to address a wider constituency.

Contemporary struggles by indigenous communities around the world for land rights and cultural-political sovereignty thus testify to the material and representational aspects of subaltern politics. Ironically, academic discussions and debates on globalization rarely include references to these struggles. Yet they epitomize in many ways the enduring structures and practices of domination and marginalization, engendered by persisting ignorance of indigenous cultures and the material realities of their existence.

Further reading

Ashcroft, B. (2001) *On Post-colonial Futures: Transformations of Colonial Culture*. London: Continuum.

Michaels, E. (1994) *Bad Aboriginal Art: Tradition, Media and Technological Horizons*. St Leonards: Allen & Unwin.

Muecke, S. (1992) *Textual Spaces: Aboriginality and Cultural Studies*. Kensington: New South Wales University Press.

San Juan, E. (1998) *Beyond Postcolonial Theory*. New York: St Martin's Press.

7 | GLOBALIZATION, IMPERIALISM AND NATIONAL CULTURE

The escalation of separatist movements in contemporary world politics testify to the rapidly shifting currents that bear witness to a further dimension of the global–local dialectic. With the constant redrawing of the world map following the redefinition of national boundaries, debates on national culture and identity take on particular relevance. Central to these debates is the constitution of national culture. For instance, separatist movements tend to justify their claims on an unstable mixture of history and cultural uniqueness that respectively legitimize an autonomous state and an independent national identity. In this context, the question arises as to whether the definition of national culture is an outcome of common identity crystallized from a collective existence over a period of time and a shared history and tradition that is common to all, or if national culture is an artificial construct imposed on the populace by national elites who are implicated in global capital, an insidious hegemonic notion. Since claims to nationhood are inevitably premised upon cultural uniqueness, are national identity and cultural identity coterminous? Do people of a nation share an ethnicity, and are they thereby able and willing to 'imagine' the national community (Anderson 1993)? Ideas of cultural coherence and territorial belonging – frequently the bases of separatist demands – have been known to contribute to internecine conflict and ethnic cleansing, as witnessed in the former Yugoslavia, as boundaries pertaining to the political, economic and cultural spheres are challenged from below. The shifts in collective identity that this indicates is not limited to the challenges to the nation-state, however, as the formation of supranational organizations of cooperations, mostly on economic or military grounds, such as NATO, the European Union, ASEAN and NAFTA, spill over into the cultural sphere, as the constitution of national culture is similarly called into question.

One of the 'hot spots' of contemporary conflicts is Chechnya, where separatist movements have been calling for independence from the Russian Federation since the dissolution of the former Soviet Union in 1991. As Tony Wood (2004) observes, whereas the demand for autonomy from other states of the former Soviet Union, such as Estonia, Lithuania and Latvia were approved by the politburo in 1991, a demand from Chechnya, invoking a similar popular mandate prefigured the Russo–Chechen conflict.

Embroiled in this conflict are several issues that are relevant to our concerns. Primarily, whether we construe of it as a Chechen resistance to Russian invasion and occupation – in other words, Chechen struggle for independence from Russian colonization – or as Russia's attempt to control Chechen terrorism, is revealing of not only our political sympathies, but more importantly, also of the debates and conflicting theories that form part of the intricate web of discourses on globalization. Demands for self-determination, based on historical and cultural, as well as political rationale and justification, collide with arguments in favour of a putative democracy and, particularly in the case of Russia, a relatively incipient capitalism.

Nor is this situation unique to Russia. India, for example, has had a long history of subnational conflicts and movements around claims of separate statehood – in Punjab, the North East, Kashmir. In Indonesia, the success of East Timorese independence movement has been followed by analogous demands in the Aceh province and elsewhere. In Sri Lanka, the civil war between government forces and Tamil separatists continues unabated after more than twenty years. The Kurds, spread across much of Turkey and Iraq, have been involved in a struggle for self-determination for a long time; the conflict in Algeria has centred around the legitimacy of the government that is supported by the French; whereas China's occupation of Tibet has had diverse responses from the West, most of which are prompted by considerations of *realpolitik*. According to Wood, the politics of necessity over ethics and moral deliberations has been typified in Western responses to the Chechen conflict: 'in the West, on the rare occasions that attention is devoted to Chechnya there has been almost total unanimity that Chechen independence is not to be countenanced for the good of Russian democracy and its nascent capitalism' (Wood 2004, p. 7), with the result that discussions of the conflict have neglected what he refers to as Russian 'brutality', instead 'preferring the state-sponsored obfuscations of the "war on terror" '.

Nationalism, in particular the form of ethno-nationalism that inspires collective identity and inter-ethnic conflict as in Sri Lanka, Rwanda, and the former Yugoslavia, has been scrutinized and debated upon. As San Juan rightly observes, nationalism is one of 'the most dangerously utilized words in contemporary discourse on culture and politics' (San Juan 1998, p. 201). He goes on to suggest two contradictory responses to the idea of nationhood: 'while some predict the demise of a "nation" (more precisely, the bourgeois and neo-colonial forms of the nation-state sprung from booty or comprador capitalism), others want "nationalism" arrested, convicted and buried; both terms however, are not only alive and well but have acquired urgent multi-accented resonance' (San Juan 1998, pp. 201–2). San Juan's reference to national separatism and capitalism are instructive, being a useful reminder of the entanglements between economy and culture, both at the global and local level, that informs nationalist politics as well as politics within the nation-state.

Jeffrey Alexander (1995) draws attention to the unpopularity of nationalism stemming from its recourse to primordial ethnic connections: 'Nationalism is the name intellectuals and publics are now increasingly giving to the negative antinomies of civil society. The categories of the "irrational", "conspiratorial", "repressive" are taken to be synonymous with forceful expressions of nationality, and equated with primordiality and uncivilized social forms' (Alexander 1995, p. 39). In a celebrated analysis on the alleged derivativeness of national discourse, Partha Chatterjee refers to the suspicion of nationalist politics among Western intellectuals: 'nationalism is now viewed as a dark, elemental, unpredictable force of primordial nature threatening the orderly calm of civilized life.... Like drugs, terrorism, and illegal immigration, it is one more product of the Third World that the West dislikes but is powerless to prohibit' (Chatterjee 1993, p. 69).

In order to examine the political validity of the claims to separate nationhood, and to explore the constitutive aspects of the rhetoric and ideology of nationalism it is necessary to locate them in a broader context. This entails an engagement with wider issues, both contemporary and historical, that provide the grounds for nationalist struggles. In its most politically persuasive avatar, nationalism is presented as a necessary component in the struggle for state sovereignty and independence from imperial domination. As demonstrated in the case of East Timor, Kurdistan, Chechnya or Sri Lanka, political domination is not always construed in terms of Western ascendency. Such cases demonstrate too, the persistence of nationalism and nationalist struggles in contemporary societies, that is, they are not merely of historical relevance. Debates on the conceptions of national culture, of cultural uniqueness, however, carry strong historical resonances from the former struggles for national liberation in the early part of the twentieth century. Yet another point is the alleged loss of sovereignty in the context or as a consequence of globalization, where the latter is perceived as a novel form of Western domination that results in the 'levelling' of local cultures and ways of life. Global media are often identified in such debates as being among the primary vehicles for the new imperial ventures.

Globalization or imperialism?

Jameson (2000) begins his discussion claiming that 'attempts to define globalisation often seem little better than so many ideological appropriations – discussions not of the process itself, but of its effects, good or bad: judgements, in other words, totalising in nature' (Jameson 2000, p. 49). In order to escape the limitations of functional descriptions of the term, or the ideological overtones of definitions of globalization, Jameson proposes tracing the interconnections between 'five distinct levels of globalisation . . . the technological, the political, the cultural, the economic, the social' as a step towards enumerating the politics of resistance to globalization. His premise as well as his main arguments both point to a particular political position with regard to globalizing processes, which he clearly identifies as sustaining different levels of inequality, a condition that demands resistance, and attempts to conceive alternatives to locate the foundations for alternatives to the 'tremendous invasive force of the new, globalized capital' (Jameson 2000, p. 67).

McChesney (2001) prefers the term 'neo-liberalism' to globalization, with neo-liberalism seen as referring to

> the set of national and international policies that call for business domination of all social affairs with minimal countervailing force. . . . Understood as one of neoliberalism rather than simply as globalisation, the current era seems less the result of uncontrollable natural forces and more as the newest stage of class struggle under capitalism.
>
> (McChesney 2001, p. 2)

How then to approach the question of contemporary global economy and culture? It would seem that the choice between 'globalization' and 'imperialism' as a term to account for the neo-liberal market economy underlying the 'liberalization' of economies and the concomitant changes in terms of flexible capital and labour often reflects different positions with regard to these changes. Broadly speaking, 'globalization' appears to reveal a tendency to either describe various global social and cultural formations in terms of inter-connectedness or the shrinking of time–space, as for instance by Robertson and Giddens, or as a celebration of the triumph of Western liberal politics and capitalist values signified by the dissolution of the Soviet Union, a historical event which is seen as a sign of the inevitability of the spread of capital.

The much-quoted Tomlinson (1991) makes his preference clear, concluding his critique of the cultural imperialism thesis by recommending that we regard the growing interrelationship between various regions of the world as globalization, since 'it is far less coherent or culturally directed' than imperialism. The 'idea of "globalisation" suggests interconnection and interdependency of all global areas which happens in a far less purposeful way' (Tomlinson 1991, p. 175). Such benign interpretations of the intensification of transnational forms of production and economic power retain their optimism regarding recent global developments and rarely address patterns of inequality. Terms like 'interconnection' and 'interdependency' suggest a process of equal exchange and partnership, which belies the fundamental inequality in the flow of media and capital, and in the international division of labour.

Those taking such issues as the starting points of their analyses however, prefer the term 'imperialism' to 'globalization'. Harvey for instance, refers to current developments as 'the new imperialism', defining imperialism as 'a contradictory fusion of "the politics of state and empire", . . . and "the molecular processes of capital accumulation in space and time" ' (Harvey 2003, p. 26). Similarly, Petras and Veltmeyer argue that the term 'globalization' must be 'counterposed with a term that has considerably greater descriptive value and explanatory power: imperialism' (Petras and Veltmeyer 2001, p. 12).

Preferring the term 'imperialism' implies a focusing on patterns of economic, political and cultural power. Harvey suggests that one of the constituents of the new imperialism is the process of accumulation by dispossession through a combination of coercion and consent enforced by the international financial system and organized state power. Coercion and consent link this process of imperialism not only to Gramsci, to hegemony, and to culture, but also to Guha's (1997) analysis of colonial power in India. The cultural imperialism thesis thus relates not merely to the spread of Western values through the media, but more significantly to a fundamental reorganization of local cultures that is linked to economic liberalization, neo-liberalism, and imperialist formations of global capital.

This is an important point, and a possible corrective to the excesses of earlier critiques of cultural imperialism which divided the world along West versus the Rest lines, and conceived of imperialism as a form of imposition by the West on the Rest. This appears far too simplistic given contemporary formations of global capital whose pathways wind in and out of both the West and the developing world, incorporating cultural and economic elites situated in different locations. The analysis of global patterns of inequality and of the relations between global media and power, therefore, has to account for both the structural aspects of global economy as well as the roles of national elites, particularly in the developing world. As McChesney argues, with regard to analysing global media, 'one has to start with understanding the global system and then factor in differences at the national and local levels' (McChesney 2001, pp. 2–3). This is mainly because of the spread of neo-liberalism as an ideology underpinning the 'liberalization' of national economies, and because 'proponents of neoliberalism in every country argue that cultural trade barriers and regulations harm consumers, and that subsidies inhibit the ability of nations to develop their own competitive media firms' (McChesney 2001, p. 6).

Unpacking the intense and as yet unresolved debate on cultural imperialism reveals certain persistent and, at times, petrified oppositions that continue to obstinately underpin the diverse positions interested academics have assumed with regard to the debate. These positions vary greatly, ranging from those for whom the term imperialism no longer holds any intellectual or political merit (see Tomlinson 1991), to those like McChesney (2001) who see the critique of cultural imperialism as an extension of the critique of the liberalization of global economy and the pre-eminence of the market as a self-regulatory system, to those for whom it is not so much a political debate as an epistemological one – for example, the political economists insisting on the primacy of the economy as a foundational category, and the cultural studies theorists for whom such foundational categories or meta-narratives are anathema.

Admittedly, this is a slight caricature of the different positions on the debate which misses their growing theoretical and empirical sophistication. It must be said, however, that caricatures often underlie the various arguments that continue to figure prominently in the debates on media or cultural imperialism. Buell (1994) provides an illustration of this rhetorical style in his introduction, where he introduces Herb Schiller's concern about the apparent homogenization or Americanization of global culture by quoting from an essay by Schiller published in 1969, and by summarizing Schiller's subsequent corpus of work on international communication (which in Buell's defence was remarkably consistent in its politics) in a somewhat throwaway phrase: 'Schiller theoretically retooled his position somewhat by grounding it in the then-emerging field of world-systems theory, but his fundamental polemic remained the same' (p. 1). Although Buell goes on to tackle fairly assiduously the different aspects of current intellectual debates on globalization and culture, as a starting premise his account of conceptualizations of cultural imperialism appears as a caricature.

The cultural imperialism thesis has come under a lot of criticism recently, so much so that it has spawned a veritable academic industry dedicated to highlighting the apparent empirical inadequacies and theoretical lacunae that are alleged to undermine the legitimacy of the critique. Such criticisms range from attacks on the putative 'purity' of local cultures that the critique is seen to promote, to empirical demonstrations of 'semiotic democracy', which show that audiences from different cultures actively engage with media texts and interpret them differently. While a few of these criticisms are valid and contribute to the refinement of the critique, others are based on a misconception of the critique.

One such critique emerges from audience research, which purports to demonstrate what is considered to be a major flaw in the argument about the media's contribution to homogenization of cultures across the globe. The few studies that have worked with audiences from different cultures (and they are relatively speaking, very few; most such critiques restricting themselves to Liebes and Katz's (1993) analysis of interpretations of *Dallas* by ethnically diverse groups) base their claim on different cultural groups 'actively' engaging with texts, bringing to bear their own cultural frameworks to engage with the television programme. This may well be the case, although the Liebes and Katz study is problematic (see Harindranath 2000, for a discussion of the problems with equating ethnicity with culture).

Limiting the argument to demonstrations of diverse interpretations by differently situated audiences is however, to miss the point. As Dan Schiller (1996) has argued, specifically in response to Liebes and Katz,

> the critique was not only, not even principally, about the purported homogenisation of interpretation, nor even about cultural consumption more generally. Rather, it centred on how structural inequality in international cultural production and distribution embodied, pervaded, and reinforced a new style of supranational domination.
>
> (Schiller 1996, p. 89)

Similarly, Boyd-Barrett (1998), focusing more narrowly on the idea of media imperialism, argues that what is of importance is not so much the apparent manipulation of audiences, but the democratization of communication: 'whose voices get to be heard, and which voices are excluded? That's all' (Boyd-Barrett 1998, p. 168).

The market, the state and the nation

Much has been written recently about the relations between states and markets in the context of globalization, most of it in terms of what exactly globalization entails. Judgements, revealing different political stances, have been made about globalization on the basis of specific positions vis-à-vis states and markets (see for instance, Boyer and Drache 1996). One of the consequences of globalization, it has been argued, is the withering away of state control particularly over national economies arising from the liberalization of global economy, the dissolution of border controls and the lifting of trade barriers. The repercussions of this development has been much debated between those who celebrate the 'free market', and those for whom neo-liberalism constitutes a neo-colonial hegemony that threatens both the economic and cultural sovereignty of nations.

Intrinsic to this are debates about state sovereignty and market efficiency, in which the role of the state is seen either as a guarantor of particular rights of citizens, including those of social welfare, or as an impediment for the untrammelled expansion and flow of the market, which is seen to facilitate economic development and equality. How does one construe the relationship between states and markets? Is it (a) the withering away of the state, even if it isn't the way in which Marx intended it?, (b) state versus the market, in which the two are presented as opposing forces, each performing the function of curtailing the otherwise unhindered power of the other?, or (c) alternatively, do markets and states work together in the creation and maintenance of global economy and society, in other words, are they equally implicated in the process of globalization?

Challenging the 'myth of the powerless state' undermined by the logic of capitalism, Weiss (1997) rightly refers to three hypotheses that contribute to versions of 'strong globalisation': '(i) strong globalisation; state power erosion [for instance K. Ohmae, 1990], (ii) strong globalisation; state power unchanged [Weiss's example is the argument presented in *The Economist* of 7 October, 1995 that states never had control over macroeconomic planning], (iii) weak globalisation (strong internationalisation); state power reduced in scope [exemplified in Hirst and Thompson, 1996]' (Weiss 1997, p. 5).

Arguing the case for a fourth proposition, that of 'weak globalisation (strong internationalisation); state power adaptability and differentiation emphasised' (*ibid.*), Weiss seeks to challenge the globalist orthodoxy. For her the stated power of global finance, which is a significant part of this orthodoxy, as well as the concomitant weakening of the state's power to form fiscal and economic policies, are vastly exaggerated. The constraints placed by the financial markets on the state's ability to address domestic economic issues are relative rather than absolute. She points out three principal weaknesses in the argument about the state's alleged 'powerlessness': it exaggerates the power of the state in the past, emphasizing its relative lack of power in the contemporary globalized world, which belies the challenges faced by policy makers for decades; it similarly overlooks the differences among states' responses to external pressures. Finally, she points to the role of political leaders to overstate their helplessness in the face of global trends. Most importantly for our purposes, Weiss argues that 'far from being victims, (strong) states may well be facilitators (at times perhaps perpetrators) of so-called "globalisation" ' (Weiss 1997, p. 20).

In a later essay (1999), Weiss asserts that neo-liberalism need not be the sole form of globalization, and points to alternatives other than either succumbing to the pressures to 'open up', or resisting them. She recommends instead, a 'managed openness', which 'implies that global and national are not necessarily competing principles of organization, that they can be – and indeed in many ways already are – complementary' (Weiss 1999, p. 127).

Weiss's argument about the complementary nature of the relations between global and national, or the global market and the nation-state, recalls Leo Panitch's (1998) contention that the 'conceptual optics of neo-classical economics' that gave the original impetus and rationale for neo-liberal globalization has obfuscated the role played by the state 'in setting the rules of the game as well as in shifting the balance of class forces as part of the process of globalization' (Panitch 1998, p. 13).

States perform the role of providing the infrastructure and juridical conditions amenable to markets, their rules facilitate capital movements, trade and investment, and instead of attempting to withdraw from the economy, they renegotiate their relationship to it in terms of regulation. '[A]ll this takes place through trial and error, negotiation and compromise, tension and contradiction. These tensions and contradictions, and the class struggle that attend them, may be displaced from one terrain of the state, only to reappear in another, where they re-emerge in new forms' (Panitch 1998, p. 14). He quotes from the 'remarkable' World Bank report of 1997, which, overturning the neo-liberal emphasis on the minimal state, advances a thesis for the role of the state as one of protecting and correcting markets. Attempting to shift the 'attention from the sterile debate of state and market to the more fundamental crisis of state effectiveness' (quoted in Panitch 1998, p. 16), it emphasizes the complementarity of the role of the state in restructuring of institutions and apparatuses in such a way that it enables 'markets to flourish' (*ibid.*). The ideological underpinning of this argument is fairly obvious, as it reinforces the notion of the state performing particular functions for the smooth operations of the market. What is central to our present concerns however, is Panitch's observation that 'a fully effective state will avoid limiting itself to these "first generation reforms" and will eventually move to restructure the executive itself as well as the judiciary, the civil service, unions, political parties, media' (Panitch 1998, p. 19) in the service of the penetration of the values of global capital into diverse dimensions of society.

Examining the role of national elites in sustaining the neo-liberal orthodoxy consequently entails two complementary moves – market versus the state, and the politics of cultural nationalism. The other side of the debate on globalization is the role of the state. While the state is seen as increasingly irrelevant by both supporters of the apologists for globalization such as Fukuyama, who celebrate its apparent demise, as well as more critical theorists such as Hardt and Negri (2000) who see its decline as an inevitable consequence of the inexorable dynamic of global capital, others such as Wood (2003) argue that the state plays a significant role in the expansion of capital beyond direct political control, whereby 'local states have proved to be far more useful transmission belts for capitalist imperatives' (Wood 2003, p. 23). She makes a similar argument in an earlier essay (1998) while distinguishing between older forms of colonialism and contemporary global economy: 'today, transnational capital may be more effective than was the old style military imperialism in penetrating every corner of the world, but it tends to accomplish this through the medium of local capital and national states' (Wood 1998, p. 45).

Implicated in this process are local elites, who are both the guarantors and the beneficiaries of market liberalization. Ahmad (1995) insists even more strongly on the complicit role of the state to the globalization of capital. For him national bourgeoisie have an ambivalent attitude to the state, as

> they wish to more or less bypass the regulatory aspects of this state (through liberalization, marketization, etc.), and yet they utilize it both for securing the domestic conditions of production favourable to capital . . . and for facilitating the articulation of domestic and foreign capitals. In other words, the new national bourgeoisie, like imperial capital itself, wants a weak nation-state in relation to capital and a strong one in relation to labour.
>
> (Ahmad 1995, p. 11)

Nationalism, then

This recognition is related to debates on nationalism and national culture as a site of resistance against imperialism. The reconstruction of national culture as possible resistance or alternative to cultural imperialism implies both the undermining of the idea that the globalization of cultures is inevitable as well as the return of agency to national cultural production. The reorganization of national media is central to the critique of cultural imperialism, as Dan Schiller suggests: 'the baseline for judgement of national culture was this: what could communications media contribute to revolutionary social transformation?' (Schiller 1996, p. 102).

National cultural formations as emancipatory projects has come under attack mainly from postcolonial critics, for whom nationalism is an elite cultural practice which appropriates the cultures of the subaltern classes, or is at best a 'derivative discourse' of Western modernity. Said (1993), building on insights from Tagore's

Nationalism (1917) and Du Bois's extraordinary *The Souls of Black Folk* ([1903] 1969) on notions of national or collective identity, identifies three 'great topics [that] emerge in decolonising resistance, separated for analytical purposes, but all related' (Said 1993, p. 259). These interrelated themes constitute, 'the insistence on the right to see the community's history whole, coherently, integrally. Restore the imprisoned country to itself'; secondly, 'the idea of resistance, far from being merely a reaction to imperialism, is an alternative way of conceiving human history', and the third constituent is 'a noticeable pull away from separatist nationalism towards a more integrative view of human community and human liberation' (pp. 260–1).

Said identifies a 'broadly *cultural* opposition' in intellectual circles, from both the Left and the Right, to anti-imperialist nationalisms from 'the formerly subject peoples'. Said declares himself ambivalent to nationalism: while he is supportive of such nationalisms that enabled the restoration of a community and assertions of identity that mobilized the anti-colonial struggles, he is also aware of the intellectual and political discomfort with post-independence discourses of nationalism, 'when new and imaginative reconceptions of society and culture were required in order to avoid the old orthodoxies and injustices' (Said 1993, p. 263).

As discussed in Chapter 3 in the context of post-apartheid South Africa, the pronouncements of national cultural formations from national elites post-independence at times obscures and comes at the expense of addressing economic disparities and sociocultural injustices. Conversely, it is also possible to sympathize with Vanaik's (1997) argument that the critique of nationalism is restricted to the representations of nationalism, and ignores the 'exceptional character of nationalism', which 'lies in its unique combination of politics and culture, of civic power (e.g. the importance of citizenship), and identity' (Vanaik 1997, p. 42). The answer to both the danger of ethnic nationalism and the elitist silencing of subaltern voices seems to lie in the recognition of vernacular cultural production as sites of popular (as opposed to elite) consciousness.

Lazarus (1999) argues that the focus on nationalism and the critique of ethnonationalism in scholarly literature is an instance of a largely 'unreflexive' engagement from a predominantly First World perspective that takes the disastrous conflicts in Rwanda, Liberia and Chechnya as indicative of an essential characteristic of all struggles for national self-determination. He quotes Worsley's observation that after 1918

> nationalism was seen as a problem, even a catastrophe; a reason for pessimism, not hope. To intellectuals, it had now become supremely illogical and supremely irrational. The subsequent emergence of fascism, which was launched upon the total elimination of dissent at home and military expansion abroad, seem the final confirmation of the inherently evil nature of nationalist thinking, pushed to its ultimate extremes.
>
> (Lazarus 1999, p. 272)

Lazarus finds this position 'deeply disingenuous' and indicative of current thinking that adamantly persists on a Western perspective, which deplores nationalist movements elsewhere. The anti-colonial independence struggles that were premised on national-ist sentiments and notions of a national culture are conveniently forgotten. This suggests two interrelated but distinct issues: the validity and legitimacy of nationalist struggles on the one hand, and the assumptions informing the dismissal of all nationalisms – both emancipatory and ethnic – on the other. They raise the question of how to adjudicate between nationalisms. References to 'irrational', 'illogical' and the tribal nature of nationalisms, as Lazarus and others like Dallmayr (1998), Chat-terjee (1986) argue, originate from a distinction between 'our' and 'their' national-isms, in which the former is 'typically classed as finished projects and are taken to have had benign effects: modernizing, unifying, democratizing'; whereas the latter is construed as still 'unfolding' nationalisms or unfinished projects, and 'are categorized under the rubrics of atavism, anarchy, irrationality, and power-mongering. . . . [I]t is taken to pose a danger to the established social order of the West' (Lazarus 1999, p. 69).

Presenting a similar argument, Dallmayr (1998) critiques Plamenatz's distinction between 'liberal' and 'illiberal' nationalisms, in effect, that '[w]hereas Western nation-alism has been mainly liberal and only occasionally illiberal, Eastern nationalism, in Plamenatz's view, has been and continues to be generally illiberal, sometimes violently illiberal' (Dallmayr 1998, p. 196). The main distinction between the two, for Plamenatz, lies in the fact that Western nationalism has been premised on a common culture among advanced nation-states, while 'Eastern' nationalism (which to him encompassed nationalist politics in Africa, Asia and Latin America) was predicated on the shakier grounds of a reaction to a Western phenomenon that was incongruous with local traditions. In this view, Eastern nationalism is tainted by the ambivalence that results from attempts to adopt Western forms of state formation and governance by native cultures whose values are fundamentally incompatible with Western political phil-osophy. To summarize an argument I have presented elsewhere (Harindranath 2000), the Indian national elite of colonial India were conscious of the irony of adopting a Western idiom in the alternative politics of the independence struggle. As pointed out by Chatterjee (1993), Indian nationalism 'produced a discourse in which, even as it challenged the colonial claim to political domination, it also accepted very intellectual premises of "modernity" on which colonial domination was based' (Chatterjee 1993, p. 30).

The legitimacy of cultural nationalism, in the form of an 'authentic' local voice, informing the struggle for national liberation was much debated by anti-colonial figures such as Gandhi and Fanon. More recently, the post-structuralist suspicion of 'essences' has inspired critiques of nationalism which, for scholars such as Said, Spivak and Hall, was a historically contingent strategy that essentialized a 'sort of collective "one true self", invoking shared histories and common roots'. Such invocations have the merit of erecting alternative paradigms that challenge the colonial hierarchization of cultures. However, for Hall (1994), such pronouncements of collective identity are a risky strategy, particularly in the current political climate. As we saw in Chapter 1, for Hall collective identity is a process of 'becoming' as well as 'being', and therefore it is wrong to turn back to a putative past that is 'waiting to be found, and which when found, will secure our sense of ourselves into eternity' (Hall 1994, p. 394).

Plamenatz's dichotomy is clearly unacceptable for Dallmayr, for whom non-Western nationalism is 'not necessarily or tendentially illiberal, even and precisely when it proceeds from a thick fabric of cultural traditions' (Dallmayr 1998, p. 199). In the case of the Indian struggle for independence, the different emphases placed on Hinduism by spiritual leaders and cultural and political figures are instructive. Whereas for the former, such as Vivekananda and Aurobindo, Indian nationalism was, at least temporarily, infused by Hindu cultural distinctiveness, for the latter, like Tagore and Gandhi, it was the very heterogeneity of religious and caste diversity that precluded any homogenizing impulse. Interestingly, there were differences even between Tagore and Gandhi: while Tagore celebrated cultural uniqueness and was cautious about political nationalism, Gandhi saw the political form of nationalism as having a necessary role in the creation of the post-independence state. What is crucial here, however, is that they recognized the profusion of religious and ethnic diversity in their conception of a culturally distinct India, and were concerned about the homogenizing impulse of state bureaucracy.

Lowe and Lloyd (1997), in their analysis of the creation of state institutions in newly independent countries, allude to the contradiction that is 'virtually constitutive of the practices of anticolonial nationalism. On the one hand, the ends of anticolonial nationalism are defined by the goal of the capture of the state, and its ideology is in large part structured in terms of liberal discourses and for liberal state institutions.' The claims to self-determination are premised on the basis of rights to sovereignty that refer to enlightenment universality, as do citizenship rights in the new country. On the other hand, however, 'within the terms of an anticolonial struggle, it is rare for a nationalist movement not to draw on conceptions of "tradition" of cultural anti-modernity. . . . In this, nationalism repeats the very distinction between tradition and modernity that colonialism institutes to legitimate domination' (Lowe and Lloyd 1997, p. 9).

Writing in the context of international communication theory, Dan Schiller (1996) points to another apparent contradiction immanent in notions of national culture. According to him, it is constituted by an inherent contradiction designated by its inescapable class character: 'on the one hand, it is an expression of the basic relations of domination as they exist in the cultural sphere, the representative of the dominant culture itself, imposed upon and inculcated in the subordinated social groups', which is at odds with national culture as 'the site for the subordinated social groups to struggle against the dominant culture' (Schiller 1996, p. 97). The various discussions of the opposing positions with regard to nationalism and national culture attest to the complex processes of hegemony and counter-hegemony that are intrinsic to national politics, assertions of cultural uniqueness and claims of sovereignty.

Stam (1991), in his discussion of Third Cinema, underlines the problematic nature in the concept of nationalism, particularly the oscillation between 'progressive and regressive poles' hinging on the political predilections of the hegemonic power bloc that mobilizes nationalism. Early conceptions of nationalism, he finds, 'took it as axiomatic that the issue was simply one of expelling the foreign to "recover" the national. . . . The simple elimination of foreign influences, it was assumed, would automatically allow the national culture to emerge in all its plenitude and glory' (Stam 1991, p. 227). This originary notion of nationalism was clearly fraught with difficulties, Stam observes, as it elided the inequalities inherent in the local societies thereby valorizing them, as in the case of patriarchy critiqued in the film *Xala*, or muffling the voices of the marginalized in the search for an alleged 'essence' of national culture.

These inherent contradictions also testify to the difficulties in adjudicating the legitimacy of nationalist projects. In what circumstances can references to national culture, for instance, be deemed emancipatory, if most calls for national sovereignty and self-rule are based on putative cultural unity? Brennan (1990) posits a possible framework as contributing towards such adjudication in his distinction between 'imperial' and 'anti-imperial' nationalisms. Imperialist nationalisms, for Brennan, have an acquisitive logic by which, seeking to subsume and exploit a regions natural resources or populations, they promote a 'project of unity on the basis of conquest and economic expediency'. Conversely, anti-imperialist nationalism, whose project is one of consolidation after or towards the separation from the colonial power, is geared in the direction of 'reclaiming community within boundaries defined by the very power whose presence denied community' (Brennan 1990, p. 58).

The expediency here is cultural rather than economic, relating to the constitution of a national community within a nation-state whose borders were drawn by the process of colonization and, particularly in the case of Africa, by the power-sharing arrangements and conflicts between various colonizing powers. It is worth remembering at this juncture Etienne Balibar's (1991) declaration that 'we have no right whatever to equate the nationalisms of the dominant with that of the dominated, the nationalisms of the dominant with that of the dominated, the nationalism of liberation with the nationalism of conquest. . . . Fichte or Gandhi are not Bismark; Bismark or De Gaulle are not Hitler' (Balibar 1991, p. 45).

Even during anti-colonial struggles, however, the constitution of national culture as a necessary move towards national liberation was a topic of constant debate and negotiation. We have already noted the differences of opinion between nationalist leaders in colonial India. In the case of Africa too, it is worth noting that pronouncements of a common project were far from being unified. A case in point is 'Negritude', conceived in the 1930s by Aimee Cesaire and Leopold Senghor as a pan-African literary and political movement. This sought to address the marginalization of Africans by Europeans both in Europe as well as in their own countries through what Appiah and Gutmann (1996) call 'color consciousness', expressions of alleged cultural unity across the continent that signified Africanness and differentiated it from European culture. As Cesaire defined it, Negritude was 'becoming aware of being black, admitting and accepting one's blackness, and taking responsibility for the history and culture that goes with it' (quoted in Schipper 1999, p. 82). Such constructions of a putative pan-African nationalism around the uniqueness of black experience and history, however, was dismissed by others such as Soyinka, who in his rejection of Negritude once declared famously that 'a tiger does not proclaim his tigritude, he pounces' (quoted in Schipper 1999, p. 82).

More recently, Appiah (1992) and Makang (1997) have raised objections to Negritude's monolithic conception of an 'African personality'. Makang objects to the cultural nationalism that exemplified the Negritude project: 'the danger of culturalism during the colonial era was in overshadowing the demand for national liberation by putting forward the demand for cultural recognition, whereas in postcolonial time it is meant to cover the problem of political oppression and of economic injustice perpetrated by autocratic African regimes' (Makang 1997, p. 331).

We shall have occasion to explore the debates on cultural nationalism in the context of globalization later, but it is worth examining briefly here, the contributions by Amilcar Cabral and Frantz Fanon on the question of national culture. In 'National liberation and culture' ([1979] 2000) Cabral declares that 'the value of culture as an element of resistance to foreign domination lies in the fact that culture is the vigorous manifestation, on the ideological or idealist level, of the material and historical reality of the society that is dominated or to be dominated' (Cabral 2000, p. 474). Culture, to him, is 'simultaneously the fruit of a people's history and a determinant of that history'. Cabral's conception, therefore, was not narrowly conceived as a superstructure removed from the material realities of the populace. 'Culture, whatever the ideological and idealist characteristics of its expression, is thus an essential element of the history of the people. . . . Like history, or because it is history, culture has as its material base the level of the productive forces and the mode of production' (*ibid*., p. 475).

In terms of national liberation, culture was to Cabral instrumental to transformations in the economic, political and social spheres. The recovery of African subjectivity in other words, implied both contributing to, and resulting from national self-governance.

San Juan (2002) argues, rightly, that for Cabral national culture was implicated in the regaining of a people's agency, from which they are deprived under colonization, and this included reclaiming control over the development of productive forces. 'For Cabral, culture is the key constituent of the productive forces in society. Culture becomes the decisive element in grasping the dialectic of subjective and objective forces, the contradiction between the productive forces and the production relations, as well as the uneven terrain of class struggles' (San Juan 2002, p. 281).

Lazarus (1999) emphasizes another element in Cabral's formulation that approximates Fanon's discussion of national culture: the coalescence of intellectual thinking and popular consciousness which is fundamental to meaningful social transformation. National culture and identity are the sites of the convergence, contributing to the national liberation movement. Assertions of national right to sovereignty in other words, transcended the Manichean dichotomy of native intellectual against the colonizing power to include the people or nation, that is, the subalterns. In his celebrated essay, 'The pitfalls of national consciousness' Fanon (1963) expressed his vehement critique of an elitist or bourgeois nationalism, which he felt, even in its anti-colonial formulations, was merely an attempt to replace one form of hegemony with another, a 'neo-colonial class consolidation' in which the elite performed the role that linked the subaltern communities in the peripheries to the metropolitan capital.

This, however, did not mean that Fanon's vision was anti-nationalist. He distinguishes between bourgeois nationalism and the national-popular that is genuinely emancipatory and anti-imperialist. In a move reminiscent of Gramsci's argument regarding the role of the intellectual, Fanon insisted on the subaltern groups' political education, elevating them from 'national consciousness to political and social consciousness' (Fanon 1963, p. 203). To him, a national culture

> is the whole body of efforts made by a people in the sphere of thought to describe, justify, and praise the action through which that people has created itself and keeps itself in existence. A national culture in underdeveloped countries should therefore take its place at the very heart of the struggle for freedom which these countries are carrying on.
>
> (*ibid.*, p. 233)

The involvement of the subaltern groups was, therefore, central to national independence, and, as San Juan (1998) argues, 'for building [a nation's] institutions of participatory democracy. . . . [T]he nation as the locus of the mobilized masses serves as the framework in which the renaissance of culture and the democratic state can occur' (San Juan 1998, p. 213).

To Lazarus, Fanon's critique of bourgeois nationalism is a sufficient reminder to contemporary theorists sceptical of any form of nationalism of the existence of other forms of insurgencies such as that of peasants, strikes and protests, which testify to an alternative history of anti-colonial struggle than the one contained in elite representations of it. He uses Guha's (1983) analysis of the 'politics of the people' – peasant insurgencies in colonial India – to demonstrate autonomy of the domain of the non-elite and the subaltern politics from that of the indigenous elite. The dismissal, by many contemporary theorists, of all forms of nationalisms as expressions of indigenous elite power, is for Lazarus negligent of such non-elite insurgencies as well as of the pronouncements and contributions of revolutionary figures who instead of fetishizing local customs and traditions, incorporated them into their formations of national culture.

Nationalism, now

Lazarus argues against what he considers the ' "strong" version of the globalization hypothesis' (Lazarus 1999, p. 47). Taking as examples claims regarding the transnationalization of trade and the apparent demise of the state, Lazarus argues his case against such conceptualizations of the process of globalization. Pertinent to our discussion is his contribution to the debate on the putative 'obsolescence of the nation-state form' (Lazarus 1999, p. 48). As an instance of 'strong' versions of globalization on the subject of the nation-state he uses Baumann's (1994) assertion that in contemporary forms of globalization, it is 'structurally impossible for individual nations to sustain independent, or even autonomous, economies, polities, and social structures' (Baumann 1994, p. 152).

While conceding the *partial* validity of Baumann's argument by acknowledging the weakening of state power, Lazarus is at pains to point out that in capitalist societies the state continues to perform the function of supporting capital. He quotes Callinicos's (1994) argument: 'private capitals continue to rely on the nation state to which they are most closely attached to protect them against the competition of other capitals, the effects of economic crisis, and the resistance of those they exploit' (Lazarus 1999, p. 54). Arguing against the notion of a weak state as professed by Ohmae (1990, 1995) and others, that considers the nation-state as an anachronism, Ahmad (1995) suggests that nation-states in former colonies in Africa and Asia have in reality been further accentuated as a site for the consolidation of national elite power and their links with global capital.

Ahmad's striking image of 'the saffron yuppies' who open local Indian stock exchange, its computer industry and its market to foreign capital even while professing cultural exceptionalism and the authenticity of national culture precisely highlights the apparent contradictions in contemporary Indian politics. Until the elections in 2004 when the right-wing Hindu nationalist party, the BJP, was removed from power, Indian society revealed near-schizophrenic aspects of xenophobic rearticulation of cultural protectionism alongside enthusiastic removal of import restrictions.

But as the rise of Hindu fundamentalism in India in the late 1980s suggests, cultural protectionist measures and the invocation of a dubious past as a foundation for a putative national culture pose problems. Moreover, resistance to transnational culture requires a transcendence of national boundaries, a concerted effort from a multiplicity of sites. As Chatterjee (1986) has argued persuasively, the discourse of nationalism derives from that of modernization, thereby adopting the latter's teleological logic. Limiting the politics of resistance to nationalism is consequently inadequate:

> the very goal of national liberation has demonstrated its won failure in its realization: any number of countries have become independent of their former colonial masters, only to fall at once into the force-field of capitalist globalization, subject to the dominion of the money markets and overseas investment.
>
> (Jameson 2000, p. 65)

It seems to me that any attempt to address the debates on the critique of cultural imperialism needs to acknowledge this argument about state-market relations. The critique of cultural imperialism, which formed the basis of a considerable body of critical literature in international communications has, especially since the early 1990s, come under strong criticism which supports calls for it to be consigned to a former period in the intellectual history of media and communication studies. What used to be a hotly-contested debate is at present seen by some as a once-useful concept now devoid of much critical purchase. As Tomlinson has declared, 'the idea of cultural imperialism has been heavily criticized and, as a result, is far less fashionable a critical position in academic circles in the 1990s than it was during the 1970s and 1980s' (Tomlinson 1999, pp. 79–80).

Critiques of the cultural imperialism thesis emanate from mainly three points: a few scholars such as Tomlinson have referred to the conceptual inadequacies that continue to bedevil the argument, even while accepting, in varying degrees, the overall need for an intellectual intervention into the relationship between international media and the continuing patterns of global inequality. The second critique emerges from international audience research, such as Liebes and Katz (1993), which challenge the assumption underlying the media/cultural imperialism thesis of a text's ideology being uncritically accepted by audiences in different locales, and the consequent Westernization of these cultures. Such studies question the correlation between the unequal flows of international media forms and texts, and imperialism, arguing that audiences were often 'read into' the media content. The third is the apparent 'gate-keeping policies' of the state that seeks to protect local national cultures. Chadha and Kavoori (2000) for instance, refer to various protectionist measures adopted by various Asian countries, including, in the case of China and India, the encouragement of domestic media production (Chadha and Kavoori 2000, pp. 418–19). In addition, they point to evidence suggesting that audiences predominantly preferred locally produced fares to outside, or Western television. Similarly, Banerjee (2002) disputes the media/cultural imperialism thesis on the basis of the dramatic increase in local and regional production benefiting from liberalization and deregulation of the media in countries such as Malaysia and Singapore, and argues for a reconceptualization of the nature and implications of global media flows.

Recent developments in countries such as India and China concerning the media, markets and the state impinge on nationalism and identity, particularly in the context of the liberalization of both national economies and the media. Seemingly paradoxical developments in India and China reveal the complexity of the issue. For instance, while in India the progressive liberalization of the national economy developed in tandem with the emergence of the nationalist Hindu party and its claim to political-cultural legitimacy, in China this apparent paradox is manifested in the adoption of 'market socialism' as the doctrine underpinning economic liberalization.

Of primary interest is the articulation of the national in the global, as in the construction on Indian television of the Hindu citizen-consumer of multinational consumer goods, and the legitimation of fundamentalist politics through the invocation of 'Hindu' moral and legal discourses, both of which have to be considered alongside the proliferation of cable and satellite channels and the putative imperial discourses of 'Westernization'. In the case of China, this includes media reforms as a balancing act between state control and commercial constraints, characterized by some as 'market authoritarianism', and the liberalization of the media including state validation of advertising as a part of economic liberalization.

Oppositions to ethnocentric Western notions of democracy have also formed the basis for the alleged 'Asian way' cultural nationalism promulgated by Malaysia and Singapore, which considers liberal democracy as inappropriate to East Asian populations. This is premised on arguments that construe East Asian populations as attracted more to the ethics and practice of communitarian values and inter-group harmony than to individual rights. Quite apart from the epistemologically suspect nature of such conceptions, while they present an alternative to Western formulations of democracy by promoting political pluralism and cultural reflection and awareness, they 'can also serve as a potent ideological refuge for authoritarian rule by providing the theoretical basis for a strongly interventionist state dominated by a political party' (Rahim 1998, p. 56).

To take the example of the complicitous relations between the media, the market, and Hindu extremism, Rajagopal's (2001) well-known study of the complex ways in which Indian television serves as the site for the revival of Hindu nationalism as well as the espousal of neo-liberalism and the apparent merits of globalization, is perhaps the most comprehensive analysis of this seemingly contradictory development in contemporary Indian political culture. Others, such as Nandy *et al.* (1997), Ludden (1996), Jaffrelot (1999) provide extensive and occasionally provocative analyses of the emergence and rise of Hindu nationalism within the democratic process in India.

In terms of the media, the market and religious nationalism in the context of globalization, however, Fernandes (2000) and Chakravarty and Gooptu (2000) make exemplary attempts at tracing the complicated lines of connection. Fernandes is interested in shifting the terms of debate on the apparent failures of the state in order to examine 'how the nation is being reformed through the processes of globalization to the question of how the production of "the global" occurs through the nationalist imagination' (Fernandes 2000, p. 611). The transformation of national political culture from the post-independence Nehruvian vision that included industralization and a steadfastly secular state to the economically liberalized contemporary India is for her marked by the deepening of the culture of consumption.

In a culture that has subscribed increasingly to the visible indicators of wealth in the form of 'foreign' products, the adoption of the global within the purview of the national is evident Fernandes argues, in the 'visual representations of newly available commodities [that] provide a lens through which we can view the ways in which meanings attached to such commodities weave together narratives of nationhood and development with the production of middle-class identity' in India (Fernandes 2000, p. 615). Her essay presents a convincing analysis of television and print advertisements of consumer goods that draw on images and narratives from a nationalist and Hindu tradition as instances of advertising strategies that successfully combine the global, in the form of the products that they sell, with the idiom of the national. The conclusion that 'the aesthetic of the commodity does not merely serve as a passive reflector of wider social and cultural processes but instead becomes a central site in which the Indian nation is re-imagined' (Fernandes 2000, p. 619) presents a different conception of the apparent paradox of economic liberalization and cultural nationalism that has been a characteristic of contemporary India, in which both developments combine to produce a particular national imaginary.

Chakravarty and Gooptu (2000) see the consolidation of Hindu nationalism in India as an antidote to a presumed peril of subsumption by 'Western culture, on the one hand, and on the other the apparent threat to national security presented by the Muslim "other" ' (p. 97). However, this essay too, focuses on the mediation of consumption and consumerism linked to specific constructions of family and national community. 'With the market driving the growth of the media', they argue, 'and the middle class forming its primary target audience, not surprisingly, media productions not only drew upon, but also reproduced and magnified middle class notions of the "Hindu" nation in a bid to promote consumerism among these classes' (Chakravarty and Gooptu 2000, p. 97).

In the context of these arguments that demonstrate the intertwining of the global market and national rhetoric, the opposition between the global and the local needs to be rethought. The nation as a site of contestation in which the forces of cultural or media imperialism are opposed appears no longer valid. This may well require a rethinking of the local culture as vernacular cultural production, which has profound implications for the idea of intercultural dialogue.

Firstly, communication across and between cultures, both within national borders and internationally across the 'third world' has be construed not merely as a problem to be overcome in order to achieve understanding between heterogeneous cultural formations, but as multiple sites of cultural struggle against what Herbert Schiller has called 'the levelling' of cultures by transnational capitalism, which suggests a common project.

Secondly, vernacular culture, conceived as localized voices expressing the material aspects of local lived experience, has to be seen as a contribution towards achieving alternative social visions which simultaneously present a different version of national cultural and economic development, and offer scope for resisting exploitation and cultural 'levelling'. It should be noted, however, that vernacular cultural production, what Dan Schiller refers to as the 'theater of liberation' goes 'unacknowledged in the mainstream discussions of how national cultural variation purportedly offsets cultural imperialism' (Schiller 1996, p. 102). Moreover, the suppression of vernacular cultural production by the state is not uncommon in developing countries.

The link between vernacular cultural practice as providing alternative visions and older forms of anti-colonial cultural practice is fairly obvious. The contributions to the debate on nationalism by such figures as Fanon, Cabral and Gandhi are, therefore, still valid, and need to be considered in a proper examination of contemporary forms of imperialism and resistance. The recuperation of such voices and the politics of 'anti-imperial' nationalism, to use Brennan's serviceable dichotomy, goes against the grain of much current academic thinking that, as we have seen, has raised significant queries about the validity of nationalism. As Shohat observes, 'third world peoples . . . must speak today in a theoretical context where the notion of a coherent subject identity, let alone a community identity, is endlessly fragmented and de-centred, even epistemologically suspect' (Shohat 1995, p. 174).

This epistemological issue has profound political implications, as noted by Kenyan feminist Debra Amory:

> Doesn't it seem funny that at the very point when women and people of colour are ready to sit down at the bargaining table with the white boys, that the table disappears? That is, suddenly there are no grounds for claims to truth and know-ledge anymore and here we are, standing in the conference room making all sorts of claims to knowledge and truth but suddenly without a table upon which to put our papers and coffee cups, let alone to bang our fists.
>
> (quoted in Shohat, *ibid.*)

Negotiating the complex politics of nationalism and its epistemological and ethical validity is thus fraught with difficulty, not least because the idea of nationalism has been tainted by its association with ethnic absolutism and the extremist politics that it engendered. As in the case of multiculturalism, nationalism too, appears an amorph-ous and contested term; and like multiculturalism, it too has to arbitrate between the notions of sameness and difference in its engagement with marginalization and collect-ive identity. The fact that multiculturalism is subsumed within the national, and often challenges the latter's declarations of cultural cohesion throws the politics of nationalism into sharper relief.

Nationalist politics consequently epitomizes, as much as multiculturalism and indi-geneity, the themes that this book is mainly concerned with, namely the marginaliza-tion and inequality – both symbolic and material – that characterize the underside of globalization. The first section touched on the silences in globalization theories, elab-orated on the 'culture wars' and how these impacted on 'race' and ethnic issues. Subalternity was presented as a potentially productive concept with which to address the intricate politics of enunciation and representation. Contemporary manifestations of indigenous politics offer a clear example of the enduring patterns of marginalization and exploitation, as well as of the potential of emancipatory politics that seeks to destabilize dominant representations. Indigeneity, along with multiculturalism and nationalism, is the site in which history, the politics of 'race', and cultural difference are imbricated. Third Cinema as an overt political project undertakes a critical interro-gation of representational politics in terms of both theory and practice. It is a project with manifest concerns that address issues of economic inequalities, exploitation and marginalization.

Writers like Benhabib are concerned with the limits of cultural difference, favouring a dialogic relationship between cultures in an effort to keep the critical engagement with universalism alive. Maintaining a balance between pronouncements of cultural difference in the name of recuperating the voice of the marginalized on the one hand, and on the other recognizing the validity of universal values and norms is a delicate issue. The reference to 'cultures' in the plural in the title of this book is a deliberate allusion to the diverse and various cultural sites in which difference, minority or peripheral status, histories of exploitation and indifference, are contested, productively disrupted, and alternative narratives are presented. This book thus, presents an attempt to not only locate such themes, but also signal locales and practices of enunciation that challenge domination.

Further reading

Barker, F., *et al.* (ed.) (1994) *Colonial Discourse/Postcolonial Theory.* Manchester: Manchester University Press.

Dissanayake, W. (ed.) (1994) *Colonialism and Nationalism in Asian Cinema.* Bloomington: Indiana University Press.

Lazarus, N. (1999) *Nationalism and Cultural Practice in the Postcolonial World.* Cambridge: Cambridge University Press.

Mishra, V. (2002) *Bollywood Cinema: Temples of Desire.* London: Routledge.

GLOSSARY

Canon: originating from ecclesiastical principles and standards as expressed in religious texts, 'canon' is used here to refer to a set of academic writing that has contributed to the formation of a common understanding of social or political issues, that is, an orthodoxy.

Connectivity: a term used in discussions of globalization to suggest the complex ways in which apparently distant geographical locations are increasingly interlinked, either through mediation, in the form of media representations, or physically, through air travel.

Cultural imperialism: this is a much debated term that initially provided a frame with which to critique the persisting and ubiquitous inequalities across the world. It proposes that earlier forms of colonial domination have been replaced by more subtle ways of exploitation that operate hegemonically. Writers such as John Tomlinson have questioned the validity of such claims, while others such as Harindranath, attempt to reformulate the central thesis of the critique.

Disaster capitalism: Naomi Klein has used this term to describe the role of international 'for-profit' companies that benefit from contract work on the reconstruction of places devastated by conflict or natural disasters, such as Iraq, Aceh, Sri Lanka or Afghanistan. She argues that local governments are rarely consulted or involved in the decision-making process.

Ethnocentrism: the propensity to engage with and evaluate other cultures from the perspective of one's own set of cultural values. Ethnocentrism is said to be the basis of the formation of racial hierarchies and constructions of the 'Other'. Fallacious assumptions regarding other cultures and peoples result from an ethnocentric perspective, which disrupts the possibility of dialogues across cultural divides.

Global culture: the cultural dimensions of globalization. What constitutes global culture is a matter of debate, as for instance whether it suggests the amalgamation of diverse cultures into one, or points to the continuing existence and even increase of cultural diversity globally.

Homogenization: those who argue that cultures around the world are being merged into one, either in terms of consumer culture, or Westernization, or modernity, use the term homogenization to describe the process by which cultural distinctions are being blurred and cultural uniqueness destroyed through globalization.

Knowledge economy: a notion that gained currency particularly in the late 1990s and emphasized the changes to global economy facilitated by developments in new information and communication technologies working together with 'intellectual capital' or knowledge. Manuel Castells, for instance, has sought to explore the ways in which economic production is linked to the ability to store and retrieve information and knowledge.

Media imperialism: a critical perspective on international communications that focuses on the ownership and control of transnational media organizations, the 'flow' of news and media products from the West to the developing nations, and on the politics of representative practices on international media.

Metropolitan: used in this book to refer to academic centres and theory generation in Europe and North America, as opposed to those from Africa, Asia and Latin America.

Postcolonial: as Stuart Hall has pointed out, this does not designate a time after decolonization as much as the continuation of exploitation and marginalization under a new guise and in a novel configuration.

Post-Fordism: Unlike the Fordist assembly-line production, post-Fordism is characterized by flexible production systems and specializations among multi-skilled workers, fragmentation (contracting out) of production and competition globally, and niche marketing. Some analysts claim that post-Fordism has transformed the way people live in advanced economies.

Time–space distanciation: Anthony Giddens uses this term to describe the 'stretching' of social relations across vast distances and time zones, enabled by advances in transport and communication technologies. For instance, advances in telephony and email technology contributes to the maintenance of personal relationships across continents.

Virtual communities: this is attributed to Howard Rheingold who used it to designate online groups who, at least for the duration of their involvement in computer-mediated communication, form relationships that constitute communities.

Westernization: the conversion of non-Western communities to the values and practices of what is considered Western cultures. Some analysts argue that globalization amounts to the imposition of Western consumer culture on the world, the homogenization of diverse global cultures into norms that are largely Western.

BIBLIOGRAPHY

Abu-Lughod, L. (1993) *Writing Women's Worlds*. Berkeley, CA: University of California Press.

Achebe, C. ([1977] 2001) 'An image of Africa; racism in Conrad's *Heart of Darkness*', in G. Castle (ed.) *Postcolonial Discourses: An Anthology*. Oxford: Blackwell.

Ahmad, A. (1987) 'Jameson's rhetoric of otherness and the "national allegory" ', *Social Text*, 17.

Ahmad, A. (1992) *In Theory: Classes, Nations, Literatures*. London: Verso.

Ahmad, A. (1995) 'The politics of literary postcoloniality', *Race and Class*, 36:3.

Alcoff, L. (1991–2) 'The problem of speaking for others', *Cultural Critique*, no: 20.

Alexander, J. (1995) *Fin de Siecle Social Theory: Relativism, Reduction, and the Problem of Reason*. London: Verso.

Anderson, B. (1983) *Imagined Communities: Reflections on the Origin and Spread of Nationalism*. London: Verso.

Anthias, F. and N. Yuval-Davis (1992) *Racialized Boundaries: Race, Nation, Colour and Class, and the Anti-Racist Struggle*. London: Routledge.

Appadurai, A. (1996) *Modernity at Large: Cultural Dimensions of Globalization*. Minneapolis: University of Minnesota Press.

Appiah, A. (1992) *In My Father's House: Africa in the Philosophy of Culture*. London: Methuen.

Appiah, A. and A. Gutman (1996) *Color Conscious: The Political Morality of Race*. Princeton: Princeton University Press.

Armes, R. (1987) *Third World Filmmaking and the West*. Berkeley, CA: University of California Press.

Ashcroft, B. (2001) *On Post-Colonial Futures: Transformations of Colonial Culture*. London: Continuum.

Bahl, V. and A. Dirlik (eds) (2000) 'Introduction', in *History After the Three Worlds: Post-Eurocentric Historiographies*. Lanham: Rowman and Littlefield.

Baldwin, J. and M. Mead (1971) *A Rap on Race*. New York: Doubleday.

Balibar, E. (1991) 'Racism and nationalism', in E. Balibar and I. Wallerstein (eds) *Race, Nation, Class: Ambiguous Identities*. London: Verso.

Balibar, E. (1994) 'Racism as universalism', in *Masses, Classes, and Ideas*. New York: Routledge.

Banerjee, I. (2002) 'The local strikes back? Media globalization and localization in the new Asian television landscape', *Gazette*, 64:6.

Banerjee, S. and G. Osuri (2000) 'Silences of the media: whiting out Aboriginality in making news and making history', *Media, Culture & Society*, vol. 22:3.

Barlet, O. (2000) *African Cinemas: Decolonizing the Gaze*. Trans. Christ Turner 2000. London: Zed Books.

Bartolovich, C. (2002) 'Introduction: Marxism, modernity, and postcolonial studies', in Bartolovich, C. and N. Lazarus (eds) *Marxism, Modernity, and Postcolonial Studies*. Cambridge: Cambridge University Press.

Battaglia, D. (ed.) (1995) 'Problematising the self: a thematic introduction', in D. Battaglia (ed.) *Rhetorics of Self-Making*. Berkeley, CA: University of California Press.

Baumann, Z. (1991) *Modernity and Ambivalence*. Cambridge: Polity.

Baumann, Z. (1994) 'Searching for a centre that holds', in M. Featherstone, *et al.* (eds) *Global Modernities*. London: Sage.

Benhabib, S. (2002) *The Claims of Culture: Equality and Diversity in the Global Era*. Princeton: Princeton University Press.

Bennett, D. (ed.) (1998) *Multicultural States: Rethinking Difference and Identity*. London: Routledge.

Bennett, T. (1992) 'Putting policy into cultural studies', in L. Grossberg, *et al.* (eds) *Cultural Studies*. New York: Routledge.

Bennett, T. (1998) *Culture: A Reformer's Science*. London: Sage.

Benzi Zhang (2002) 'Re-siting the global/re-siting the local: the politics of cultural diaspora', in K. Tam, *et al.* (eds) *Sights of Contestation: Localism, Globalism, and Cultural Production in Asia and the Pacific*. Hong Kong: The Chinese University Press.

Beteille, A. (1998) 'The idea of indigenous people', *Current Anthropology*, vol. 39, no. 2.

Beverley, J. (1999) *Subalternity and Representation: Arguments in Cultural Theory*. Durham: Duke University Press.

Beverley, J. (2004) *Testimonio: On the Politics of Truth*. Minneapolis: University of Minnesota Press.

Bhabha, H. (1989) 'The commitment to theory', in J. Pines and P. Willemen (eds) *Questions of Third Cinema*. London: BFI.

Bhabha, H. (ed.) (1990) *Nation and Narration*. London: Routledge.

Bhabha, H. (1998) 'Culture's in-between', in D. Bennett (ed.) *Multicultural States: Rethinking Difference and Identity*. London: Routledge.

Bhatt, C. (1997) *Liberation and Purity: Race, New Religious Movements and the Ethics of Postmodernity*. London: UCL Press.

Boyd-Barrett, O. (1998) 'Media imperialism reformulated', in D. Thussu (ed.) *Electronic Empires: Global Media and Local Resistance*. London: Arnold.

Boyer, R. and D. Drache (1996) *States Against Markets: The Limits of Globalization*. London: Routledge.

Braham, P., *et al.* (eds) (1992) *Racism and Antiracism: Inequalities, Opportunities, and Policies*. London: Sage.

Brennan, T. (1990) 'The national longing for form', in H. Bhabha (ed.) *Nation and Narration*. London: Routledge.

Brennan, T. (1997) *At Home in the World: Cosmopolitanism Now*. Cambridge, Mass: Harvard University Press.

Brennan, T. (2003) 'The empire's new clothes', *Critical Inquiry* 29 (Winter, 2003).

Buell, F. (1994) *National Cultures and the New Global System*. Baltimore: Johns Hopkins Press.

Burawoy, M. (2000) 'Grounding globalization', in Burawoy, M. *et al.*, *Global Ethnography: Forces, Connections, and Imaginations in a Postmodern World*. Berkeley: University of California Press.

Burton, J. (1985) 'Marginal cinemas and mainstream critical theory', *Screen*, vol. 13:3.

Butler, J. (1990) *Gender Trouble*, New York: Routledge.

Butler, J. (1995) 'Collected and fractured', in K. Appiah and H. Gates (eds) *Identities*. Chicago: University of Chicago Press.

Butler, J. (1996) 'Universality in culture', in M. Nussbaum (with Respondents), *For Love of Country: Debating the Limits of Patriotism*. Boston: Beacon Press.

Cabral, A. (1973) *Return to the Source: Selected Speeches of Amilcar Cabral*. New York: Monthly Review Press.

Cabral, A. (1979) 'The role of culture in the liberation struggle', in *Communication and Class Struggle. Vol. 1, Capitalism, Imperialism*. New York: International General.

Cabral, A. ([1979] 2000) 'National liberation and culture', in *Unity and Struggle: Speeches and Writings*, reproduced in D. Brydon (ed.) *Postcolonialism: Critical Concepts in Literary and Cultural Studies*. New York: Routledge.

Callinicos, A. (1994) 'Marxism and imperialism today', in A. Callinicos, *et al.* (eds) *Marxism and the New Imperialism*. London: Bookmarks.

Carter, S. (2005) 'The geopolitics of diaspora', *Area*, 37:1.

Castles, S., *et al.* (1996) 'Australia: multi-ethnic community without nationalism?', in J. Hutchinson and A. Smith (eds) *Ethnicity*. New York: Oxford University Press.

Chadha, K. and A. Kavoori (2000) 'Media imperialism revisited: some findings from the Asian case', *Media, Culture & Society*, vol. 22.

Chakrabarty, D. (1998) 'Modernity and ethnicity in India', in D. Bennett (ed.) *Multicultural States: Rethinking Difference and Identity*. London: Routledge.

Chakraborty, D. (2000) *Provincializing Europe: Postcolonial Thought and Historical Difference*. Princeton: Princeton University Press.

Chakravarty, R. and N. Gooptu (2000) 'Imagi-nation: the media, nation, and politics in contemporary India', in E. Hallam and B. Street (eds) *Cultural Encounters: Representing 'Otherness'*. London: Routledge.

Chanan, M. (1997) 'The changing geography of Third Cinema', *Screen*, 39:4, Winter.

Chatterjee, P. (1986) *Nationalist Thought and the Colonial World: A Derivative Discourse?* London: Zed Books.

Chatterjee, P. (1993) *The Nation and its Fragments: Colonial and Postcolonial Histories*. Princeton: Princeton University Press.

Childs, J. and Guillermo-Delgado, P. (1999) 'On the idea of the indigenous', *Current Anthropology*, vol. 40, no. 2, pp. 211–12.

Clifford, J. (1997) *Routes: Travel and Translation in the Twentieth Century*. Cambridge: Harvard University Press.

Comaroff, J. (1996) 'Ethnicity, nationalism, and the politics of difference in an age of revolution', in E. Wilmsen and P. McAlister (eds) *The Politics of Difference: Ethnic Premises in World Power*. Chicago: University of Chicago Press.

Corner, J. (2001) ' "Ideology": a note on conceptual salvage', *Media, Culture & Society*, vol. 23.

Cubitt, S. (2005) *The Cinema Effect*. Cambridge: MIT Press.

Dallmayr, F. (1998) *Alternative Visions: Paths in the Global Village*. London: Rowman and Littlefield.

de Certeau, M. (1986) *Heterologies: Discourse on the Other*. Minneapolis: University of Minnesota Press.

Diawara, M. (ed.) (1993) 'Black American cinema: the new realism', in *Black American Cinema*. Routledge.

Diawara, M. (1999) 'Toward a regional imaginary in Africa', in F. Jameson and M. Miyoshi (eds) *The Cultures of Globalization*. Durham and London: Duke University Press.

Didur, J. and T. Heffernan (2003) 'Revisiting the subaltern in the new empire', *Cultural Studies*, 17 (1).

Dirlik, A. (1994a) 'The postcolonial aura: third world criticism in the age of global capitalism', *Critical Inquiry*, 20 (Winter 1994).

Dirlik, A. (1994b) *After the Revolution: Waking to Global Capitalism*. Hanover, New Hampshire: Wesleyan University Press.

Dirlik, A. (1996) 'The global in the local', in R. Wilson and W. Dissanayake (eds) *Global/Local: Cultural Production and the Transnational Imaginary*. Durham, NC: Duke University Press.

Dirlik, A. (1997) *The Postcolonial Aura*. Boulder, Co: Westview Press.

Dirlik, A. (2000a) 'Introduction', in V. Bahl, and A. Dirlik (eds) *History After the Three Worlds: Post-Eurocentric Historiographies*. Lanham: Rowman and Littlefield.

Dirlik, A. (2000b) 'Is there history after Eurocentrism? Globalism, postcolonialism, and the disavowal of history', in V. Bahl, and A. Dirlik (eds) (2000) *History After the Three Worlds: Post-Eurocentric Historiographies*. Lanham: Rowman and Littlefield.

Dissanayake, W. (1994a) 'Nationhood, history, and cinema: reflections on the Asian scene', in W. Dissanayake, (ed.) *Colonialism and Nationalism in Asian Cinema*. Bloomington: Indiana University Press.

Dissanayake, W. (ed.) (1994b) *Colonialism and Nationalism in Asian Cinema*. Bloomington: Indiana University Press.

Dissanayake, W. (1996a) 'Introduction/Agency and cultural understanding: some preliminary remarks', in W. Dissanayake (ed.) *Narratives of Agency: Self-making in China, India, and Japan*. Minneapolis: University of Minnesota Press.

Dissanayake, W. (1996b) 'Introduction', in R. Wilson and W. Dissanayake (eds) *Global/Local: Cultural Production and the Transnational Imaginary*. Durham: Duke University Press.

Downing, J. (ed.) (1987) *Film & Politics in the Third World*. New York: Praeger.

Du Bois, W. ([1903] 1969) *The Souls of Black Folk*. New York: New American Library.

Dwyer, R. and D. Patel, (2002) *Cinema India: The Visual Culture of Hindi Film*. London: Reaktion Books.

Espinosa, J.G. (1983) 'For an imperfect cinema', in M. Chanan (ed.) *Twenty-five Years of Latin American Cinema*. London: BFI, reprinted in M. Martin (1997) (ed.) *New Latin American Cinema. Vol 1. Theory, Practices and Transcontinental Articulations*. Detroit: Wayne State University Press.

Fanon, F. ([1961] 1979) *The Wretched of the Earth*. Trans. C. Farrington. Harmondsworth: Penguin.

Fanon, F. (1963) *The Wretched of the Earth*. London: MacGibbon and Kee.

Featherstone, M. (1996) 'Localism, globalism, and cultural identity', in R. Wilson and W. Dissanayake (eds) *Global/Local: Cultural Production and the Transnational Imaginary*. Durham: Duke University Press.

Featherstone, M. (1995) *Undoing Culture: Globalization, Postmodernism and Identity*. London: Sage.

Fernandes, L. (2000) 'Nationalizing "the global": media images, cultural politics and the middle class in India', *Media, Culture & Society*, vol. 22.

Ferguson, K. (1993) *The Man Question*, Berkeley, CA: University of California Press.

Forgacs, D. (1984) 'National-popular: genealogy of a concept', in T. Bennett (ed.) *Formations of Nations and Culture*. London: Routledge.

Foucault, M. (1977) *Language, Countermemory, Practice* (ed.) D. Bouchard, New York: Cornell University Press.

Foucault, M. (1980) *Power/Knowledge*. London: Harvester.

Fraser, N. (1997) *Justice Interruptus: Critical Reflections on the 'Post-Socialist' Condition*. New York: Routledge.

Frow, J. (1998) 'Economies of value', in D. Bennett (ed.) *Multicultural States: Rethinking Difference and Identity*. London: Routledge.

Fusco, C. (1989) 'About locating ourselves and our representations', *Framework*: 36.

Gabriel, T. (1982) *Third Cinema in the Third World: the Aesthetics of Liberation*. Ann Arbor, MI: UMI Research Press.

Gabriel, T. (1989) 'Third cinema as guardian of popular memory: towards a third aesthetics', in J. Pines and P. Willemen (eds) *Questions of Third Cinema*. London: BFI.

Geertz, C. (1973) *The Interpretation of Cultures*. New York: Basic Books.

Gellner, E. (1985) *Relativism and the Social Sciences*. Cambridge: Cambridge University Press.

Giddens, A. (1999) *Runaway World: How Globalisation is Reshaping Our Lives*. London: Profile.

Gillespie, M. (1995) *Television, Ethnicity, and Cultural Change*. London: Routledge.

Gilroy, P. (1987) *There Ain't No Black in the Union Jack*. London: Hutchinson.

Gilroy, P. (1993) *The Black Atlantic: Double Consciousness and Modernity*. Cambridge: Harvard University Press.

Gilroy, P. (1994) 'Diaspora', *Paragraph* 17 (1).

Gilroy, P. (2000) *Against Race: Imagining a Political Culture Beyond the Color Line*. Cambridge: Harvard University Press.

Ginsburg, F. (1991) 'Indigenous media: Faustian contract or global village?', *Cultural Anthropology*, 6 (1).

Ginsburg, F. (1995) 'Production values: indigenous media and the rhetoric of self-making,' in D. Battaglia (ed.) *Rhetorics of Self-Making*. Berkeley: University of California Press.

Ginsburg, F. (2003) 'Embedded aesthetics: creating a discursive space for indigenous media', in L. Parks and S. Kumar (eds) *Planet TV*. New York: New York University Press.

Giroux, H. (1994) 'Living dangerously: identity politics and the new cultural racism', in H. Giroux and P. McLaren (eds) *Between Borders: Pedagogy and the Politics of Cultural Studies*. London: Routledge.

Goldberg, D. (ed.) (1994) *Multiculturalism: A Critical Reader*. Oxford: Blackwell.

Gramsci, A. (1971) *Selections from the Prison Notebooks*. New York: International Publishers.

Gramsci, A. (1985) *Selections from Cultural Writings*, ed. and trans. Q. Hoare and G. Smith, New York: International.

Gray, H. ([1995] 2001) 'The politics of representation in network television', in D. Kellner and M. Durham (eds) *Media and Cultural Studies Key Works*. Oxford: Blackwell.

Griffiths, T. (1996) *Hunters and Collectors: The Antiquarian Imagination in Australia*. Melbourne: Cambridge University Press.

Gugelberer, G. (1999) 'Stollwerk or Bulwark? David meets Goliath and the continuation of the Testimonio Debate', *Latin American Perspectives*, issue 109, vol. 26, no. 6.

Guedes-Bailey, O. and R. Harindranath (2005) 'Racialised "othering": the representation of asylum seekers in the news media', in S. Allan (ed.) *Journalism: Critical Issues*. Maidenhead and New York: Open University Press.

Guha, R. (1982) 'On some aspects of the historiography of colonial India', in R. Guha (ed.) *Subaltern Studies*, vol. 1, Oxford University Press, reprinted in R. Guha and G. Spivak (eds) (1988) *Selected Subaltern Studies*. New York: Oxford University Press.

Guha, R. (1983) *Elementary Aspects of Peasant Insurgency in Colonial India*. Delhi: Oxford University Press.

Guha, R. (1988a) 'Preface', in R. Guha and G. Spivak (eds) *Selected Subaltern Studies*. New York: Oxford University Press.

Guha, R. and G. Spivak (eds) (1988b) *Selected Subaltern Studies*. New York: Oxford University Press.

Guha, R. (1996) 'The small voice of history', *Subaltern Studies*, 9.

Guha, R. (1997) *Dominance Without Hegemony: History and Power in Colonial India*. Cambridge, MA: Harvard University Press.

Guneratne, A. (2003) 'Introduction: rethinking third cinema', in A. Guneratne and W. Dissanayake (eds) *Rethinking Third Cinema*. NY: Routledge.

Gupta, A. (1999) *Postcolonial Developments: Agriculture in the Making of Modern India*. Delhi: Oxford University Press.

Gupta, A. and J. Ferguson (eds) (1997a) 'Culture, power, place: ethnography at the end of an era', in *Culture, Power, Place: Explorations in Critical Anthropology*. Durham: Duke University Press.

Gupta, A. and J. Ferguson (eds) (1997b) – 'Beyond "culture": space, identity, and the politics of difference', in *Culture, Power, Place: Explorations in Critical Anthropology*. Durham: Duke University Press.

Hage, G. (2003) *Against Paranoid Nationalism: Searching for Hope in a Shrinking Society*. Annandale: Pluto Press.

Hall, S. (1980) 'Race, articulation and societies in structured dominance', in *Sociological Theories: Race and Colonialism*. Paris: UNESCO.

Hall, S. (1981) 'The whites of their eyes', M. Alvarado and J. Thompson (eds) *The Media Reader*. London: BFI.

Hall, S. (1982) 'The rediscovery of "ideology": return of the repressed in media studies', in M. Gurevitch, *et al*. (eds) *Culture, Society, and the Media*. London: Routledge.

Hall, S. (1988) 'New ethnicities', in K. Mercer (ed.) *Black Film/British Cinema*. ICA Document 7. London: BFI.

Hall, S. (1989a) 'The morning discussion', *Framework*, 36.

Hall, S. (1989b) 'Introduction to the afternoon discussion', *Framework*, 36.

Hall, S. (1989c) 'Cultural identity and cinematic representation', *Framework*, 36.

Hall, S. ([1993] 1999) 'Culture, community, nation', reproduced in D. Boswell and J. Evans (eds) *Representing the Nation: A Reader*. London: Routledge.

Hall, S. (1994) 'Cultural identity and diaspora', in P. Williams and L. Chrisman (eds) *Colonial Discourse/Postcolonial Theory*. New York: Columbia University Press.

Hall, S. (ed.) (1997a) *Representations: Cultural Represenations and Signifying Practices*. London: Sage.

Hall, S. (ed.) (1997b) 'The work of representation', in *Representation: Cultural Representations and Signifying Practices*. London: Sage.

Hall, S. (2000) 'Conclusion: the multi-cultural question', in B. Hesse, (ed.) *Un/Settled Multiculturalisms: Diasporas, Entanglements, 'Transcriptions'*. London: Zed Books.

Hall, S. and D. Held (1990) 'Ethnicity: identity and difference', in S. Hall and M. Jacques (eds) *New Times: the Changing Face of Politics in the 1990s*. London: Verso.

Hamilton, A. (1990) 'Fear and desire: aborigines, Asians, and the national imaginary', *Australian Cultural History*, 9.

Hardt, M. and Negri, A. (2000) *Empire*. Cambridge: Harvard University Press.

Hardt, M. and Negri, A. (2004) *Multitude: War and Democracy in the Age of Empire*. New York: Penguin.

Harindranath, R. (2000) 'Theorising protest: the significance of social movements to metropolitan academic theory', *Thamyris*, vol. 7, nos 1 & 2.

Harindranath, R. (2005) 'Ethnicity and cultural difference: some thematic and political issues on global audience research', *Participations: International Journal of Audience Research*, Vol. 2(2).

Harvey, D. (1990) *The Condition of Postmodernity: an Enquiry into the Origins of Cultural Change*. Oxford: Blackwell.

Harvey, D. (2003) *The New Imperialism*. Oxford: Oxford University Press.

Held, D. *et al*. (1999) *Global Transformations: Politics, Economics and Culture*. Oxford: Polity Press.

Hesse, B. (2000) 'Introduction: Un/settled multiculturalisms', in B. Hesse (ed.) *Un/Settled Multiculturalisms: Diasporas, Entanglements,'Transruptions'*. London: Zed Books.

Hirst, P. and G. Thompson (1996) *Globalisation in Question*. Cambridge: Polity.

hooks, b. (2001) 'Eating the Other: desire and resistance', in *Black Looks: Race and Representation*, reproduced in M. Durham and D. Kellner (ed.) *Media and Cultural Studies: Key Works*. Oxford: Blackwell.

Hutton, W. and A. Giddens (eds) (2000) *On the Edge. Living with Global Capitalism*. London: Vintage.

Independent Commission on International Humanitarian Issues (ICIHI) (1987) *Indigenous Peoples: A Global Quest for Justice*. London: Zed Books.

Jaffrelot, C. (1999) *The Hindu Nationalist Movement and Indian Politics: 1925 to the 1990s*. New Delhi: Penguin.

Jameson, F. (1986) 'Third World literature in the era of multinational capitalism', *Social Text*, 15.

Jameson, F. (1991) *Postmodernism, or the Cultural Logic of Capitalism*. London: Verso.

Jameson, F. (2000) 'Globalization and political strategy', *New Left Review*, 4, Jul/Aug.

Jhally, S. and J. Lewis (1992) *Enlightened Racism: 'The Cosby Show', Audiences, and the Myth of the American Dream*. Boulder, Colorado: Westview.

Julien, I. and K. Mercer (1988) 'Introduction de margin and de centre', *Screen*, vol. 29.

Kellner, D. (1995) *Media Culture*. New York: Routledge.

Khare, R. S. (1992) 'The Other's double – the anthropologist's bracketed self: notes on cultural representation and privileged discourse', *New Literary History* 23.

Klein, N. (2005) 'The rise of disaster capitalism', *The Age*, 14 May 2005.

Kohli, A. (1990) *Democracy and Discontent: India's Growing Crisis of Governability*. Cambridge: Cambridge University Press.

Kureishi, H. (1997) *My Son the Fanatic*. London: Faber & Faber.

Laclau, E. and C. Mouffe (1985) *Hegemony and Socialist Strategy: Towards a Radical Democratic Politics*. London: Verso.

Lal, V. (2002) *Empires of Knowledge: Culture and Plurality in Global Economy*. London: Pluto.

Langton, M. (1993) *Well, I Saw It on Television and I Heard It on the Radio*. Sydney: Australian Film Commission.

Langton, M. (1994) 'Introduction', in E. Michaels, (1994) *Bad Aboriginal Art: Tradition, Media and Technological Horizons*. St Leonards: Allen & Unwin.

Lazarus, N. ([1992] 2001) ' "Afropop" and the paradoxes of imperialism', reprinted in G. Castle (ed.) *Postcolonial Discourses: An Anthology*. Oxford: Blackwell.

Lazarus, N. (1994) 'National consciousness and the specificity of (post)colonial intellectualism', in F. Barker, *et al.* (eds) *Colonial Discourse/Postcolonial Theory*. Manchester: Manchester University Press.

Lazarus, N. (1999a) *Nationalism and Cultural Practice in the Postcolonial World*. Cambridge: Cambridge University Press.

Lazarus, N. (1999b) 'Charting globalization', *Race & Class*, 40.

Lazarus, N. (2002) 'The fetish of "the West" in postcolonial theory', in C. Bartolovich, and N. Lazarus (eds) *Marxism, Modernity, and Postcolonial Studies*. Cambridge: Cambridge University Press.

Lewellen, T. (2002) *The Anthropology of Globalisation: Cultural Anthropology Enters the 21st Century*. Westport: Bergin and Garvey.

Liebes, T. and E. Katz, (1993) *The Export of Meaning*. Cambridge: Polity.

Loomba, A. (1998) *Colonialism-Postcolonialism*. London: Routledge.

Loshitzky, Y. (2000) 'Orientalist representations: Palestinians and Arabs in some postcolonial film and literature', in E. Hallam and B. Street (eds) *Cultural Encounters: Representing 'Otherness'*. London: Routledge.

Lowe, L. and D. Lloyd (eds) (1997) 'Introduction', in *The Politics of Culture in the Shadow of Capital*. Durham: Duke University Press.

Ludden, D. (ed.) (1996) *Making India Hindu: Religion, Community, and the Politics of Democracy in India*. New Delhi: Oxford University Press.

Makang, J.-M. (1997) 'Of the good use of tradition: keeping the critical perspective in African philosophy', in E. C. Eze (ed.) *Postcolonial African Philosophy: A Critical Reader*. Cambridge, Mass: Blackwell.

Malik, K. (1996) *The Meaning of Race*. London: Macmillan.

Manning, P. (2003) 'Arabic and muslim people in Sydney's daily newspapers', *Media International Australia*, no. 109, November 2003.

Martin-Barbero, J. (2002) 'Identities: traditions and new communities', *Media, Culture & Society*, vol. 24.

McChesney, R. (2001) 'Global Media, neoliberalism, and imperialism', *Monthly Review*, March, 52:10.

McClintock, A. (1995) *Imperial Leather: Race, Gender, and Sexuality in the Colonial Context*. New York: Routledge.

Mehta, B. (2003) 'Emigrants twice displaced: race, color, and identity in Mira Nair's *Mississippi Masala*', in E. Shohat and R. Stam (eds) *Multiculturalism, Postcoloniality, and Transnational Media*. New Brunswick: Rutgers University Press.

Menchu, R. (1984) *I, Rigoberta Menchu: An Indian Woman in Guatemala*. E. Burgos-Debray (ed.), trans. A. Wright. London: Verso.

Merelman, R. M. (1995) *Representing Black Culture: Racial Conflict and Cultural Politics in the United States*. New York: Routledge.

Michaels, E. (1994) *Bad Aboriginal Art: Tradition, Media and Technological Horizons*. St Leonards: Allen & Unwin.

Michell, K. (1997) 'Different diasporas and the hype of hybridity', *Environment and Planning D: Society and Space*, 15.

Miles, R. (1989) *Racism*. London: Routledge.

Minh-ha, T. (1989) 'Outside in inside out', in J. Pines and P. Willemen (eds) *Questions of Third Cinema*. London: BFI.

Mishra, V. (1996) 'The diasporic imaginary: theorizing the Indian diaspora', *Textual Practice*, 10:3.

Mishra, V. (2002) *Bollywood Cinema: Temples of Desire*. New York: Routledge.

Mohanty, C. T. (1994) 'Under Western eyes: feminist scholarship and colonial discourses', in P. Williams and L. Chrisman (eds) *Colonial Discourse and Postcolonial Theory: A Reader*. New York: Harvester.

Mohanty, S. (1998) *Literary Theory and the Claims of History: Postmodernism, Objectivity, Multicultural Politics*. New Delhi: Oxford University Press.

Montgomery, M. (2005) 'Talking war: how journalism responded to the events of 9/11', in S. Allan (ed.) *Journalism: Critical Issues*. Maidenhead and New York: Open University Press.

Morley, D. and K. Robins (1995) *Spaces of Identity: Global Media, Electronic Landscapes and Cultural Boundaries*. London: Routledge.

Morrison, T. (1987) *Beloved: A Novel*. New York: Plume.

Mowitt, J. (2005) *Re-Takes: Postcoloniality and Foreign Film Languages*. Minneapolis: University of Minnesota Press.

Mudimbe, V. Y. (1994) *The Idea of Africa*. Bloomington: Indiana University Press.

Muecke, S. (1992) *Textual Spaces: Aboriginality and Cultural Studies*. Kensington: New South Wales University Press.

Muecke, S. (2004) *Ancient and Modern: Time, Culture and Indigenous Philosophy*. Sydney: University of New South Wales Press.

Myers, F. (1988) 'Locating ethnographic practice: reality and politics in the outback', *American Ethnologist*, 15.

Myers, F. (1991) 'Representing culture: the production of discourse(s) for Aboriginal acrylic paintings', *Cultural Anthropology*, 6:1.

Nandy, A. (1995) *The Savage Freud and Other Essays on Possible and Retrievable Selves*. Delhi: Oxford University Press.

Nandy, A., *et al.* (1997) *Creating a Nationality: The Ramjanmabhumi Movement and the Fear of the Self.* New Delhi: Oxford University Press.

Naficy, H. (1993) *The Making of Exile Cultures: Iranian Television in Los Angeles.* Minneapolis: University of Minnesota Press.

Naficy, H. (2003) 'Narrowcasting in diaspora: Iranian television in Los Angeles', in L. Parks and S. Kumar (eds) *Planet TV.* New York: New York University Press.

Narismulu, P. (2003) 'Examining the undisclosed margins: postcolonial intellectuals and subaltern voices', *Cultural Studies*, 17 (1).

Nussbaum, M. (with Respondents) (1996) *For Love of Country: Debating the Limits of Patriotism.* Boston: Beacon Press.

Ohmae, K. (1990) *The Borderless World: Power and Strategy in the Interlinked Economy.* New York: HarperBusiness.

Ohmae, K. (1995) *The End of the Nation-state: The Rise of Regional Economics.* New York: HarperCollins.

Panitch, L. (1998) ' "The state in a changing world": social-democratizing global capitalism?', *Monthly Review*, vol. 50. no. 5.

Petras, J. and H. Veltmeyer (2001) *Globalization Unmasked: Imperialism in the 21st Century.* New York: Zed Books.

Pines, J. and P. Willemen (eds) *Questions of Third Cinema.* London: BFI.

Radhakrishnan, R. (2003) *Theory in an Uneven World.* Oxford: Blackwell.

Rahim, L. Z. (1998) 'In search of the "Asian Way": cultural nationalism in Singapore and Malaysia', *Commonwealth & Comparative Politics*, vol. 36, no. 3.

Rajadhyaksha, A. (1996) 'Indian cinema: origins to independence', in G. Nowell-Smith (ed.) *The Oxford History of World Cinema.* Oxford: Oxford University Press.

Rajagopal, A. (2001) *Politics After Television: Hindu Nationalism and the Reshaping of the Public in India.* Cambridge: Cambridge University Press.

Ray, M. (2000) 'Bollywood down under: Fijian Indian cultural history and popular assertion', in S. Cunningham and J. Sinclair (eds) *Floating Lives: The Media and Asian Diasporas.* St Lucia: University of Queensland Press.

Rocha, G. ([1982] 1997) 'An esthetic of hunger', reprinted in M. Martin (ed.) *New Latin American Cinema. Vol 1. Theory, Practices and Transcontinental Articulations.* Detroit: Wayne State University Press.

Rosen P. (1991) 'Making a nation in Sembene's *Ceddo*', *Quarterly Review of Film & Video.* vol. 13 (1–3).

Safran, W. (1991) 'Diasporas in modern societies: myths of homeland and return', *Diaspora* 1.1 (Spring).

Said, E. (1978) *Orientalism.* Harmondsworth: Penguin.

Said, E. (1993) *Culture and Imperialism.* London: Vintage.

San Juan, E. (1998) *Beyond Postcolonial Theory.* New York: St Martin's Press.

San Juan, E. (2002) *Racism and Cultural Studies: Critiques of Multiculturalist Ideology and the Politics of Difference.* Durham, NC: Duke University Press.

Schiller, D. (1996) *Theorizing Communication: A History.* New York: Oxford University Press.

Schipper, M. (1999) *Imagining Insiders: Africa and the Question of Belonging.* London: Cassell.

Seed, P. (2001) 'No perfect world: aboriginal communities' contemporary resource rights', in

I. Rodriguez (ed.) *The Latin American Subaltern Studies Reader*. Durham: Duke University Press.

Sen, K (2003) 'What's "oppositional" in Indonesian cinema?' in A. Guneratne and W. Dissanayake (eds) *Rethinking Third Cinema*. NY: Routledge.

Shohat, E. (1995) 'The struggle over representation: casting, coalitions, and the politics of identification', in R. Campa, *et al.* (eds) *Late Imperial Culture*. London: Verso.

Shohat, E. ([1997] 2000) 'Post-Third-Worldist culture: gender, nation, and the cinema', in J. Alexander and C. Mohanty (eds) *Feminist Genealogies, Colonial Legacies, Democratic Futures*, reprinted in D. Brydon (ed.) *Postcolonialism: Critical Concepts in Literary and Cultural Studies, vol. V*. London and New York: Routledge.

Shohat, E. and R. Stam (1994) *Unthinking Eurocentrism: Multiculturalism and the Media*. New York: Routledge.

Shohat, E. and R. Stam (1996) 'From the imperial family to the transnational imaginary: media spectatorship in the age of globalization', in R. Wilson and W. Dissanayake (eds) *Global/Local: Cultural Production and the Transnational Imaginary*. Durham: Duke University Press.

Shohat, E. and R. Stam (eds) (2003) *Multiculturalism, Postcolonialism, and Transnational Media*. New Brunswick: Rutgers University Press.

Sivanandan, A. (1990a) 'All that melts into air is solid: the hokum of New Times', *Race & Class*, 31:3.

Sivanandan, A. (1990b) *Communities of Resistance: Writings on Black Struggles for Socialism*. London: Verso.

Solanas, F. and O. Getino ([1983] 1997) 'Towards a Third Cinema: notes and experiences for the development of a cinema of liberation in the third world', in M. Chanan (ed.) *Twenty-five Years of Latin American Cinema*. London: BFI, reprinted in M. Martin (ed.) *New Latin American Cinema. Vol 1. Theory, Practices and Transcontinental Articulations*. Detroit: Wayne State University Press.

Sommer, D. (1991) 'Rigoberta's secrets', *Latin American Perspectives: Voices of the Voiceless in Testimonial Literature*, part. 1, 18:3 (issue 70).

Sommer, D. (2001) 'Slaps and embraces: a rhetoric of particularism', in I. Rodriguez (ed.) *The Latin American Subaltern Studies Reader*. Durham: Duke University Press.

Spivak, G. (1988a) 'Can the subaltern speak?' in C. Nelson and L. Grossberg (eds) *Marxism and the Interpretation of Culture*. Urbana: University of Illinois Press.

Spivak, G. (1988b) *In Other Worlds: Essays in Cultural Politics*. New York: Routledge.

Spivak, G. (1993) *Outside in the Teaching Machine*. New York: Routledge.

Spivak, G. (1999) *A Critique of Postcolonial Reason: Toward a History of the Vanishing Present*. London: Harvard University Press.

Spivak, G. (2001/2) 'Mapping the present: interview with Gayatri Spivak. By Meyda Yenenoglu and Mahmut Metman', *New Formations*, 45.

Spivak, G. (2003) 'Righting wrongs', in N. Owen (ed.) *Human Rights, Human Wrongs: Oxford Amnesty Lectures 2001*. Oxford: Oxford University Press.

Stam, R. (1990) '*The Hour of the Furnaces* and the two avant-gardes', in J. Burton (ed.) *The Social Documentary in Latin America*. Pittsburgh: University of Pittsburgh Press.

Stam, R. (1991) 'Eurocentrism, Afrocentrism, polycentrism: theories of Third Cinema', *Quarterly Review of Film & Video*, vol. 13 (1–3).

Stam, R. (1999) 'Eurocentrism, polycentrism, and multicultural pedagogy: film and the quincentenial', in R. de la Campa, *et al.* (eds) *Late Imperial Culture*. London: Verso.

Stoll, D. (1998) *Rigoberta Menchu and the Story of All Poor Guatemalans*. Boulder: Westview.

Tagore, R. ([1917] 1985) *Nationalism*. New York: Macmillan, Madras: Macmillan.

Tam, K., T. Siu-han Yip, and W. Dissanayake, (eds) (2002) *Sights of Contestation: Localism, Globalism, and Cultural Production in Asia and the Pacific*. Hong Kong: The Chinese University Press.

Taylor, Clyde (1989) 'Black cinema in the post-aesthetic era', in J. Pines and P. Willemen (eds) *Questions of Third Cinema*. London: BFI.

Taylor, C. (1989) *Sources of the Self*. Cambridge: Harvard University Press.

Taylor, C. (1994a) 'The politics of recognition', in A. Guttman (ed.) *Multiculturalism: Examining the Politics of Recognition*. Princeton: Princeton University Press.

Taylor, C. (1994b) *Multiculturalism and 'The Politics of Recognition'* (edited and introduced by A. Guttman). Princeton: Princeton University Press.

Tharoor, S. (1997) *India: From Midnight to the Millenium*. New Delhi: Penguin.

The United Nations (1994) *International Covenant on the Rights of Indigenous Nations*. New York: UN Publications.

Thomas, R. (1989) 'Sanctity and scandal: the mythologising of Mother India', *Quarterly Review of Film and Video*, 11/3.

Thompson, J. (1990) *Ideology and Modern Culture*. Cambridge: Polity.

Tomlinson, J. (1991) *Cultural Imperialism: A Critical Introduction*. London: Pinter.

Tomlinson, J. (1999) *Globalization and Culture*. London: Polity.

Tomlinson, J. (2000) 'Globalised culture: the triumph of the West?', in T. Skelton and T. Allen (eds) *Culture and Global Change*. London: Routledge.

Turner, V. (1990) 'Visual media, cultural politics, and anthropological practice: some implications of recent uses of film and video among the Kayapo of Brazil', *Commission on Visual Anthropology Review* (Spring).

Turner, V. (1992) 'Defiant images: the Kayapo appropriation of video', *Anthropology Today* 8 (6).

Valaskakis, G. G. (2002) 'Remapping Canada's north: Nunavut, communications, and Inuit participatory development', in R. Harris and M. Pendakur (eds) *Citizenship and Participation in the Information Age*. Aurora, Ontario: Garamond Press.

Vanaik, A. (1997) *The Furies of Indian Communalism: Religion, Modernity, and Secularization*. London: Verso.

Wallerstein, I. (1991) *Geopolitics and Geoculture: Essays on the Changing World-Sytem*. New York: Cambridge University Press.

Waters, M. (1995) *Globalization*. London: Routledge.

Wayne, M. (2001) *Political Film: The Dialectics of Third Cinema*. London: Pluto.

Wayne, M. (2002) 'The critical practice and dialectics of Third Cinema', in R. Areen *et al.* (eds) *The Third Text Reader on Art, Culture and Theory*. London: Continuum.

Weiss, L. (1997) 'Globalization and the myth of the powerless state', *New Left Review*, 225.

Weiss, L. (1999) 'Managed openness: beyond neoliberal globalism', *New Left Review*, 238.

West, C. (1990) 'The new cultural politics of difference', reprinted in During, S. (ed.) (1993) *The Cultural Studies Reader*. London: Routledge.

Willemen, P. (1989) 'The Third Cinema question: notes and reflections', in J. Pines and P. Willemen (eds) *Questions of Third Cinema*. London: BFI.

Willis, A.-M. and T. Fry (2003) 'Art as ethnocide: the case of Australia', in R. Araeen *et al.* (eds) *The Third Text Reader on Art, Culture and Theory*. London: Continuum.

Wilson, R. (1994) 'Melodramas of Korean national identity: from *Mandala* to *Black Republic*', in W. Dissanayake (ed.) *Colonialism and Nationalism in Asian Cinema*. Bloomington: Indiana University Press.

Wilson, R. and W. Dissanayake (ed.) (1996) *Global/Local: Cultural Production and the Transnational Imaginary*. Durham: Duke University Press.

Wolf, E. (1982) *Europe and the People Without History*. Berkeley: University of California Press.

Wood, E. M. (1998) 'Modernity, postmodernity, or capitalism?', in R. McChesney *et al.* (ed.) *Capitalism and the Information Age: the Political Economy of the Global Communication Revolution*. Monthly Review Press.

Wood, E. M. (2003) *Empire of Capital*. London: Verso.

Wood, T. (2004) 'The case for Chechnya', *New Left Review*, 30.

Worsley, P. (1984) *The Three Worlds: Culture and World Development*. Chicago: University of Chicago Press.

Yudice, G. (1991) 'Testimonio and postmodernism', *Latin American Perspectives: Voices of the Voiceless in Testimonial Literature*. Part 1, 18:3 (issue 70).

Yue Daiyun, (1998) 'Cultural discourse and cultural intercourse', in M. Akiyama and Y. Leung (eds) *Crosscurrents in the Literatures of Asia and the West*. Newark: University of Delaware Press.

Yue, M.-B. (1998) 'Visual agency and ideological fantasy in three films by Zhang Yimou', in W. Dissanayake (ed.) *Narratives of Agency*. Minneapolis: University of Minnesota Press.

Zhang, Y. (1994) 'Ideology of the body in Red Sorghum: national allegory, national roots, and third cinema', in W. Dissanayake (ed.) (1994) *Colonialism and Nationalism in Asian Cinema*. Bloomington: Indiana University Press.

INDEX

IDENTITY AND CULTURE
NARRATIVES OF DIFFERENCE AND BELONGING

Chris Weedon

- Where does our sense of identity and belonging come from?
- How does culture shape and challenge identities?

Identity and Culture looks at how different forms of cultural narratives and practices work to constitute identity for individuals and groups in multi-ethnic, 'postcolonial' societies.

- Uses examples from history, politics, fiction and the visual to examine the social power relations that create subject positions and forms of identity
- Analyses how cultural texts and practices offer new forms of identity and agency that subvert dominant ideologies

This book encompasses issues of class, race, gender and sexuality, with a particular focus on the mobilization of forms of ethnic identity in societies still governed by racism. It a key text for students in cultural studies, sociology of culture, literary studies, history, race and ethnicity studies, media and film studies, and gender studies.

Contents
Preface – Introduction – Subjectivity and identity – History, nation and identity – History, voice and representation: Aboriginal women's life writing – Narratives of identity and difference: Voicing black British history – Identity, origins and roots – Diasporic identities: South Asian British women's writing – Visualizing difference: South Asians on screen – Competing cultures, competing values – Concluding reflections – Notes – Glossary – Bibliography – Index.

192pp   0 335 20086 9 (Paperback)   0 335 20087 7 (Hardback)